OUT OF THE FIRING LINE... INTO THE FOYER

MY REMARKABLE STORY
BRUCE COPP
WITH ANDY MERRIMAN

The
History
Press

To my sister Diana,
who is still at my side

Unless otherwise credited, images are from the author's collection

Cover illustrations: front: a publicity pose for The Players', 1948. (Athol Skipsey); back: with the great and the good of 'The Establishment'. (Bryan Wharton)

First published 2015

The History Press
The Mill, Brimscombe Port
Stroud, Gloucestershire, GL5 2QG
www.thehistorypress.co.uk

British Library Cataloguing in Publication Data.
A catalogue record for this book is available from the British Library.

ISBN 978 0 7509 6134 9

Typesetting and origination by The History Press
Printed and bound in Malta, by Melita Press

CONTENTS

ACKNOWLEDGEMENTS

I am extraordinarily indebted to Philip Paxman for all his support and for persuading me to undertake this adventure. Also much thanks to the delightful Becky Duncan for all her hard work. I'm appreciative to all at South Farm for their kindness.

Many thanks to the following for their contributions: Alan Bennett, Wendy Cook, Dame Judi Dench, Violetta Farjeon, Phyllida Law, Emma Malin, Joan Le Mesurier, Robin Le Mesurier, Donald Macleod, Penelope Niven, Jane Nye, Philippa Potts, George Potts, Maroussia Richardson, Carol Lindsay-Smith, Margot Lovatt-Smith, Peter Tatchell and Francesc Mas Vidal.

A special mention to Eliza Benge for her unbridled enthusiasm and invaluable assistance with her father's material, as well as Maryvonne and Alfreda for their participation.

We have had valuable archive material provided by Sara Hodson (manager) and Sue Garwood (volunteer) at the Ilfracombe Museum and Tappan Wilder, Literary Executor of the Thornton Wilder estate.

And thank you to the National Portrait Gallery for their assistance with The Establishment image.

To all the staff at The History Press, especially Mark Beynon and Naomi Reynolds.

Grateful appreciation to my surviving siblings, my brother Tom Copp and my sister Diana Dodds, for their love and kinship.

I simply couldn't manage without the ministration of my dear friend and carer, Danny Duch. In fact, I feel sure he's keeping me alive!

And finally, of course, I am very grateful to Andy Merriman for putting my story together so skilfully and for making all my anecdotes and memories come alive.

Apologies to anyone I've forgotten – it's my age you know …

FOREWORD
BY DAME JUDI DENCH

I am absolutely delighted to be able to contribute a foreword to this autobiography, for if ever a man deserved to have his story told then it is dear Bruce. He is a terribly modest man, and whereas there are those who indeed do have a lot to be modest about, Bruce is not one of them.

A reluctant war hero, he survived the North African campaign, thanks to a series of fortunate escapes in what he describes as 'my charmed life'. Bruce then embarked upon a career in catering, which, although clearly not as dangerous as combat, occasionally found him in an atmosphere of conflict in the form of temperamental chefs, wayward waiting staff and naughty busboys.

Bruce is a quite wonderful cook, very much home on the range, and he went on to run a number of highly successful eating establishments. He was acknowledged nationwide for his expertise in managing theatrical restaurants and became something of a backstage legend. Bruce's address book contains the names of more actors and actresses than *Spotlight,* and being the most sociable character, he has created lasting friendships with luminary writers, artists and performers.

We first met well over fifty years ago through my parents, who had connections with the lovely old York Theatre Royal where Bruce ran the restaurant. We have remained fast friends since then. Charming, generous and kind to a fault, he is the most adorable company, although it's sometimes difficult to get a word in! Bruce is coquettish by nature, gloriously camp and a dreadful flirt with both men and women, but always utterly reliable and honourable.

Despite his protestations to the contrary, Bruce has led the most extraordinary life, and I am thrilled that he has finally committed his exploits and experiences to paper. I have no doubt that you will enjoy this deeply engaging book, which not only tells his astonishing story but also charts a personal, social history of nearly 100 years.

PREFACE

It was during the Battle of Sedjenane in early 1943 that I tried to commit suicide. I thought I could just walk into some machine-gun fire and have done with it. I could die very nicely and that would be that …

The Tunisian campaign had been going on for several months and we were making an assault on one of the mounts, east of the town, which dominated the skyline. This was called Green Hill. A place I'll never forget. The attack had continued for two days and nights and I simply couldn't take any more. Despite being somewhat battle hardened by now, the idea of war still puzzled me. I couldn't understand what we were doing to each other. I'd seen friends and comrades shot, blown up and maimed. How could men do this?

I was lying down behind a little clump of grass and suddenly thought, 'What am I doing here? I can't go on like this. I don't want to be part of it any more, it's too much.' It was as simple as that. Machine-gun bullets were going all over the place and the light was fading. There were so many tracer bullets fizzing around at all angles. And I thought if I walk into the line of fire, I'd get it all over with. I stood up and strode forward expecting to be hit at any moment … but I wasn't touched at all. I carried on for about 50 yards unscathed when I heard a voice calling out for help.

I looked to where the cries were coming and saw, lying on the ground, a seriously wounded man, very distressed and needing immediate attention. He had a terrible wound in his side. I couldn't leave him like that. All thoughts of my own fate were forgotten and I went to help him. I remember putting both his and my field dressings into his wound and, at that moment, the cry went up to retreat.

Later they gave me a medal for my actions. I told them that I was actually in the middle of a suicide attempt. They didn't believe me. I didn't think of myself as a hero. I was never much of a soldier. Looking back I never really wanted to hurt anyone – I always aimed to miss and believe me, some of those great big German brutes were difficult to miss.

ONE

CHARABANCS, MARIGOLDS AND SCRUMPIES

'Childhood is measured out by sounds and smells and sights, before the dark hour of reason grows.'

John Betjeman

I'd better warn you, dear reader, before you start to tuck into my story, that there is an awful lot about food and restaurants in the book, and you might begin to feel a little peckish. I suggest, therefore, that an accompaniment of an *amuse-bouche* or a little nibble of some sort might help you digest the following couple of hundred pages. G.K. Chesterton once wrote, 'Poets have been mysteriously silent on the subject of cheese.' I am by no means a poet, but I am certainly never silent on the subject of cheese or other kinds of foodstuff.

When I was a young boy, father used to send me on my bicycle down into the town – a good 1½ miles away – to a butcher friend of ours, Mr Greenland, to purchase home-cured bacon for breakfast. It really was the most delicious bacon, and I've never had anything like it since. I'm afraid that I have to say that nothing tastes the same as in the old days. I suppose that you assume it's because of my age that I think this way, but it's not – I'm only saying it because it's true!

My childhood was dominated by food as my parents ran a small hotel in Weston-super-Mare and I used to spend a lot of time in the kitchen with the chefs. I'd watch them working, and they would let me do little jobs like washing the vegetables, slicing tomatoes and other things like that to help them. My father, although not a chef, was a very good amateur cook, and he turned the hotel's restaurant into a place where people used to come for miles to dine. I was always amazed how the dining room was full of people day after day. This was the first time I saw how people reacted to food and how much enjoyment they took from the experience. When I was very young I'd be sitting on some-body's lap and he'd tell me he had come all the way from Bristol to eat at The Lake Hotel. I used to marvel at that, as up until then it had never occurred to me that people were interested in what they ate. It was pretty straightforward food, but the ingredients were the best my father could provide for his customers.

I'm getting a little ahead of myself here. I do apologise. Let's go back a little: I was born George Charles Bruce Copp on 27 January 1920 in the Railway Hotel, Penarth, in the Vale of Glamorgan. I was given my middle name, Charles, after an uncle, Lance Corporal Charles Copp, who had been killed in Iraq in the First World War at the age of 28 (his brother Ernest also lost his life in that war) and 'Bruce' was a family name, which was given to all my siblings – whatever their gender. My sister Di, who is twenty months younger than me, once asked my mother why all family members, irrespective of gender, were given the middle name of 'Bruce'. My mother simply replied, 'Because I adore your father.' I was actually one of six siblings: another sister, Joan, and three brothers, Reginald, Jack and Tom.

The Copps can be traced back to the seventeenth century, and my stock derives from yeoman farmers in North Devon. My grandfather, Thomas Bruce Copp, owned the Royal Coach Company. The Copps ran all the buses and coach trips in the area and had been in the busi-ness for years, since the days of the horse-drawn buses; they actually owned the first charabanc in the West Country. Barnstaple was origi-nally their base, and later on they opened up the transport businesses in Ilfracombe and throughout Devon. I sometimes travelled in one of Grandpa Copp's coaches if there was ever a spare seat.

We used to go to Woolacombe on occasions, and it was at the town's lovely beach that I learned how to surf. Grandpa Copp was one of the last great gentlemen from quite a well-known family in north Devon and was also a local dignitary, being the first chairman of the Ilfracombe Urban District Council. I remember being with him when he used to walk to his office in Ilfracombe's High Street and everyone came out of their homes to say hello, doffing their caps and proffering good wishes. There were abundant handshakes all round, and grandpa would brandish his walking stick and raise his top hat to one and all. His wife, Edith, my grandmother, was the daughter of a Biddeford shipbuilder, John Cox.

My father also went under the name of Thomas Bruce Copp and was equally known in Torrington and Ilfracombe. Strikingly handsome and charming, he was a racing man, an expert horseman, who had served in the First World War as a sergeant in the Yeomanry. His duties were to select suitable horses for the Front. Unlike his two brothers mentioned previously, he survived the Great War and was retired from the Yeomanry in 1917 on account of a heart valve defect caused by his having contracted rheumatic fever in childhood. Father was very kind, a great gentleman and more than a little disappointed that I wasn't more interested in the equine world. In my early years, I accompanied him to some stables where I became nauseated by the smell and threw up.

My mother, Florence Emily Holbrook, was born in Swansea: her father was Welsh and her Irish mother had graduated from Trinity University, Dublin. She was younger than my father and tremendously warm and witty. Di recently told me that she had never met anyone like her: 'Mother was beautiful, the perfect mother – always loving and encouraging.'

My mother was one of four rather beautiful sisters – she was, in my opinion, the most beautiful – but was the only one that didn't marry into money. The others had all become involved with rich men. One sister, Kate, was the mistress of the Greek shipping millionaire Embericos, who was a kind of Onassis of his time and had his own family in Greece. Kate used to quite fancy my father. She was a wonderful woman, extremely witty, chic and quite lovely. She was the first really sophisticated lady I'd ever met, and I've loved those sorts of women all my life. In fact, I'd go as far as to say she was another Marlene Dietrich …

My parents originally lived in a small house in Ilfracombe before moving into a little house on the outskirts of Weston-super-Mare when I was a small child. Father was the eldest of his siblings and was expected to run the transport business, but he just wasn't interested – he was much more of 'a devil may care' character and wanted something else for himself and my mother.

For many years Weston was just a small village of about thirty houses, until the hamlet became popular as a seaside resort. Its location, situated behind a number of sand dunes, was perfect, and by the middle of the eighteenth century doctors began to exalt the merits of drinking and bathing in sea water; for residents of Bath and Bristol, Weston was the nearest coastal village. The first hotel was opened in 1810, and Brunel's Bristol and Exeter Railway reached the town thirty years later. In the 1880s Weston became a centre for thousands of visitors, and the pier offered 'a theatre of wonders, an alpine railway, a shooting gallery, park swings, merry-go-round, switchback, helter-skelter and bandstand'.

A second pier, which was more in the centre of the town and brought day trippers nearer the shops, was built in 1904. One of the piers burned down a few years ago; there was another time when it caught fire. I remember seeing it. It was in 1930, and we had workmen decorating the front of the hotel, so there was a ladder against the wall. I climbed halfway up and watched the fire. It was quite an exciting event for an inquisitive 10 year old.

Two years earlier, the Winter Gardens and the Pavilion were created, and the open-air pool, famous for its arched concrete diving board, was built. The mid-1930s saw the addition of the Odeon cinema, and I remember standing in the road, waving a flag, when the Duke and Duchess of York visited Weston in 1934 to open the hospital.

The Marine Lake was built to provide a safe shallow beach where the tide was always in, and it was here, on the seafront, that Grandpa Copp 'staked' my father by providing funds for him to run a small hotel. It was inevitably called The Marine Lake Hotel, and adjacent to the hotel was a very grand ice-cream parlour, run by a lovely Italian family. It was a special treat to go there, and it was where I had my first ever Knickerbocker Glory.

Mother and father adored each other, and they loved attending the West End theatre. They used to travel to London regularly and would stay at the Strand Palace Hotel. Both were food connoisseurs and had knowledge of everything on the menu; in fact, all the family were obsessed with quality fare. Because of the nature and character of my parents and growing up in a hotel, I enjoyed an idyllic and unconventional upbringing.

My parents were devoted to us and gave us as much time as they could, although all the while they were being kept busy by the business. To encourage our independence, they also gave us all the freedom that we needed and never criticised us unfairly. They would put us right on things and correct us when necessary but always did it in a kindly way. They were the most wonderful couple, and I can't compare them with anybody else's parents because they were so special.

I had a little canoe, a sort of kayak, which I loved. One day I decided to paddle to Steep Holm, which is a little island, a bird sanctuary, halfway between us and Cardiff. It's about 25 miles across the channel, and about halfway I gave up and turned back, realising I couldn't make it the whole way across to the island. I didn't know until the next day that my mother had been on the balcony of the hotel watching me through a pair of binoculars and becoming more and more horrified as I went further and further away. But she never said a word to me when I returned. That's a perfect example of what my parents were like. They never made you feel as if you'd done something wrong. All she would say is, 'I'm so glad you enjoyed yourself. You're very good in that canoe. You went a long way out and came back. Very clever!' That's how my parents reacted. We were never on the receiving end of serious admonishment such as 'Don't you ever do that again' or that sort of stuff.

I can remember riding in the back of my father's horse and trap, which he drove into Weston in the early 1920s. By the time I was 5 years old we had a car; we were the only people in the whole area that had one. It was a funny little snub-nosed Morris with a dicky seat, which I always used to occupy when we went out for a spin. There was no heating, and my mother used to have a big foot muff to put her feet in and another for her hands. In those days the roads were so clear and it was very pleasant – not like now when no one goes for a leisurely spin because the traffic is unbearable and petrol so expensive. I think the term 'Sunday Driver' is no longer pertinent. I remember many special car trips to Cheddar Gorge. We ate cheese and then devoured the strawberries that grew on slopes near the gorge. They were the best in the world.

Another thing I recall was the harvest festival, and I remember one year in particular. There was a park nearby, and a slope led uphill to the church. Everyone was carrying things up to the church, and I was hauling something too – I don't know what … probably a cucumber or the like. Anyway, there was a boy who was a little bit older than me, and his family had given him a huge marrow as an offering, and he'd tied string to it as a handle and was pulling the lengthy squash along the grass as if he was walking a dog. I've never forgotten that image, and the memory has affected me all my life – to the extent that I have since felt that marrows should be always treated with such disdain.

During the summer, when the hotel was always full, our family lived in the basement area where the kitchens were located, and we created our own family sitting room. We slept in bunk beds in two tiny bedrooms, and from mine I could climb out of the window, cross the lawn and walk down to the beach and sea. I remember having mumps when quite young and having to be separated from the rest of the family. I had to sleep downstairs while everyone else was upstairs, and I will never forget that awful feeling of isolation: it was the first time I ever felt lonely, I suppose.

I was generally in good health during my childhood, although I did faint once during a church parade. We were all lined up, ready to march to the local church for a service that I didn't want to go to. I wasn't religious, although I had been confirmed, and all the family, although not over zealous, were regular churchgoers and went to communion. The officer in charge of the parade was a friend of mine: one of the only army officers I knew in those days. Just before being called to attention and marching off, I suddenly fell down in a dead faint and couldn't participate. I expect it was psychological ... or the work of Satan.

We had very little pocket money, and it wasn't just given out: we had to earn it by doing odd jobs. I used to mow the lawn or paint the railings or whatever, and my father would reward me. I remember having to save for a few months when I did want to ride and needed a new racing costume. Even in those days an outfit cost about 30s as they were made from silk. I remember roller skating along Weston seafront with my friends; none of us had much money, but we used to go into the fish and chip shop and get a bag of scrumpies, which were the scraps of leftover batter. We used to get four bags for 1d.

We prepared tea trays for the holidaymakers, and people would come from the beach across the road to the hotel and get a laden tea tray and carry it back to the beach. We had a little tent we used to erect at the end of the lawn next to the hotel's railings, and we would take quite a big deposit to make sure the customers brought everything back. A tray for a whole family would cost about 2s. We provided teapots and hot water, milk and sugar, cups and saucers and teaspoons – the lot. Food would be extra, of course! I used to love doing that with my brother Jack. It was my first experience of 'service'.

We were also very big on family teas. Our various nursemaids were usually teenagers from the mining valleys, and on one occasion we had a Welsh girl who had never ever seen sugar. When she was given her cup of tea and told to help herself to sugar, she put so much in the cup that it overflowed. We had to teach her how to use it. It's extraordinary when you look back at how simply most people lived in those days and how privileged some of us were. Sugar was a luxury for some people. Far too many people had very little food in those days, and it shames me to think that we were living so comfortably when there was so much poverty.

My sister Joan was a bit older than us and very much the organiser. When we were young we always used to put on some kind of entertainment for our parents. I remember one year, when Joan was about 16, she was directing us in our most ambitious production: an elaborate musical show, which included the song 'We'll All Go Riding on a Rainbow' from the film *Aunt Sally*, starring Cicely Courtneidge. The lyrics seemed to sum up our happy childhood:

Sing brothers, and sing sisters
We're all leaving today
And we'll all go riding on a rainbow
To a new land far away

Get started, be light hearted
There's no time for delay
And we'll all go riding on a rainbow
To a new land far away

Everyone playing in the sun
Without a worry or care
Children dancing through fields of daisies
With rose buds in their hair, ah-ah-ah

We made all our own costumes, and Joan choreographed the dance routine but became very annoyed when those of us in the chorus line messed up our steps. I remember her wielding a stick and letting us have it when we got things wrong. I think she thought she was Busby Berkeley. Despite her autocratic nature while in 'show business' mode, Joan was always agreeable and quite lovely. The pillar of the family, she later became an officer in the ATS and worked at their HQ in Nottingham, dishing out the pay.

In fact there was very little sibling rivalry of a serious nature, and I don't recall any dramatic scenes or fallings out, as we all got on very well together and respected each other. I think it was largely down to the most marvellous parenting and the fact that there was absolutely no favouritism. Di was the closest in age to me, and we used to go for long walks together. She was always … and still is … incredibly intelligent and sensible. Father used to say, 'Di's the one with the money – if you ever need to borrow £100, Diana will have it stashed somewhere.'

My father taught me how to swim at a very young age, and I used to go to the beach early every morning. I joined the Weston swimming club, which at that time was a noted institution and produced lots of champion swimmers. I spent a lot of time in the water from the age of 7, and I entered into the annual mile race in the sea when I was 10.

Knightstone was a little promontory that went out into the sea opposite the hotel, and we used to go on the rocks at the back and dive into the sea and pretend we were in trouble to people who were looking over the wall! Very naughty ... it was actually dangerous there, but we knew exactly what we were doing; huge waves used to crash us against the rocks, but we were always ready to regain our balance. Terrible, some of the things we used to do.

When I was at school, I had a lot of special training and wasn't allowed to participate in any other competitive sports in case the activity affected the muscles I used for swimming. I was Western Counties Champion, and I was in the initial trials for the 1936 Olympic Games but sadly didn't quite make the grade. I was second in a mile race to John Holt, who went on to represent Great Britain at swimming at the 1948 Summer Olympics in London.

I used to go all over England by train to various events with the sports master. My father was also always there to support me. Whenever I was about to dive in, at the start of all these events, I'd see him there on the side, cheering me on. And if we won a cup he used to fill it with champagne and pass it round to everyone in attendance. I have always loved swimming, but I finally had to give it up at the age of 93 when it became too much for me. It's heartbreaking when age prevents you from doing the things you have done all your life, but it's simply inevitable. Still, I try to be positive and live life as fully as I can. I am reminded of that quote of George Bernard Shaw: 'You don't stop laughing when you grow old, you grow old when you stop laughing.'

The world famous American diving champion Pete Desjardins, who won a number of gold and silver medals in the 1924 and 1928 Olympics, gave an exhibition of his diving skill at a swimming gala in the open-air pool in Weston. There followed competitive races in which I participated, and I actually won one of the races. Desjardins, who later went on to appear with Johnny Weissmuller (famous for the *Tarzan* films) in global swimming exhibitions, wasn't the only famous person present, because I was introduced to none other than Haile Selassie, the Emperor of Ethiopia, who presented me with my cup and shook my hand.

Haile Selassie is revered by the Rastafarian movement as the returned messiah and God incarnate. Many years later I was running an old people's home, and on my way to work I used to walk past a Rastafarian community. I happened to do this on the very day that Bob Marley had died. It was a very hot day in May, and there were about thirty dreadlocked Rastas outside their houses – clearly very upset and mourning the great reggae musician's death. I stopped and thought I'd go and tell them something that would cheer them up. So I approached them. They looked very surprised at this middle-aged white chap coming up the path, but I went up to the first man there, shook his hand and said, 'How do you do? My name is Bruce Copp, and I've come here to say how sorry I am about Bob Marley. But I must tell you that this very hand also shook hands with Haile Selassie.' They were amazed and incredibly excited. There was lots of whooping and hollering and much 'high fiving'. I was the toast of the day, and my street credibility rose sky high!

I was once left alone in the hotel with a nursemaid in charge while my parents had to go somewhere. Everyone else was out, and it was wintertime, so the hotel wasn't open to the public. I was in the kitchen, having decided I needed a snack. There was a bread machine, which you slid up and down against the loaf. My hand slipped, and I nearly cut off the top of my thumb. The young nursemaid put me on the bed and placed a bowl under my thumb so that blood would just run into it. She didn't do anything else. I suppose she thought she was doing the right thing, but I could have bled to death.

Luckily, Aunt Terry, one of my mother's sisters, who owned the Douglas Hotel on the other side of Weston, had gone out for a walk and decided to pop in. Terry found me in my bedroom, took one look at me – I was still bleeding – and shouted at the nursemaid, 'You stupid girl! You can't leave him like that!' She then struck her, and the poor girl went hurtling right across the room. Terry immediately bound up my thumb, called a taxi and took me to the hospital, where my wound was stitched. Terry was wonderful and rescued me that day, although she probably shouldn't have knocked the nursemaid for six.

Terry was married to Philip Grey, who came from a very good family, rather grand and rich, but he spent it all on various vices and was an alcoholic. He was the only man I've ever seen with the DTs – delirium tremens. I remember him sitting on the end of his bed, hallucinating, shaking and pale and calling out, 'Take them away. Take them away!' I don't know what he was imagining, but it was horrible to witness his desperate suffering. I've never been much of a drinker, and it's quite possible that experiencing this scene at a young age made a lasting impression on me.

Some years later Philip and Aunt Terry, who were very fond of each other, moved to Gloucestershire, a village called Frampton Cotterell in the heart of the countryside. They lived in the old converted Millhouse, which was lovely, and my cousin Lena stayed with them. Lena was born with a club foot and also had some sort of learning disability: she was what we used to describe as 'simple'. Lena always lived with one of the family but mainly with Terry, who she used to help with the housework. Early morning we used to pick mushrooms in a nearby field, which shone like snow with all the white-capped fungi. Lena would simmer them in fresh milk, and we would devour them for breakfast. Absolutely delicious.

The Greys' principal pastime most days was backing horses. Terry loved horse racing, and she used to be given wonderful tips from a friend of hers called Lord Glanely, a Welsh shipowner and thoroughbred race-horse owner and breeder. During the Spanish Civil War he supported the Republicans and helped open a home in Caerleon, South Wales, for fifty Basque child refugees.

I recall Terry being a very successful punter, thanks to these tips. She backed these horses regularly and won quite a lot of money. One day, Philip was sitting on the little wall of the mill, having had too many drinks in the local pub, and he fell over backwards into the stream, and being too inebriated to swim, he drowned. That was the demise of poor old Philip: the drink did get him in the end. Lord Glanely fared little better, as he was killed in 1942 in an air raid on Weston-super-Mare.

We used to spend every summer with my grandparents in Ilfracombe, and when we arrived at the station, we were collected by one of the Copps' silver buses. The seaside town was a lovely place to visit, and we took great pleasure in pottering about on the beach. The town crier used to announce the fishing boats bringing in the herring catch, and for 1s, the townspeople could fill a vessel to the top with herrings. They would drag the largest containers they could find to the harbour. I remember seeing dustbins being filled to the top with the fish. For those that were very poor, this was a lifesaver, and the herrings could be cured and last a whole winter.

We would also visit this wonderful old lady who made the most delicious treats for us. 'Cut Rounds' were a kind of scone that she baked. On top she would spread 'thunder and lightning' – a very Devonian tradition and term for huge amounts of homemade jam and clotted cream. Oh, it was scrumptious! She used to make the most wonderful lardy cake and other specialities I've never had since, which probably explains why I am mainly in good health!

Grandfather and Grandmother Copp lived in a lovely house called Moortown on the Barnstaple Road on the outskirts of Ilfracombe. Just beyond a bend in the road was a smallholding – a chicken farm that they owned. We had fresh eggs every day, and in the yard there were derelict traps and buses, in which we loved to play, from Grandpa's transport days. To add to the excitement we were also employed as rat killers. We used to wait for the rodents and bludgeon them with bricks. I think we were paid 6d for every dead rat! That was quite a lot of money in those days.

Grandpa planted a tree when each of his grandchildren was born, and mine was a copper beech. I've often wanted to go and have a look at it and see how large it's grown by now. Grandma Copp used to show us how to make Japanese gardens with old plates and mirrors, and when I was back in Weston she would send me newly picked primroses in the post.

We used to breakfast with Grandpa every day before he went to his office. The use of hot plates was quite common then, although you don't see them much now. This was a plate that had a well underneath it and a little nozzle on the side into which you could pour boiling water. I used to carry it on a clean napkin down to my Grandfather's office, as he had a hot lunch every day.

All the children and my grandparents would sit down to a proper Sunday lunch, which was always roast beef. Mrs Heddon, the house-keeper, used to do all the cooking. The meal was always quite delicious, with all the trimmings and beautifully served with silver service. I always remember there was a little silver trough on tiny feet, and on it was a scraper for putting the horseradish on to your meat. The horseradish had been prepared, the black part removed, and you just had to grate it on to your meat. That was the only way you ate horseradish in those days.

Grandfather Copp used to have to make speeches at various events and functions, and there was usually entertainment in which we, the grandchildren, would participate. It was at one of these events that my sister Joan and I won the Charleston competition. The Charleston was a popular dance at the time. I was about 7, and my sister was two years older than me. Grandpa was such a character, and I remember that Moortown had an upstairs balcony from which he used a pair of strong binoculars to watch the countryside. At least that was his story, as I later discovered it overlooked the local 'Lovers Lane' and he was actually observing courting couples!

Dear old Grandpa had been suffering from dementia for some years but was still physically in good health. One afternoon in 1935 he wan-dered out into the outskirts of the town for a walk. His bedtime was usually 5.30 p.m., but he didn't return after tea, and at 10.30 p.m. the alarm was raised. A search party, initiated by his son Harry, was unable to find him, and it wasn't until the following morning that his naked body was found in a field. He was 79 and had died from heart failure due to exposure. It was such a tragic end to such a wonderful and produc-tive life. Ilfracombe had been quite grand in the mid-1850s, but it had become a little faded, and Grandpa had spent much of his life wanting to put the town 'back on the first line of Devon resorts'. According to his obituary in the *Ilfracombe Chronicle*, he had 'ploughed a dignified but lonely furrow in urging progressive ideas'.

I had been furrowing my own field, but in a completely different way. As you will no doubt have gleaned by now from reading the blurb on the cover, I am gay. I have never been overly political or strident about it. I've never jumped up and down about it or made an issue of it. It's just the way I am and have always been. I was born gay, and it didn't take me long to realise that this was just a fact of my life.

My first homosexual experience occurred when I was just 7 years old. Another of mother's sisters, Auntie Maude, lived in Maida Vale, London, and married a man named Jones. Their son, Charlie Jones, was a traveller for Huntley & Palmers Biscuits, and he used to go all over the West Country. When he was in Weston he stayed in our hotel, usually in the winter. As incredible as it sounds now, he used to ask my mother and father if I could sleep in the same bed as him.

Believe it or not they agreed, and they would send me to bed before dear Charlie to warm up the bedclothes for him; they never thought there was anything strange about it. He never made a move, but I did. Even at that ridiculously early age, I was gay enough, or interested enough, for a sexual adventure. I went to bed hours before he did and used to pretend to be asleep when he came up to the bedroom and watch him undress. I wanted to see him naked, and when he got into bed I used to snuggle up to him and put my bum in his crotch and try and excite him. Unbelievable. I'm even shocking myself writing this. He wasn't gay, and he later married and had a number of children. It was the first time I was aware of the sexual thing, and it developed very quickly from that. I am convinced that people are definitely born gay, not 'persuaded or corrupted' as some ignorant people would have it. I knew at the age of 7 that I was homosexual.

My only sexual experience with a girl was actually with my cousin Dorothy, known as 'Tiny', who was Charlie's sister. Tiny contracted scarlet fever when she was a child and went deaf. She used to help out at the hotel. One day, when I was about 15, we were alone together and she suggested we went to bed together. I agreed, and she seduced me. It was the first time I had sex, and I didn't enjoy it very much, which wasn't just because she was a girl but because she was a virgin too, and the blood on the sheets mystified and alarmed me.

A few years later, I was befriended by an assistant in the local chemist's shop; he used to love taking me on his motorbike on the pillion. He used to take me all over the place. I was quite a pretty boy, and I'm sure he fancied me, but he never laid a hand on me. Years later when I thought about it, he definitely liked me in that way; he was a very nice man and kind to me but he never tried to get into my pants. Again, my parents never thought that this was odd you know. It sounds as if they were very naïve, and maybe they were in that way, but those were very different times.

When I was a teenager, a gay friend of mine used to write to me. He was very naughty and wrote all sorts of things in his regular correspondence – much of it with gay sexual references and homosexual gossip. Unfortunately, my father opened one of these letters by mistake, thinking it was for him, and he wanted to know what it was all about and the nature of the relationship, and he questioned me about some of the gay references. He didn't confront me or accuse me of being 'queer', but of course he knew about my sexuality. I think he quietly accepted who I was as long as I didn't disgrace myself or bring shame on the family. In fact, I think he might have been slightly bent himself, as he often admired beautiful young men and was a regular customer at the local Turkish baths!

I never discussed the fact that I was gay with my mother. She knew, of course, but it was never talked about with her or my siblings. My brother, Tom, told me that the fact I was gay only became apparent to him much later, by which time the climate had changed and my sexual orientation was of no great consequence. He said, 'I can't recall it being discussed among the family in any way other than as acceptable.'

Tom had polio as a child and was in hospital in Bath for four years. At that time, very little was known about polio, or infantile paralysis as it was then named. The recommended treatment was complete immobilisation to stop the paralysis spreading further (the complete opposite of current practice), and so poor Tom was clamped to an upholstered board and placed in an isolation ward as he was considered infectious. His fellow patients were almost all bone tuberculosis sufferers and were mainly from the slum areas of Bristol where TB was then rife. Our family weren't allowed to visit, and so his only communication was with these Bristolian and Bath residents with whom he conversed on a daily basis. It wasn't surprising that when he was finally discharged from hospital he had acquired the local accent and the 'Lingua Franca'.

I attended the local infant school. It was in a sweet little house in Weston, and the woman that ran it was called Miss Marigold, and her home was surrounded by beds of bright orange and yellow … marigolds! I've loved them all my life because of that particular connection and have always grown them. One of my earliest and worst memories at school was wetting myself. I had to take my trousers off and, as Miss Marigold didn't have a spare pair of trousers, she put me into a pair of girl's knickers. I remember feeling so terribly ashamed – even at no more than 4 years old. And before you jump to conclusions – no, this experience did not turn me into a cross dresser.

In 1926, after graduating from Miss Marigold's academy, I was put into a very ordinary school called St John's, which was about a mile from the hotel, along the seafront. I had to walk to school and would then return home for lunch before going back for the afternoon classes. I completed that mile walk four times a day in all weathers: in snow, rain and storms, and with sea spray blowing over me. No wonder we grew up strong and healthy. I can't imagine many kids doing that nowadays: most children of that age aren't allowed out alone.

My brother Jack wasn't very academic and had trouble with exams, so my family paid for him to have a tutor to come to the hotel, and the crammer turned out to be my favourite master, Mr Day, from St John's. He taught English, and I used to love him. He liked me too because I spoke rather better than most of the working class boys in the school, and he used to make me read my essays out to the school and recite in public. We called him Ginny Day for some reason.

I was sitting in the window of the hotel dining room when I saw him coming up the garden path for the first time. I knew that a teacher was coming to work with Jack, but I had no idea who it would be. And then I saw dear Ginny coming up the path looking rather sad and poor and with slightly frayed trouser ends. I thought, 'This isn't right: he shouldn't have to do this extra work to supplement his earnings after a long day teaching.' I was horrified, and I think it was the first socialist feeling that I experienced. The differences between rich and poor in those days were appalling; as far as I'm concerned, they still are.

The depression in the 1930s affected my brother Reginald to the extent that, like many others, his life might have turned out very differently. Before the war Reginald went to Australia as part of the Big Brother movement, which was a scheme whereby eminent Australian businessmen would sponsor well-educated and enthusiastic young men from Britain to emigrate down under. The young migrant, or 'Little Brother', would be provided with an adult person, the 'Big Brother', who would provide encouragement, advice and support during the émigré's early adjustment period in the new country. There was also the hope that the Big Brother movement would appeal to middle-class families and attract educated boys to Australia. The Big Brother would act as a mediator between the young person and his employer.

The Little Brother was intended to be 'a physically fit, upright, clean-cut, well-mannered British young man who was determined to work hard on the land'. Reg was allocated to work on a sheep farm and stayed with a very nice Aussie farmer and his family, but unfortunately the farmer experienced financial difficulties during the depression and the Big Brother organisation was unable to keep him in employment. In fact, during the 1930s, nearly 400 Little Brothers returned to Britain.

When Reg first returned, he couldn't find a job, despite being well educated, full of life and very handsome; this was frustrating for him as he never had any money to take girls out! Then, just before the war, Reg returned home after a couple of job interviews much more optimistic: 'I've got the chance of two jobs. Either a bus conductor or sweeping the floors at Woolworths.' He decided to take the Woolworths job and within three months had become assistant manager before being promoted to being one of the company's top executives.

Reg survived the war, despite being a rear gunner on a bomber, which was the most dangerous place to be. He returned to work for Woolworths and ended up in their London head office in the Marylebone Road, but sadly died in 1959 from a massive brain haemorrhage, resulting from very high blood pressure. Later, Woolworths took some responsibility for putting so much stress on their top executives and changed their employment practices.

I left St John's school at 14. I didn't want to continue my studying any more, and I suppose I was a little confused that while all my siblings had been afforded private education, I hadn't. My sisters were both educated privately, and my two brothers had attended Wellington school, but by the time it was my turn to attend school, my parents had run out of money to pay the large fees. I was the only one that went to a council school. I was a bit miffed about that but, according to my brother Tom, I ended up being the best educated of all my siblings!

The financial situation was, however, a reality, and the hotel went bust in 1938. The building was later demolished and replaced by a block of flats. I pleaded with my parents to let me go to work, and luckily they were sympathetic. I found employment at the United Bill Posters Company, which was located at the approach to Weston-super-Mare's railway station. The company was owned by a Mr Broomfield, who had once 'trod the boards', but was run very efficiently by an Irishman, Mr O'Connell. I was the office boy, making tea and undertaking menial administrative duties but also charged with keeping Mr Broomfield's office clean and tidy. In fact, he was quite insistent that it was kept in an immaculate condition, which I endeavoured to do.

Because of his theatrical leanings, Mr Broomfield kept a stack of *Theatre World* magazines, which featured play reviews and articles about the acting profession. Whenever the coast was clear and I had completed my duties, I would throw myself into the thespian world. On one occasion, I was engrossed in the magazine when Mr Broomfield came into his office. I jumped up feeling guilty and expecting to be admonished at my dereliction of duty. I started to apologise, but instead of ticking me off, Mr Broomfield said, 'I'm delighted that you're interested. Read them whenever you wish. Very good!' I was extremely lucky that Mr Broomfield was so kind, and I'm absolutely positive that it was here, while immersing myself in *Theatre World* and listening to Mr Broomfield's stories, that I developed my love of the theatre.

The posters were of an advertising nature and were put up by a group of about five men, who would collect them from a yard at the back of the offices and would then climb on bicycles, clutching pots of paste with which to hang the posters. They would cover the whole town and some of the county.

The work was very physical, and so the men were all pretty tough. One of them must have been gay, because he seemed to be very fond of me, and every time I used to go out into the backyard he would call me over and give me a great big hug. I remember feeling terribly thrilled by it. It was all so exciting that this great big, muscular, butch man wanted to cuddle me. I was in heaven. I was only 14 and, I have to admit, rather pretty. I must have appeared quite glamorous to him, although he never went further than a hug and a squeeze. In a way, I wish we had gone a little further, and if I'd been older I would certainly have made a pass at him!

I stayed at the company for three years and was still living in the hotel with the family, but soon an opportunity arose for me to leave the safe environs of Weston for a more adventurous existence. I was on my way to the town that Sir Arthur Conan Doyle described as 'that great cesspool into which all the loungers and idlers of the Empire are irresistibly drained'. And, no, I'm not referring to Shepton Mallet.

TWO

A MODERN BABYLON

'I can resist everything except temptation.'

Oscar Wilde

Towards the end of my schooldays at St John's I made friends with a boy called Roy Huxley. He came from a family rather like ours – 'bohemian' I suppose is the word. Actually, I hate that word – let's say both our families were 'unconventional'. I used to love going to his house. His parents were divorced, but Roy's father, a lovely musician, used to visit the family regularly. It always ended in tears: not because the father was difficult or temperamental but because his ex-wife invariably became furious with him for using the antimacassar to blow his nose. I was both horrified and amused.

The Huxleys had three stunning daughters, and one of them, Rita, was the celebrated beauty with whom my brother Reg fell in love. In fact, he left a packet of condoms on her bathroom shelf by mistake, and Rita found them. She was furious, and she came storming into the sitting room and said to me, 'I found these on the bathroom shelf, and they belong to your brother Reg. Just go and stuff them in his mouth!' I didn't know what she was talking about, and at the age of 14 I'd never seen condoms before. I didn't know what they were.

Roy Huxley had found employment with Cook & Sons (the merchants, not the travel agents). The company had a huge warehouse at the side of St Paul's Cathedral. He wrote to me and explained that a firm in the area called Hitchcock, Williams & Co. were looking for new staff and suggested that I apply. Although Roy wasn't gay, we were close friends, and he said he missed me and that I would love living in London. He suggested I write a letter to Hitchcock and Williams, which provided window dressing for departmental stores and shops in the West End. He advised me that finding lodgings would not be a problem, as the firm had their own hostel for employees.

My parents weren't at all surprised at my decision to leave home. My siblings had all left the Copp nest, and it was expected that I would follow suit. In fact, they encouraged me to move on and weren't the type of parents to worry about what might happen to me in London. I always had unconditional love and support from my parents.

The history of Hitchcock, Williams & Co. was fascinating in that it was a well-established firm of drapers in the city of London's Cheapside. Before the West End became the centre of fashionable department stores, Cheapside was the most well known of London's shopping streets. The original owner was George Hitchcock, a devout Christian who had become involved with some of the more radical movements of the time, including the Early Closing Association, the Ragged School Union and the anti-slavery campaign.

George Williams, who hailed from Bridgwater in Somerset, joined the firm as a buyer and subsequently married into the Hitchcock family. Like his father-in-law, he was also a Christian radical, and on his arrival in London he was horrified by the terrible working conditions and decided to do something about it. He organised a number of his fellow drapers together with the objective of 'the improvement of the spiritual condition of the young men engaged in houses of business, by the formation of Bible classes, family and social prayer meetings, mutual improvement societies, or any other spiritual agency'.

In 1844 this group became known as the Young Men's Christian Association (YMCA) and is now an organisation active throughout the world. Williams later took over the firm, and by 1900 he had established Hitchcock, Williams & Co. as a hugely successful international business.

He was knighted by Queen Victoria in 1894, died in 1905 and is buried in St Paul's Cathedral – in close proximity to where Hitchcock, Williams & Co. thrived.

Within a few weeks of my letter of application, and after a brief interview, I was offered a job and digs. The firm were wholesale suppliers to shops for all kinds of things, and each floor of the building sold different goods. I went to work as a packer on the 'Flowers and Feathers' floor. Well, let's face it, where else would they put me? Our section sold decorations for shop windows. I later graduated to the sales department and met lots of the customers that came to the firm to select window dressings for their outlets.

In those years I was still known by my given name, George, but when I started work I was told by my foreman that they already had two employees named George and it would be too confusing to have another one in the department. I was asked if I had another name, and so I replied, rather proudly, 'I've got three. I'm George Charles Bruce.' It was decided they would call me Bruce, and so from then on I became 'Bruce'. My entire new set of friends and acquaintances got to know me as Bruce, and the name gradually caught on; now everybody, even my siblings, calls me Bruce.

Thus began a love affair with London that was to last nearly fifty years. I arrived soon after the coronation of George VI, which had taken place in May 1937. It was a shame I missed all the excitement and bunting. I do like bunting. The capital city already had a population of over 9 million and was continuing to increase in numbers as the city spread creating new suburbs. People complain about too much traffic congestion and the discomfort and frustration of public transport, but even during those days London was terribly congested. Roads, constructed for use by hansom cabs and sedan chairs, were already clogged with traffic and struggling to cope with cars and buses. Commuters and visitors alike were packed like sardines on the underground and on buses.

London's theatre was thriving; it had survived the worldwide depression, initiated by the 1929 Wall Street Crash in New York, the arrival of 'talkies' (talking films), the BBC's radio broadcasts of live theatre on the radio and, by 1936, the first television broadcasts in the London area. Sadler's Wells actually reopened, and John Gielgud, Laurence Olivier, Ralph Richardson, Alec Guinness and Peggy Ashcroft, who I absolutely adored, were all making their mark on the London stage while shows by Ivor Novello and Noël Coward lit up the city. In fact, I went to see my first Coward show during this period. It was a musical called *Operette* at His Majesty's Theatre. I loved it, but the production wasn't a success and only ran for a few months; however, it did feature that lovely number 'The Stately Homes of England', which, of course, made mention of a 'Lord Camp'.

I loved living in London in those days and used to walk to most places so that I could see the sights properly and soak up the atmosphere. Being a mere provincial it was so exciting to be part of this extraordinary metropolis, which Benjamin Disraeli described as 'a modern Babylon'. Although, imagine my disappointment when I discovered that Big Ben was a clock ...

I would walk right up from the City, down Ludgate Hill and up Fleet Street and along the Strand to Trafalgar Square and into Covent Garden. I loved travelling by shank's pony and enjoyed the solitary nature of that mode of transport, although I took in everything I saw. Along the way I would pass The Savoy Hotel, and I would always turn in there because you look down through a fan light into The Savoy Hotel kitchens. It was fascinating to watch the chefs preparing the food and cooking. But if you looked very closely, just behind the cooking ranges, on a sill or a ledge, there lurked a seething mass of cockroaches. I know that this isn't unusual in kitchens, but I had never seen anything like it before. I thought, 'Here is one of the best known and smartest hotels in the world, and it is absolutely heaving with cockroaches.'

As Roy had said, Hitchcock, Williams & Co. did provide accommodation in a nice hostel, very close to St Paul's and right behind the Old Bailey in Paternoster Row. I could actually see the Scales of Justice from my window. There were two or three of us sharing a room, and we used to go across from there to the main building where the canteen was situated. We used to have all our meals there, and quite good they were too. We had to be there by a certain time or we weren't given any-thing to eat, and so I remember running down there in the mornings for breakfast. The hostel was run by a matron, a trained nurse, who was called Miss Dingle, and if you were ill there was a small ward for the sick boys that she attended.

We had discovered that Miss Dingle used to go through our belong-ings when we were at work. I don't know whether she was looking for some kind of contraband or if she was just being nosy. Anyway, I didn't take kindly to this and so produced a series of notes and leaflets with pointed messages for her such as 'Fuck off Dingle', and we put them under our socks and underwear in our chests of drawers. I hope she found them, although nothing was ever said.

All my companions were roughly the same age as me – between 17 and 20 – and we had a ball there. Two of the hostel's residents were brothers, who were – how should I describe it? – very obliging. There was thus inevitably something of what we might now call 'a gay scene' at the firm. George Williams had three sons who all worked for Hitchcock Williams, and on his death they took over the running of the company. One of them, also named George, was openly gay and often used to take out the most handsome male staff to lunch at expensive restau-rants, which caused not only some amusement but also a little jealousy. The Dean of St Paul's Cathedral also used to invite some of the chaps for lunch. I think he was homosexual, although he never made any advances. Perhaps he was just being kind …

I shared a room with a young man called Henry Parkinson. He was also gay, but we didn't have an affair. He was Cornish, and every week his mother used to post him a huge Cornish pasty. Although we never shared a bed, we did share his pasty, which was enormous, and there was plenty for both of us. It was the most delicious pasty I have ever tasted, and at the risk of repeating myself, I've never tasted one like it since. It was one of the highlights of our week!

Eventually Henry Parkinson left the hostel. He was a little older than me, and when you reached the age of 20 then you could, if you wanted to, go out and get your own digs. It was all so wonderfully paternalistic in those days. Henry found a place in Penywern Road, Earls Court. I was still living in the hostel, but I used to spend my days with Henry when we weren't working. He had a very good record player, and I had built up a little record collection, which I kept at his digs along with some other possessions. I never got around to collecting all of my belongings, and when the house was bombed during the war, some of my stuff was destroyed, including my record collection. Funnily enough, the house was only one of about three places destroyed in the locale.

I managed to keep up my swimming habit despite living in the city. The firm arranged a competitive mile race in the Thames at Richmond, in which I participated, and because George Williams had also founded the YMCA, every young man in the company was given a free membership to the organisation. The YMCA had a wonderful hostel and facilities in Great Russell Street in Bloomsbury, and so I used to go there frequently. They had a lovely swimming pool there, and I used to take part in all the galas and races. I was just 17, with practically no money, and if I didn't have the fare I could walk there from the City as it wasn't that far. I met a little chap called Billy Jay at the YMCA; he was a screaming queen, but not a lover.

Soon after we made friends, Billy asked if I was interested in the ballet. I told him that I had never actually seen a proper production, and so he obtained tickets for us to go to the Russian Ballet at Covent Garden. I have never forgotten the first time I went. It was the most marvellous experience and turned me on for life to classical dance. The company was then undoubtedly the greatest in the world. It was a wonderland to me.

Billy and I used to attend regularly. We used to get up early in the morning, walk over to the Royal Opera House and book a stool. Yes, a stool! In those days the stage doorman would let you have one for 6d, and in the evening the little wooden stools would be put out outside the door to the gallery in the order that they had been reserved so you didn't have to wait for hours in the queue. Billy and I always managed to procure the first two stools right at the front, and we would sit on them until the gallery was opened, at which point we would then dash up the stairs to claim our seats. Of course, being young, we could leap up the stairway, and we always got the front row of the upper circle, which is actually one of the best places to watch ballets – better than the dress circle.

One of my first firm friends that I made in London was Rupert Mansell Woodhouse. He actually lived in Brighton and worked at the Royal Pavilion. The Royal Pavilion, which was built towards the end of the eighteenth century as a seaside retreat for George, the Prince Regent, later to be George IV, is a remarkably ornate building. Its exterior appearance is Indianesque, and during the First World War it was utilised as a hospital for Indian soldiers. There are some wonderful photographs of resplendent, ornate and chandeliered rooms housing Sikhs, Muslims and Hindus convalescing in rows of hospital beds.

Anyway, Queen Mary, George VI's mother, used to go to the Brighton exhibition, which Rupert organised. He designed it in Regency style, but in order to make it appear as 'authentic' as possible, he and his staff had to put reproductions in certain places where the antiques were missing, and they used to recreate it as it was. Queen Mary would go around with her parasol, and every time she came across a replica antique, she'd point her parasol at the offending artefact and state in a voluminous voice, 'That's a fake. There's another. That's not right.' She knew the fakes from the genuine ones just by looking at them. Anything she fancied she used to admire so loudly that the antique dealers would give it to her.

I had always felt very strongly about the Spanish Civil War; it had really affected me because of the German involvement that began days after fighting broke out in July 1936. The Nazis supported the Nationalists, and they sent in powerful air and armoured units to assist Franco's forces. In fact, they used the war to test their latest technology as well as provide combat experience for their armed forces. German operations included targets by air, and the bombing of Guernica in April 1937 was responsible for the death of nearly 300 civilians. I was so outraged by this barbaric act that, when I was 17, I applied to join the International Brigade to fight against Fascism. Unfortunately – or perhaps, in hindsight, fortunately – I was told I was too young to enlist. If I remember correctly, recruits had to be aged 18.

As an alternative, someone suggested I join the police force as an 'auxiliary', a sort of volunteer. Looking back I can't see the connection, but in any case there was a young copper who trod the local beat, and so I thought I would ask his advice. I approached him one evening and asked him a few questions about what it would entail. His suggestion was that I join him 'walking the beat', and we wandered around the city at night. He advised me against joining, 'I shouldn't bother if I were you. I find it very boring.'

We chatted for a while and eventually found ourselves in a shop doorway. It soon became rather obvious there was a mutual physical attraction, and ... well ... one thing led to 'the other'. We could, of course, have been in big trouble if we'd been discovered out in the open, if you'll pardon the pun, but I knew at least he was unlikely to arrest me! The city was deserted at night, and the only people around were caretakers or janitors. It was exciting, but funnily enough the sexual encounter also felt safe. We continued our illicit liaison for a little while, but I decided that although the police force had some attractions, it wasn't for me!

By the summer of 1939, we were all very conscious of the storm clouds gathering over Europe. My particular friends were intelligent and aware of the political upheavals. However, we were still teenagers, and at that age one doesn't dwell on worst possible scenarios. The younger employees couldn't imagine what lay ahead. I suppose we were more optimistic and perhaps naïve. It was the more mature workers, who had experienced some of the horrors of the war twenty-five years earlier, that were affected by Germany's incursions into Czechoslovakia and Poland and more aware of the meaning of yet another war.

It thus wasn't actually much of a surprise to us when war with Germany was declared at 11.15 a.m. on that Sunday morning of 3 September 1939, as there'd been talk of conflict for some time. On the day that war broke out, unlike in comedian Robb Wilton's wonderful monologue, I wasn't bound for the Home Guard. I was actually on a train bound for Bristol Temple Meads and surrounded by pregnant women.

Hitchcock & Williams had closed the previous week and had dismissed all their employees. I collected my belongings from the hostel and bid farewell to my friends. I knew I would be called up at some stage, and until then there was only one place to go and that was the family home. My parents had sold the hotel in Weston and had now moved just up the coast to Clevedon. I had spoken to my father, who told me that all the family would be congregating there as soon as they could. Mother wanted us all to be together because the pre-war uncertainty and then subsequent declaration of war had brought back her memories of losing family members in the First World War. The thought of going through it all again with her children was horrifying. Although she seemed to be very calm and collected, I know she was terribly upset about what lay ahead.

It was, however, difficult for me to leave London immediately because the authorities were already using all the trains to evacuate women and children. I therefore volunteered to help escort the evacuees out of the city and ended up at Paddington station, where an official put me in charge of a group of six pregnant ladies who were being evacuated to Bristol. At 19 I was 'in charge'. Ridiculous when you think back. The women were all cockneys, and one of them was about to drop anytime. In fact, halfway to Bristol she went into labour prematurely and we had to get her off the train and into the nearest building.

Luckily someone found a local midwife, and I hovered about and handed things to people, but the poor woman gave birth in the waiting room. Once the baby had been delivered safely, the rest of us continued our journey. When we arrived in Bristol the women all piled out and were directed to their various evacuation billets, and I caught the bus to Clevedon.

I was the last one to arrive at the new flat, overlooking the sea, where my parents now resided. All the family were ensconced and chattering away to each other. It was lovely to see them all. They had already eaten, and there was a rather pretty girl serving my lunch. Everyone was chattering away apart from this young woman, who never said a word to me. I had no idea who she was and no one had introduced me. I thought she was a maid or somebody my mother had employed. Anyway she was very sweet and looked after me, and it wasn't until later that I discovered that she was a Welshwoman called Joan who turned out to be my brother Jack's fiancée.

Jack wanted to be an architect, but he could never pass the exams and so became a draughtsman. He never had much money, but he was always incredibly generous. Jack and Joan later moved to a council house in Bristol and had three children. Poor Jack died quite young, at the age of 47, from a quite rare blood disease, possibly a form of leukaemia.

Anyway, I spent the first few months of the war in Clevedon, awaiting call up. All the rest of the family returned to their own homes and occupations while I stayed with my parents. The town was close to Weston, and so I was able to see lots of my friends. I used to cycle for miles around the Somerset villages and developed an interest in churches – for architectural interest rather than spiritual reasons.

One thing I do remember during this time is how anxious my mother was. I'm sure I tried to reassure her and tell her that everything would be fine. I don't remember feeling apprehensive or fearful.

I should have been.

THREE

KISS ME GOODNIGHT, SERGEANT MAJOR

'I am sure that if the mothers of various nations could meet, there would be no more wars.'

E.M. Forster

I was called up in February 1940 and stationed in the county town of Taunton with the Somerset Light Infantry. Even at that stage, it was all a bit of an adventure, and I held no fear. I had no idea what to expect, but true to form, one of my first memories of army life involved food. I had gone into breakfast on my second day and sat down at one of the great long enamel-top tables when a hugely obese ATS (Auxiliary Territorial Service) girl came out of the kitchen with an apron full of hard-boiled eggs. She stood at the top of the table and threw the eggs at us, and we had to catch them as they flew past. I pouched mine, cracked it open, but the shell contained a half-formed, tiny bird. It was an absolutely vile sight, and I rushed out on to the parade ground outside where I threw up. I don't throw up easily, but it was really horrible.

I knuckled down to the rules and regulations pretty quickly and initially coped very well with my new life in the army. There were a few ridiculous conventions, but most of them made sense, and I soon realised that it was the only way the army could run. I was a bit of a goody-goody actually and never disobeyed orders. Being gay, I had to be extra careful not to rock the boat or draw attention to myself. I had always been very good in social situations, and although this wasn't exactly like an extended cocktail party, I made sure that I was friendly, sociable and one of the boys. I was very good at mixing but obviously couldn't be as open as the other men. I had to keep very quiet about my sexuality.

Training was pretty tedious, and the general drills mainly consisted of route marches and singing songs like 'Roll Out the Barrel', 'Run Rabbit Run' and 'South of the Border (Down Mexico Way)'. Another tune I remember was 'My Love is for a Soldier Boy Who Sailed Away Across the Sea'. Of course it's meant to be sung by a woman, but I have to say a number of the boys were happy to join in! Later on, in my Intelligence section, the seven of us used to belt out 'The International'. Surprisingly, the subaltern in charge seemed quite happy for us to croon the Communist hymn, and that was even before the Russians joined in.

Bayonet practice was quite disgusting. We had to plunge the blade into a sack full of straw, which was hanging from some kind of a clothes line. We were supposed to scream at great volume and look very aggressive. Perhaps the top brass thought that our foes would be so terrified by the screaming they would drop their weapons and run. I never did stick it in the sack properly and hoped that I would never have to.

We had one middle-aged man who shouldn't have been with us, and his posting must have been some sort of clerical error. I recall him bayoneting the sack with suitable aggression and one of our typically upper-class officers calling out, 'Well done that man with the bald head.' I still think it's hilarious after all these years and remember his phrase as if it was yesterday. The 'bald man' was soon sent elsewhere when they discovered how old he was.

In June 1940, while still training, I was one of 100 Somerset Light Infantry lads that were sent to Scotland to join the West Kents. The 6th Battalion of the West Kents had been decimated in France and lost so many men that their numbers had to be increased by drafting soldiers from other outfits. We were thus pooled with 100 or so survivors and evacuees of Dunkirk, who were put on a train and taken all the way from Maidstone to Northumberland. It was typical of the army to move them the whole length of the country!

There were about fifty of us Somerset boys, and the train was packed full. At every stop local women would arrive with goodies for the Dunkirk evacuees. Everyone was leaning out of the train windows to receive all these lovely things that they had brought, which included homemade cakes, biscuits and even some omelettes! Of course, we were all greeted like heroes because the women didn't know that not everyone on the train had been rescued from Dunkirk. We were all soldiers together, although I have to say we had yet to see any action and so we were in better spirits and our uniforms were much cleaner!

For security reasons the Somerset contingent hadn't been told our destination, and at that time all the road and railway signs had been removed to confuse the enemy if they did ever invade. When we did finally disembark, we had no idea where we were. On the platform, when we were lining up, I asked a passing elderly porter about our whereabouts. He replied, 'Aaaaark.' I said, 'Pardon?' and he repeated, 'Aaaark!' It was unintelligible – he sounded as if he was doing an impression of a seagull. It turned out he was telling us we were in Wark, a town in Northumberland, which was situated was on the banks of the River Tweed just across the border from Scotland.

The march to the camp was hilarious. The Somerset Light Infantry were renowned for being the quickest marching soldiers in the British Army, whereas the 6th West Kents were supposed to be the slowest of marchers! Well, after you have been training for several weeks at a fast pace and then suddenly have to march slower, it's total chaos; men were striding along the country lanes at different speeds. We must have looked like something out of *Dad's Army*.

The camp was high up on the hill, and on a clear spring day we could see Newcastle from the top. It was at Wark that I first met a man who was to be a close friend and play a huge part in my life for nearly seventy years. Ronald Benge had been called up about the same time as me and was serving with the Royal West Kent Regiment. Ron's upbringing had been very interesting. He was born in Fulham, but his father, Charlie, a colonel's batman during the First World War, was a valet to the Astor family at their pile in Kent, where his mother was the cook. Ronald thus spent half his childhood in south-west London and the other half in Kent. He attended the noted Judd grammar school, Tonbridge, before being employed at the Tunbridge Wells library, and he later joined the Peace Pledge Union, whose members work for a world without war and promote peaceful and non-violent solutions to conflict.

Ron turned out to be a very brave soldier and was later decorated for his actions, but was never seduced by the idea of being a hero. He maintained his socialist ideals throughout after the war and was an avowed anti-Nazi. One of the things that he wrote in his autobiography, *Confessions of a Lapsed Librarian*, still resonates: 'As an ex pacifist I was impressed to find that nobody hated the war more than the soldiers.' My experience of men in the services was the same, and the fact that so many of them are reluctant to talk about their wartime experiences is all too common.

The day after our arrival at the camp, we assembled, waiting for them to decide what to do with us. The orderly room sergeant, the man who was in charge of the administrative side of the company, asked if anyone who had any 'knowledge of typewriting' would volunteer for special duty. I wasn't very good at typing but thought it might be a bit more interesting than the square-bashing and menial duties I had previously been subjected to. In fact, it turned out to be quite traumatic.

I was dispatched immediately to the orderly room and directed to a huge pile of mail and parcels, which almost reached the ceiling. The sergeant addressed me: 'These packages are the belongings of the West Kents who have been killed in action in France. They also contain letters from their families. I want you to go through each one and return the parcels and letters to the families with a suitable letter of condolence.' I must have looked a bit bewildered because he continued, 'There are four different types of response letters and you have to choose the most appropriate one for each family depending on what has happened to their loved one. The CO will sign them.'

And that's what I did for weeks: sorting out the correspondence and packages – some of which had been sent by relatives to the dead or missing men but never received. I opened them up and discovered the full address and names of the family and enclosed a sympathetic letter in the package, which I then posted to the poor relatives. Although I hadn't gone anywhere near any fighting, I was already witnessing the tragedy of war and the terrible effect on families.

After Wark, the battalion was joined by other men so that the West Kents were now at full strength. We were then transferred to Haverfordwest in south-west Wales, where I was again consigned to work in the orderly room, although this time my duties were more mundane and not nearly as heartbreaking as my previous posting.

Ron and I were now fast friends, and we had some fun in likening the local population with the frenzied creatures of *Cold Comfort Farm*, Stella Gibbons' minor classic. Ron later wrote, 'We identified the quivering brethren at public prayer and Effie the fey heroine wandering in water meadows, watched over by Big Basness the bull. In fact most of the ladies there were not at all fey and although cautious, were most lascivious.' I wouldn't know …

During this time an invasion of Britain was considered very likely, although the German plan, Operation Sea Lion, never got beyond its initial gathering of forces. Following Dunkirk, there was a huge scale military and civilian mobilisation and over 1 million men were enrolled as part-time soldiers in the Home Guard. On 15 December 1940, *The New York Times* ran a story claiming that tens of thousands of German troops had been 'consumed by fire' in two failed invasion attempts. It was reported that Winston Churchill gave orders for gallons of petrol to be poured on the English Channel and then set alight, causing an inferno in which the German troops perished. The invasion force supposedly got halfway across the Channel; in fact, there has never been any evidence of such an attack, although there is at least one eyewitness account of burned bodies being dragged out of the sea.

By the beginning of 1941 I was now in Malvern, Worcestershire, and we were on high alert in case of invasion. In the early hours of one morning I recall a number of drunken officers leaving the mess – most of them absolutely pissed – when sirens went off, causing us to think the German offensive had started. One of the more inebriated officers climbed on top of what he thought was his motorbike, and when it failed to start, he became very angry in his attempts to get it going. There was a huge commotion followed by loud animal noises, and he fell off; it turned out he had been trying to kick-start a sheep.

We spent a few months in the Malvern Hills, which was very pleasant at times, and I enjoyed being in the lovely rolling countryside. We were able to play records in the drill hall and enjoyed musical soirées. This somewhat idyllic slice of service life was, however, sometimes disturbed by a somewhat temperamental Irish sergeant, who took his responsibilities very seriously and was keen on drilling us to exhaustion. He was completely eccentric in his methods of instilling military discipline. In fact, he once, for no apparent reason, stuck his penis into Ron's ear. I think it was a done for a bit of a lark, but Ron was much exercised about the insertion and hit the sergeant with a chair.

One day I was on my way to the mess, which was a bit of a distance from the orderly room. Malvern was a lovely town, and I was walking down the road past these grand houses with large grounds. I looked over a gate, and there was an elderly man putting things into a wheelbarrow and sort of doddering around in the garden. I recognised him. It was George Arliss, the famous actor, who in those days was quite a star and had appeared in a number of films both in the UK and in Hollywood.

He approached me and I said, 'You're George Arliss, aren't you?' He nodded but replied, 'Please don't make it known to everybody. I live here quietly and don't want a fuss. But I do have a lot of magazines about films, not only the trade magazines but all sorts. Do you think the men would like them?' I told Mr Arliss that they would love them. He also told me that he had far too many apples in his garden for his own use and so proposed, 'You come here with a couple of chaps any time today and take fill these two wheelbarrows – one for magazines and I'll fill the other one with apples.' We did just that, and I must say I was quite popular with the boys after this chance meeting.

In 1941 the well-known pianist Moura Lympany came to a concert hall in Malvern to entertain the troops – at least the ones that would appreciate classical music. I think it was put on by Entertainment National Service Association's 'good music section'. The concert hall was full to bursting, but it was bitterly cold, and of course in those days there was no heating or anything of that kind. Everybody was huddled up in their overcoats and scarves, and Moura Lympany, then in her 20s, came on stage wearing an off-the-shoulder dress. She sat at the piano, and she had an assistant who brought her a hot-water bottle, which Miss Lympany put on her lap, and every so often she would warm her hands on the hot-water bottle. In her later years she gained a reputation for being very difficult, but I have to say she was a bloody good pianist, and it was a great treat for everybody and one that, despite the conditions, lifted the spirits.

Sir Edward Elgar was born nearby and walked in the Malvern Hills, and one of the pieces he composed (to my mind, one of the best pieces of music that has ever been written) was the Violin Concerto in B minor, Op. 61. There was quite a well-known viola player who lived in Malvern, and I used to sit on the steps at the bottom of his house listening to him practicing. He came out one day, and I talked to him, and he was so pleased that I knew about the great composer's work. He told me that Elgar had given him a transcription of the violin concerto for viola that he was now learning to play.

While stationed in Worcestershire I was taken ill with acute tonsillitis and admitted to a military hospital, part of which had been converted from an old asylum. I could look out of the window and see some of the patients, then referred to as 'lunatics', walking around the paddock grounds. Some of them were very ill and behaved bizarrely. It wasn't the most conducive place to convalesce from illness.

It was while I was recovering from illness that something happened that was to have a traumatic effect on me. I foolishly made a pass at one of the other patients. The young man had actually encouraged my interest; however, as soon as I had made my move, he told some of his friends, who then confronted me on the ward. They cornered me, called me 'a fucking queer', 'a pervert' and 'Nancy boy' before kicking and punching me.

Homophobia was very common then, but it was the first time that I had been attacked for being gay, and I was shocked. On the whole, homosexuals were accepted without much comment except for some ribbing, which on occasions could be unkind but was mainly affectionate, and even then it was only the obviously 'effeminate' types of homosexuals who were noticed at all. There was a feeling that we were all in it together, and as long as gay men did their bit and didn't let their fellow soldiers down, their sexual orientation was irrelevant. During my time in the army I was naturally constantly in the company of attractive young men, but after that incident I never took a chance or made a pass at someone who I wasn't sure would reciprocate. I had misjudged the situation, but I would never say that I had brought in on myself. There was no excuse for their violent behaviour. I was very careful after that and luckily was never beaten up again for being gay.

I had several trips home on leave while serving in the West Kents, but there was one visit that was particularly sad. I was in Weston with a group of friends, including a swimming pal of mine who had actually been selected for the 1936 Olympic Games in Berlin. It was suggested that we go and have a look at a new motorbike that one of them, Harry English, had just purchased. Harry was the son of the local baker, and I knew him and his family very well because we used to get our bread and cakes from them.

For some reason – and to this day I don't know why – I didn't want to join them and went off to do something else. Anyway they all walked up to Grove Park, which was about ¼ mile away. Almost immediately an air-raid siren sounded. They were out in the open outside the Pavilion and studying the motorbike when they were blown to bits by a direct hit from a German bomber. I remember Harry English's mother, totally hysterical, screaming and running around. She lost her mind as well as her son and never ever recovered from this tragedy. This was my first lucky escape, of which there were to be a few during the course of the war.

Weston wasn't actually the safest of spots, as the town was on the return route of bombers returning from raids on Bristol and suffered from attacks by the Luftwaffe for the first few years of the war. The first bombs fell in June 1940, but the worst attacks were in January 1941 and June 1942, causing extensive damage. At the beginning of 1941 nearly 20,000 incendiary bombs were dropped on Weston. I've already mentioned Lord Glanely, Aunt Terry's racing chum, who was killed with members of his family. They had moved from London and taken this great big house in Weston, which was hit by a bomb just two weeks after they had left the war-torn capital.

One night, while visiting my parents in Clevedon and during a particular heavy air raid on Bristol, we were listening to a Chopin nocturne. My mother seemed somewhat unsettled and asked me, 'Do you think it's the right thing to do? Listening to Chopin during an air raid?' 'On the contrary,' I replied, 'I think we should turn it up and try and drown out these explosions.'

It's so interesting to think that she was more concerned with doing 'the right thing' than the dangers of the bombs dropping around us. As soon as war broke out my mother used to fill flour bags with sand, which in those days were made of cloth. I can still picture her in a nightgown trying to extinguish flames by throwing the bags on the flames during a huge air raid.

During the Blitz, Queen Mary was evacuated from London to Badminton House in Gloucestershire, where her niece, the Duchess of Beaufort, resided. She was apparently reluctant to leave London, and there are lovely stories of her being accompanied by over fifty servants and even more pieces of luggage. While in the West Country, in order to support the war effort, she visited troops and factories and became involved with schemes to gather scrap materials.

While driving around, she and her driver used to pick up hitchhiking soldiers; in later years they were often American GIs who had no idea who she was, and when they were dropped off at their destination, she would give them a little medal that had been made specially and was inscribed with something like, 'You have travelled in this car with Queen Mary'. I'd love to have seen their faces when they discovered they had been in the company of English royalty.

One day her car broke down in a country lane near Weston. The chauffeur was tinkering with the engine, and some friends of mine were having a picnic nearby. Unlike the GIs, they recognised Queen Mary and offered their help, and one of the party said to her husband, 'Go and ask if the queen would like a cup of tea.' So he walked up to the chauffeur and asked the man, 'Would you ask the queen if she'd like a cup of tea?' The chauffeur immediately relayed the offer to Queen Mary, who replied, 'Is it China or Indian?' My friend didn't know and so traipsed back to the picnic, where he asked his wife, 'Queen Mary would like to know, is it Indian or China?' She replied tartly, 'You should know it's Indian. We only ever drink Indian.' So he went back to the chauffeur and gave him the news. The chauffeur duly advised the queen of the derivation of the tea leaves, 'It's Indian, Ma'am.' Her reply was a rather regal, 'Well in that case, I'd rather not then. Thank you.' Lovely! I know that she had a reputation of being rather austere, but I've never thought of her response as being snobbish, it was just that she never drank Indian tea. I think she was a dear old girl, really.

The choice of infusions wasn't so much of a dichotomy while living in Nissen huts in Pollokshaws, Glasgow, where I recall some very weak tea and inedible meat pies while enduring a bitterly cold winter. Training in Scotland was quite gruelling. I was in the Intelligence Section, consisting of sergeant, five men and a subaltern, and we were doing what the army described as 'a scheme', which involved a mountainside exercise. Our job was to man an outpost as if on the battlefield. When the real thing came along, my Intelligence Section would be sent to a viewpoint where we would observe the enemy and pinpoint their machine guns, estimate manpower and obtain any other information that was important.

It was freezing cold and although snowing slightly when we started, the weather deteriorated and the snow started to fall much more heavily. I had been allotted to a grand house, which the army had more or less commandeered, where I was to have telephone communication.

I was greeted by a lovely lady, who told me she was a descendant of Edvard Grieg, one of my favourite composers. He had, apparently, once owned this house and composed quite a lot of his work there in Scotland. I was immediately interested, and she was amazed that this ordinary English private had some knowledge of classical music. We had a lovely conversation, and she produced a big tray of sandwiches and cakes, and we sat there chatting for ages. My duties that day were not too onerous: all I had to do was sit there and answer the phone when it rang. I think it rang once! As I was so interested in Grieg, she took me into the music room and showed me the piano, which she told me was left just as it was before he died and with the very music he had been playing shortly before his death. It was wonderful. Unfortunately, it was also nonsense, as I have since discovered that this was all either whimsical or a big mistake. Grieg died in 1907, and though he did indeed have Scottish ancestry, he never lived in Scotland and only ever spent a few nights in Edinburgh.

While I was still basking in the memories of Edvard Grieg, the telephone rang again and I was informed that I should stop my telephone duty and rejoin the unit. I said goodbye to this delightful lady, mounted my bicycle and started wheeling my way into the snow, which was very heavy by then, and the visibility was poor. Inevitably, I got lost and I couldn't find my way back to the unit. It was dark by now, and a blizzard had created deep drifts. I couldn't ride the bicycle and had to push it along the road. I had no idea where I was, and the terrain was absolutely deserted: there was no one to find me or help. I became really quite frightened, and I thought, 'I'm going to die up here.' Then, fortunately, in the distance, I saw this little gleam of light and made my way towards it. The light came from a remote farmhouse, which I eventually reached and where the residents took me in and telephoned my unit.

Meanwhile, search parties had been sent out with soldiers, police and volunteers looking for me. I could have easily died of exposure if I hadn't spotted this little light, but I survived to tell the tale. It was another close call.

While I was in Glasgow, I was sent on an army Intelligence course in Edinburgh. I'd never been to the city before and stayed in some very pleasant civilian lodgings. I used to attend a lecture place every day.

It was like a sort of holiday in a way because I enjoyed the talks and walking around Edinburgh, which is a wonderful city. You see, the army can be really very agreeable in some ways, especially if you happened to be in an Intelligence section.

However, any pleasant times in Edinburgh were soon forgotten when we found ourselves in some tough and serious training with British and American commandos: there was time spent at a camp in the grounds of Inveraray Castle, home of the Duke of Argyll, and we were then posted to the Crieff Hydro in Perthshire. The Americans, bless their hearts, were lovely to be with, and we were only too delighted to have them on our side.

The training to support the commandos demanded the use of live ammunition, and so our drills suddenly became very much more serious and challenging. We hiked through soggy and muddy bogs, and laden down with our kit, any progress was exhausting. We then found ourselves at sea in combined operations, participating in beach landings that seemed to go on for weeks. We mounted confused and mock 'attacks' on the Hebridean islands of Harris and Rùm and Egg in landing craft. And these exercises turned out to be dangerous. We had been training for too long and were getting exhausted, and the navy had become a little lax in their navigations and preparations. We were sometimes directed to the wrong beaches and expected to wade ashore in shallow water that turned out to be not shallow at all, causing mayhem and with near tragic consequences.

We didn't know where or when, but it was clear that a real invasion was imminent and, wherever it was to take place, we were to be in the firing line.

FOUR

AN ACCIDENTAL HERO

What passing-bells for these who die as cattle?
Only the monstrous anger of the guns.
Only the stuttering rifles' rapid rattle
Can patter out their hasty orisons.
No mockeries now for them; no prayers nor bells,
Nor any voice of mourning save the choirs, –
The shrill, demented choirs of wailing shells;
And bugles calling for them from sad shires.
What candles may be held to speed them all?
Not in the hands of boys, but in their eyes
Shall shine the holy glimmers of goodbyes.

'Anthem for Doomed Youth', Wilfred Owen

There had been an intention for the Allies to invade northern France in 1942, but instead it was decided to land in North Africa where the Vichy Government had been installed. The countries of Algeria, Tunisia and Morocco were the initial targets, with the subsequent plan to attack the Germans and Italians in the Western Desert and consequently open up the Mediterranean to Allied shipping.

Operation Torch was the first time that the British and Americans had worked jointly on an invasion plan, and the Supreme Commander of this invasion was General Dwight D. Eisenhower. Initially, the Americans couldn't understand why Winston Churchill wanted to focus on North Africa, but he wanted to clear all the Axis troops out of that region and then sweep through Italy. And so on 26 October 1942 I found myself aboard the Dutch passenger liner the *Marnix van St Aldegonde*, sailing from Gourock, a Scottish seaside town and slipway to the Clyde, on our way to North Africa.

The hundreds of hammocks that we slept in were crammed together with no space between us. To get through from one end of the cabin you had to force them apart. It was incredibly claustrophobic in the bowels of the ship, and there was also the worry of being attacked by German submarines. I saw one ship, in the distance, that had been hit by a U-boat.

Although it was forbidden, Ronald Benge and I would clamber out of our hammocks most nights and go up on deck. It was just so awful down there with the noise, the heat and everybody farting. We found a way up that was unseen by the sentries and would lean on the rail and gaze at the sea with the wind whipping around us. One night, we heard a cry of 'Help! Help!' coming from somewhere in the waves below. We looked down and saw someone clinging on to a raft or a large piece of driftwood. I remember Ronald, who had a wicked sense of humour, remarking, 'I hope he's got some figs.' We'd been given figs on board ship as part of our diet and were told that they sustained life. We heard the strains of the poor man calling out as he disappeared into the blackness. We never knew who he was or what happened to him. I hope somebody picked him up, although it was unlikely. Poor soul. It was horrible, and we were helpless to do anything about it.

Of course we didn't just have to rely on figs for our nourishment. There was other sustenance to be had; at mealtimes fourteen men would sit to a table and one of us had to go down to the galley and collect the food. So many of the boys were seasick and couldn't possibly eat a proper meal. I was lucky in that I was a good sailor and didn't miss my grub once! I remember they served tripe once and there were very few takers, so I really stuffed myself that day.

Our particular convoy consisted of fifty-two ships protected by thirty warships, but we were just part of a huge fleet, which was made up of nearly 700 ships and 70,000 troops, coasting through the mountainous ocean waves. The coast of Algeria was our destination. Algeria was then a French colony, and there were over 100,000 French and French colonial troops under Pétain's Vichy Government, supported by 500 aircraft and a large Naval fleet at Toulon, which because of its firepower posed a great menace to the invasion force. Fortunately, the French Vichy troops defected and an attempt by the Germans to commandeer the French fleet was foiled when it scuttled itself rather than be taken. Other threats included the Italian fleet, although it suffered from low morale and a lack of fuel. Most of the danger to the Allies came from the Luftwaffe.

There were to be three landings divided into three task forces: western – a US force sailing direct from Virginia to Casablanca in French Morocco; central – an American force from the Clyde to Oran in Algeria; and eastern, which I was part of – a joint British and US force to Algiers. The British general in command was Harold Alexander, but the Task Force was led by Lieutenant General Kenneth Anderson and consisted of the US 34th Infantry Division, two brigades of the British 78th Infantry Division, and British and American commando units. I was attached to an American commando unit.

Initially I was given the job of sitting up on the bridge with a radio. I listened to Winston Churchill's wonderfully inspiring speech on my earphones as some of the assault boats sped to the shoreline. Then it was my turn, and I climbed into one of the landing craft. We were naturally all frightened at what lay ahead and how much fire we would have to face when we landed, but had experienced so many years of training that we knew exactly what we had to do. The tough commando regime had made us capable of doing almost anything. It was only afterwards that I thought about it.

However, it so terrified one poor chap that he lost his nerve and jumped overboard before we hit the beach. We were carrying 90lb of equipment on our backs, and of course he sank like a stone and drowned. It was horrifying, but there was nothing anyone could do. It turned out that he needn't have died so unnecessarily, because our part of the beach was unopposed and, to our relief, there was no enemy to face. In the dim light we thought what we saw were corpses on the sand, but they turned out to be soldiers grabbing some sleep.

We were lucky, because in other landings our boys were being mown down left and right. It was a piece of the good luck that was to follow me throughout the war. In fact, we only got as far as the beaches. The Germans had scarpered because there was so many of us, and after marching around for a short while, the decision was taken to attempt another landing further along the coast. We didn't return to the *Marnix*, as it couldn't come close to the shore, and so we were taken back by boat to a destroyer, which zigzagged for a while as we prepared ourselves for another assault.

The second landing was at a place called Bougie. We had been advised that there would be stiff opposition there and what one of the officers referred to as 'an unfriendly reception'. We came ashore at dawn and, yet again, were unopposed. For the week while at Bougie we helped unload equipment and supplies from ships in Bougie Harbour but came under attack from the Luftwaffe and the Italian Air Force. We had no air cover from the RAF, which was short of fuel and ammunition.

We were warned that the third landing would be different and that we 'were going were going where the action was'. But there was no resistance from the Germans or the Vichy French forces. I was in luck again. It seemed yet again that nobody wanted to shoot me and that I was immune from danger. Perhaps I should have told all the West Kents, and they could have all been right behind. Everywhere I went I would have had hundreds of men following me ... in other circumstances I would have been quite happy with that arrangement.

This time, we didn't re-embark but remained on land and were ensconced in a fort just outside a town called Philippeville (now known as Skikda). The liner we had travelled from Scotland on, the *Marnix*, had sailed up, and we could see it from the fort. There were four trained

Alsatian dogs, which had remained on board; apparently they dived off the liner and swam ashore, which was a journey of about a mile or more. They must have sensed that we were there.

A single plane came over from the island of Pantelleria, which was an island in the Strait of Sicily and which housed an Italian airbase. These 'spotters' were always the prelude to a raid. The Italians used to send these spy planes out, and when they saw something worth attacking they would report it to the Germans, who would then bomb the targets. The Stuka dive-bombers had screamers on the wings and made a noise like a police car does in the street: a terrible sound, which used to frighten you to death. We used to dig little holes and take cover in them, although these trenches actually offered little protection.

The townspeople of Philippeville had greeted us with great warmth when we first landed. They lined the streets, gave us presents and dates and figs and were cheering our arrival. It was wonderful, and we felt we had achieved something, although my part, to say the least, had been minimal up until now. My friend Derek Nottidge, a signaller and radio operator in my Intelligence unit, and I were sent to a fort up on the hill; it was an observation post that the Germans had previously been using, so it had been marvellously built in solid concrete. We couldn't have been safer, but the same could not be said for the poor residents of the town, who suffered heavy casualties when the German air raids began soon after. We watched this town being plastered with bombs, and the *Marnix* was also hit two or three times, causing irreparable damage. The huge liner sank, and all of our trucks and transport went down with the ship. We had to remain in Philippeville for a few days while some transport was sorted out and came under pretty constant bombing and strafing from the air and shelling on the ground.

One day I was alone in a slit trench, and we'd been having a bit of shelling, which was really quite nasty, but we were now experiencing a quiet period. Suddenly, a young soldier appeared from nowhere, and I asked him, 'What are you doing? Where are you meant to be going?' He replied, 'I've been told to report here. I'm a reinforcement.' 'On your own?' I asked, 'A single reinforcement?' 'Yes, I just came over on a boat,.

and I was ordered to come up here. I don't know why.' It all seemed a bit odd, but that's the sort of thing that happened on the front line. Anyway, I told him to get in the trench until we decided what he should do.

A couple of minutes later Derek Nottidge turned up. As we worked together, he shared the trench with me, so this boy had to get out. I said, 'Look there's another trench over there. Get in there, and after a while I'll take you to battalion headquarters.' So the boy did as I suggested. We suddenly had to take cover as we came under attack from enemy shelling. When it subsided I looked over to the trench where I had directed the boy. It had received a direct hit, and he was dead. Was it my fault? What should I have done? He'd only just arrived and hadn't done anything wrong. He was just another innocent victim, and I thought, 'I don't even know his name.' I hadn't even asked him his name.

Two days later Derek and I were dug in another slit trench. We were supposed to be maintaining radio silence, but instead of shutting his down, Derek started fiddling with the channels and tuned in to a civilian station, which we weren't allowed to do. He then told me that they were going to broadcast Beethoven's *Emperor Concerto* (Piano Concerto No. 5). It was a favourite of ours, and when we were on long dreary route marches we used to sing or whistle it together and try and remember all the different parts. Derek gave me another pair of earphones, and we sat together and listened to *The Emperor* from beginning to end.

Soon after the end of the broadcast, we were suddenly under an explosive attack, with shells exploding everywhere. Derek called over to me, 'Bloody hell the battery has run out!' We were near to the store, so he said he'd go and get another battery. I told him not to go, but he replied, 'I've got to. We can't have radio silence in the middle of an attack!'

Derek made a dash for the store, but he had only just got out of the trench when an anti-personnel shell burst right over his head. He was blown to pieces right in front of me. I sat there too shocked and distraught to move. If we hadn't listened to the *Emperor Concerto*, the battery wouldn't have run out and he would still be alive. This still haunts me, and I could never listen to the piece until long after the war ended.

About ten years ago I met and became friends with a woman in Spain called Una; she loved music. She told me she had two tickets for a concert in Barcelona, a piano recital, and asked if I would like to accompany her. I happily agreed but discovered, to my horror, that the opening piece on the programme was Beethoven's *Emperor Concerto*. I turned to Una and said, 'I'm sorry, but I don't think I can stay here for this.' She looked extremely discommoded and asked, 'Why on earth not?' So I told her the story, and having heard my tale, she said, 'Come on. It's time you faced up to it. I'll help you through it.'

I listened to it all the way to the end without breaking down. I suppose, in a way, it was therapeutic. Dear old, lovely Nottidge. Of course, I had felt guilty for years to a certain extent, but we were both responsible; we should never have used a civilian channel: it was strictly forbidden. If only Derek had kept a spare battery with him.

From Philippeville the plan was to force the Germans out while advancing along the coast in the direction of Tunis. We were supposed to be motorised, but we had no transport and had to commandeer trucks and coaches from the locals. There was no petrol, so the vehicles had to be fuelled by charcoal burners behind the driver's cabin. Don't ask me how that worked. I'm no mechanic. All I can remember is that progress was slow, the burners smoked a lot and the flames gave us away to enemy planes.

I remember acting as lookout when our coach was travelling. We had to have one person on the roof to keep a watch for enemy aircraft, and on one occasion, when I was on duty, I saw an Italian spotter plane near a bridge we were about to cross. We stopped and set up our anti-air-craft equipment all around as we knew this was the prelude of an attack on the bridge. Sure enough, Stukas appeared, and we took cover in a gulley by the side. They attempted to bomb the target and dive bomb us, but they didn't destroy the bridge because somehow we were able to shoo them off. Sometimes we were machine gunned by low-flying Stukas, and I remember Ron saying that the only way to stop himself shaking with fear was to fire weapons in the air in the vague direction of the planes. It was futile, but it made him feel better.

Some of the boys weren't as lucky as us. We used to bury people in temporary shallow plots on the side of the road so they could be picked up later by army officials and taken to a proper military grave. We buried them with any identification and with their helmets. We couldn't do anything else. It was grotesque. There was something terribly poignant about one boy we buried, which I recall very vividly. The book of matches that was supplied in our ration boxes had a 'V FOR VICTORY' cover. The front had a large 'V' on it and this young soldier had torn out the 'V' and had placed it carefully under the net of his helmet. We buried him just like that – with the 'V' right next to his head. He would never witness the victory.

It was the town of Sedjenane that had become of strategic importance, and two battles were fought in 1943 resulting in territorial stalemate for the following several months. Slow progress consisted of advances to positions that the enemy had sensibly abandoned and vice versa. By February of that year, the British General Harold Alexander was in charge of the Allied land forces in North Africa under the 18th Army Group, which reported to General Eisenhower, who served as Supreme Allied Commander in the Mediterranean. Until the combative General Patton was appointed by Eisenhower, Alexander was critical of our inexperienced American Allies and their fighting methods. They had failed to hold the Kasserine Pass and had lost 200 tanks. This was a common criticism; I loved the Americans as people but they were not as well trained as us and were, at times, quite hopeless. They weren't as fit and strong as we were and seemed to tire much quicker than our boys.

On a couple of occasions, the Americans actually fired at us twice. They got their range wrong and shelled us instead of the enemy further away. They also used to drop bombs in the wrong places. They were a very incompetent army, and to this day I can't understand why because it is such a wonderfully efficient country in other ways. Of course later on they found their fighting feet, and in Europe they were wonderful. Without them we really wouldn't have won the war.

The GIs also hated their food and claimed they were still eating bully beef from the First World War! I know most people in the army disliked their grub, but ours wasn't so terrible, and the supplies section, which was always in a safe place in a tunnel or somewhere sheltered, was always within a 2- or 3-mile walk. Every day one of us would be assigned to collect a box of food with rations for fourteen men. We got to know the codes on the boxes and so used to be able to choose Irish stew or steak and kidney pie instead of bully beef. The box was quite heavy as it contained food, water, Camel cigarettes, matches and lavatory paper – everything you could possibly need for one day.

It wasn't until January 1943, a couple of months after our landings, that we actually encountered German resistance on the ground. The Germans 'Ox Head' offensive was an attempt to outflank us in Sedjenane and on the high ground with an attack on the mountainous coastal band to the north. These hills were known as 'Green Hill', 'Baldy' and 'Sugarloaf' and had to be taken to allow us to keep moving on. We came under fire from a few tanks and took up positions near a place called Mateur for a battle.

There were regular skirmishes, and by now we had some protection from the Stukas in the skies from Allied air support and also from tanks, although they weren't very effective on the steep slopes. Shells were going over our heads, but mortar explosives were far more frightening. A sudden 'whoosh' overhead could be immediately followed by a direct hit, and that was curtains for you.

Ronald Benge recalled:

We advanced up the hills with more enthusiasm than our Scottish rehearsals. One of our young officers led the way blowing his hunting horn. He was never seen again and when full daylight came, we discovered that our objectives were far away and we were sitting on the open hillside in full view of the enemy machine-gunners opposite.

Ronald had a near miss when a fusillade of bullets shattered his rifle. We were pinned down, and we sent coded messages to the effect that we were serving no useful purpose maintaining our position and needed to retreat. In return we received this extraordinary command, 'Gentlemen, shall we join the ladies?' We took this as a 'yes' and scarpered down the hill as quickly as we could.

But we knew that Green Hill had to be taken eventually, and the full-scale attack began at midnight. We swept up the hill into the chaotic darkness, lit frequently by flares, tracer bullets and burning grass. The cacophony of warfare is beyond belief: the noise was deafening as shells exploded and machine guns crackled, all underpinned by the barking of orders and warnings and the wailing and groaning of the wounded. We were pinned down by enemy fire; the fighting had become confused. The battle went on for forty-eight hours, and for all the death and destruction, no progress had been made.

I simply couldn't take it any more.

We are supposed to be civilised human beings. How could this – firing guns at each other and blowing people up – be right? It was a complete puzzle to me. I just didn't want to be part of this inhumane slaughter. It didn't feel like I was having a breakdown or being cowardly, I just didn't want to be implicated in this brutality any more. I'll die very nicely and I'll get it all over with. It was just as simple as that.

I stood up, leaving my cover and just walked towards the enemy fire, almost hypnotised by the light of the tracer bullets that were fizzing in my direction. There may have been warning cries and shouts of disbelief from my comrades, but I never heard them. I walked slowly, but with intent, for what seemed like miles but was, in fact, only about 50 yards. I can't remember bracing myself for the impact of a bullet hitting me, but I must have done.

Even though I must have been a sitting duck, not one bullet found their target. I walked on unscathed until I heard the agonised cries for help of a wounded man. His name was Macdonald. He was in terrible shape and blood was pouring from his side. I couldn't leave him like that. Helping him was more important than my own destructive urge. I hurried to Macdonald, leaned over him and stuffed dressings into his wound and gave him words of encouragement. Here I was trying to be positive to this poor soldier while only seconds ago I had given up all hope and had tried to kill myself.

As I was tending to him, the cry for the retreat came. It was ordered by Major Fearnley-Whittingstall, who I knew quite well and who, incidentally, I think may be related to the eponymous television chef Hugh. Anyway, the top brass had decided that this bloody attack, which had been going on for two days and two nights, wasn't going to be successful and we were to return down the hill.

I climbed down to another gulley to safety, where stretcher-bearers were already carrying the wounded, and I called their attention to Macdonald. I saw him being carried away. He was still conscious and waved at me. I later discovered that they had taken him to a military hospital on the coast. The hospital, although clearly marked, was later bombed and Macdonald was killed. After all that. So unfair. Awful. Apparently the Germans sent a message, apologising for bombing that hospital and stating that the pilot and crew responsible had been severely dealt with. That didn't do poor old Macdonald much good.

I had survived three landings, been strafed, dive bombed and seen friends and comrades blown to pieces. I had buried boys younger than me and hadn't been touched. I had attempted suicide, and even then I had somehow miraculously survived. I was only 23 and had already seen so much death and tragedy. It seemed to me that whatever happened I was going to survive the war. I never thought of trying to kill myself again.

The extraordinary irony was that they decorated me after this incident, and I was mentioned in despatches (I was also mentioned again later in another action). I received the single bronze oak leaf emblem, given for both merit and bravery, which I then used to wear on my battle dress. I was actually nominated to receive the military medal, but apparently the number they could give out in each battle was rationed.

My CO told me how brave I'd been and said I had been commended for courage in walking through fire to help a wounded man. I tried to tell him it was ridiculous as I was trying to commit suicide at the time! He looked aghast and said, 'Don't talk nonsense Copp!' I told him that I really wasn't talking nonsense. It was the truth. I'd really wanted to put an end to it all. It was all so terrible I couldn't take any more. He didn't believe me but agreed when I said, 'It was pretty awful wasn't it?' He nodded and replied, 'Yes it was. You're quite right.'

I was supposed to be a hero, and yet the only person I ever came close to killing was myself. I couldn't bear the thought of killing anyone and always aimed to miss. I never thought about it. It was purely instinctive. The hill was later taken in another counter attack, but it was disastrous in terms of the many casualties, and we later discovered that only one third of our unit had reached the top of the hill.

I had survived but for what? More of the same. Somehow I found the mental strength to carry on. There was actually no alternative. Maybe I would be lucky again. And I was ...

It was dusk, and I was on an advance lookout, positioned in a slit trench to spy out a German machine gun nest and reporting back prior to an attack by our battalion. I was with the sergeant. He was called Bill, and he'd been a cartoonist in civilian life. A few minutes previously, our command-ing officer had allowed two visiting top brass officers to come and see the lookout posts. These officers insisted on talking to us, and it made me very nervous as the Germans were very close and these stupid idiots would give our position away. I pleaded with them to go, which they did eventually.

But it was too late. They had exposed our hiding place. Up on the ridge, we suddenly saw a German carrying something heavy, and we realised it was a mortar. I thought, 'They've seen us.' And soon after they were shelling us with mortars. The explosions were getting closer and closer, and one of the shells burst on the side of our trench and covered us with earth and debris. I wasn't hurt, but Bill suffered a slight wound. That one had been so close; we were convinced that the next mortar bomb would kill us. We didn't know what to do – breaking cover would have been dangerous, but if we remained in the trench we would be sitting ducks. While we were paralysed with fear and blind panic, another shell should have been fired. But it wasn't. And still several minutes later there was no further shelling. The Germans had run out of ammunition.

We now had to run the risk of getting out of there before they restocked. Bill decided to try and make his way back to HQ, but I decided on something else. There was a little hut about 100 yards away, which probably belonged to a local farmer. I thought I would try and get there – it might afford some safety. It was getting dark by now, and I managed to crawl over the distance to the little wooden building. By the time I got inside I was totally exhausted. I hadn't slept for two nights, and I went straight to sleep in the middle of some rubbish. When I woke up I was covered with lice.

The next morning Bill returned with some of the chaps and took me back to HQ. I was feeling really ill by then. I had a terribly sore throat, and it was decided I should see the medical officer, who was holed up in a railway tunnel a mile further back. I went on my own and could barely walk; how I got there I don't know. I practically crawled there on my hands and knees. There was a steep incline down to the tunnel, and in trying to gain a foothold over the edge, I slipped and went head over heels, falling to the bottom of the incline at high speed. No bones broken, but I certainly saw stars! I was brought to my senses by a sentry, who aimed his gun at me and barked out, 'Halt! Who goes there?' I could barely speak, and I didn't know the password, which was changed every day. I grunted, 'Black Velvet.' The sentry paused and remarked, 'That was yesterday's, but I suppose it will do.' And he let me through.

I was placed on a stretcher, and the MO examined me. He saw the lice and announced I had all the symptoms of typhus. I was kept on the stretcher at the end of the railway tunnel and isolated from the others. It was freezing cold, and I was there for a long time before eventually being taken in an ambulance to the hospital by the docks. The dockside hospital, in which poor Macdonald had been killed, had been rendered inoperative by the bombing and had now been replaced by a field hospital.

And that's where I now found myself, although my stretcher was put down on the side of the road, and I remained there for a night and a day before they found me a bed in a tent. Wherever I looked there were dozens and dozens of men on stretchers. There were just two surgeons operating for twenty-four hours and taking each surgical procedure in turn. Each doctor would stagger out of the operating tent, absolutely exhausted, and lie down on the ground until it was his turn to go in and operate.

There was a wonderfully camp male nurse in charge. He was completely over the top, extravagantly gay and he would have definitely been a drag queen in civilian life. I think we called him 'Fanny' or 'Gladys' or something like that. He was responsible for about fifty wounded or sick soldiers – twenty-five on each side of the tent. He looked after us all, tending to us, bringing us food and providing so much care. He was quite wonderful, and everybody adored him – even though he was so camp. He made no secret of being homosexual, but the boys all accepted him because he was such a marvellous nurse. When I needed to go to the toilet, I simply couldn't use a pan. I told him I needed to go to the latrine, which was about 100 yards away across the field. It was dangerous as there was always the risk of aircraft coming over and machine-gunning us.

He'd put his arm round my shoulder and I'd put mine over his and he'd say, 'Come on darling, run as fast as those gorgeous pins will go!' And then we'd hurry across to the latrines! There were times when the German aircraft would spray the tent with machine-gun fire, and we would put on our helmets and hide under our beds. The ones that couldn't move out of bed would just lie there and pray they wouldn't be hit. The Germans were appalling. Having bombed that hospital and killed all those people, they now strafed the tent, which was clearly marked with Red Cross insignia.

In fact I didn't have typhus. It was simply that my old throat infection had flared up again. When they got rid of the lice and I felt better I was able to help this queen in the ward for a while before I was discharged. I'll never forget him. He was wonderful.

While I was still recuperating, Ronald, who had previously been promoted in the field to an NCO (non-commissioned officer), was awarded the Military Medal at Djebel Bou Diss in Tunisia. (In 1944 he was awarded the Military Cross at Monte Cassino while still serving with the 5th Buffs.) The decisive battle of Longstop Hill took place in April 1943 when the enemy surrendered opening the road to Tunis, which was recaptured by the Allies the following month. Over 230,000 Axis soldiers surrendered, and it was at this point that General Eisenhower began to plan the invasion of Sicily.

Following my recovery, instead of being sent back to the battalion, I was stationed in Algiers, where I was informed that I was to be posted to Italy for officer training. I really didn't know why they thought I was suitable for such a promotion, but at the same time I was proud of myself.

It was in Algiers that I actually saw Marlene Dietrich perform at the city's opera house. She wore a uniform that she had designed herself; it was much more glamorous than the usual USO (United Service Organizations) outfits, although I remember her shoes were standard issue. God she was wonderful. Before the war, Marlene had been approached by representatives of the Nazi Party and offered lucrative contracts to return to Germany and become an iconic entertainer for their regime. Being staunchly anti-Nazi, she refused and became an American citizen in 1939, becoming one of the first stars to raise money for the Allied war effort. She worked tirelessly, performing a multitude of concerts for the USO on the front lines. Little did I know that our paths would cross again after the war.

I remained in Algiers for some time, and I did have some fun. You could get anything you wanted in Algiers. Marvellous place. I was nearly 24, which, let's face it, is an age when sex is very important. It was also all very casual. If anybody was gay or bisexual they tried to hide it, unless you could really trust your comrades or wanted to use your sexuality as a way of being drummed out the army. And of course they weren't all gay. I was once stationed in a camp full of commandos near Algiers. They were the toughest men in the army, but we were sleeping in pup tents, which housed two soldiers each. Well, every tent was heaving about and bursting at the seams, and you could hear everything that was going on.

Ron later wrote that 'our battalion (The Buffs) was taken over by a fifth column of homosexuals – a higher percentage than average. They were good soldiers and devoted to their comrades. One was either a good fellow or not and prejudices disappeared and gays were accepted without reservation.'

I'm not sure about 'a fifth column' – I think that that might have been a slight exaggeration – but it's true that the Buffs were famous for having more than their fair share of gay men. Our company commander, a courageous man and much admired by those under him (sorry, I really didn't mean that, but you know what I mean), was very open about his homosexuality, and once he inspected us on horseback while wearing a lot of slap! In fact, I don't think he joined the army so that he could see the world; he was so conceited that he actually signed up so the world could see him!

Occasionally when we afforded some time away from the front line, a basic officers' mess would be created, and Ron recalled that 'some of the batmen, who were transformed into temporary waiters, wore make-up and were given appropriate names like "Nellie" or "Lucy" and would flounce in with vermouth in enamel mugs'.

While patrolling the hill villages we had to make contact with Moroccan soldiers, 'Goums', who had been drafted to fight all over North Africa. They were incredibly brave, stealthy and ruthless fighters and were much feared. I was told they were paid a bonus based on the numbers of enemy ears they could deliver. They were also meant to be very good at sex, although I never partook. We were, of course, lectured about not having sex with 'the natives'. The art critic Brian Sewell, who did his national service some years after me, was advised, 'If you must have it, take your best mate round the back of the barracks and bugger him.' He also kept a condom in his wallet in case anyone asked him if he was 'queer'.

The top brass were always concerned about fraternising with the natives, firstly for security reasons – in case you might reveal some secret information, presumably in a moment of uncontrollable passion – but also the dangers of contracting a sexually transmitted disease.

From Algiers I was sent to Naples for officer training. Well, I was actually in a village called Paolisi, which is about 35km north-east of Naples. During the winter of 1943 I went to Ischia for a weekend, but while we were sunning ourselves there was an outbreak of typhus on the mainland, and we were all given an extra fortnight on the island. The epidemic had gone unchecked since the Germans had departed from the occupied city following a 'scorched earth' policy in which they had destroyed buildings, water and sewer systems. Much of the population sought refuge in bomb shelters, which was a perfect breeding ground for typhus among the louse-infested occupants.

Ischia is a lovely little place. There are hot springs everywhere and you can actually take eggs down to the beach, bury them in the sand and boil them. I loved it there. I had a gaggle of American friends, and we all used to strip off and go swimming. I went out in a boat in Ischia and dived in the water – about half a mile out to sea – and suddenly I was surrounded by black fins. I thought they were sharks, so I swam like Johnny Weissmuller, and when I got back to the boat the others were all laughing because they were dolphins – a whole school of them!

There was a little hotel reserved for sergeants, and the young waitress fell for me. Every time I came down for breakfast I'd open my napkin and inside she'd placed a small rose. I didn't like to let her know that I was unobtainable! When we did receive the okay to return to the mainland, we parted very lovingly, and I kissed her on both cheeks and hugged her. She was a lovely girl and would have made someone a lovely wife. But obviously with me she was barking up the wrong tree.

When we returned to Naples, conditions had steadily deteriorated, and in the first week of January 1944, the mortality rate from typhus rose to 700 cases. The cemetery was up a long hill going out of the city, and all the way – about 1½ miles – were hearses, nose to tail, transporting the bodies to the cemetery.

It was here that I made very good friends with John Buckmaster, who was also on officer training and with whom I shared a billet. He was put in charge of battalion entertainment, and I would help him out sometimes.

The famous San Carlo Opera House, which had been damaged but miraculously survived the Allied bombing, reopened in the previous November thanks to ENSA and, in the main, to an English lieutenant, Peter Francis, who was influential in making the building fit for use. On Boxing Day 1943 the first opera, *La bohème*, was produced, and the San Carlo was to see another thirty opera productions and many orchestral performances in the next two years. Naples had become a centre for rest and recuperation, so, to cope with the numbers, there were often two performances a day.

John and I were keen to attend a matinee performance of *Madame Butterfly* and so one day found ourselves standing in a queue to purchase our tickets. There were actually two queues: our queue was reserved for the military and the other was for civilians, who the opera house allowed 100 tickets. In this other line was this beautiful girl. John couldn't take his eyes off her, and I said, 'Why don't you go and talk to her?' John replied, 'Oh no. I couldn't possibly, but perhaps if she gets a seat she might be near us.' In fact, she didn't get a ticket: all the civilian tickets had been sold. This lovely girl was about to leave when I told John he must go and talk to her. He summoned up his courage, shot across and asked her very politely to wait. John went to the manager of the opera house and explained that he really wanted this girl to come in with him. Would it be possible for her, although a civilian, to join us? The manager took one look at her, could see why John was so enraptured and, being Italian, he readily agreed. The girl's name was Gilda Maltese, and she was delighted. Gilda sat with us and was the only girl in the stalls surrounded by hundreds of soldiers.

This was the first full-scale operatic production I'd ever seen in an opera house, and I found the whole experience absolutely breathtaking. John and Gilda were equally knocked out. When we came out Gilda was so grateful that John had got her a ticket and was also rather taken with him, so she asked us if we would come to her house and meet her mother. She was concerned that if anyone had seen her be picked up and taken to the opera by two strange English soldiers, her mother would kill her. Of course, I think this was all a ruse to get to know John better!

Gilda's mother, a widow with two daughters, was an absolute darling. And we met Gilda's sister, who later married an English officer. I always remember it was the first time I saw pasta being made. Gilda's mother showed us around the house and took me into the kitchen where, hanging from a laundry line, were a number of pasta strips.

It transpired that Gilda was a classically trained pianist, and she used to play on the radio once a week. Later we went to see her perform, and she was marvellous. But that day we didn't know her: she was just a young woman on her own, who wanted to see an opera and who struck up an immediate rapport with my friend John. Oh and by the way, reader, he married her. John and Gilda came to live in London after the war and resided in Earl's Court.

On 18 March 1944, John and I went into Naples to procure some records from the army entertainment bureau, after which we popped into the warrant officer's canteen in one of the main streets. While we were lunching, there was an inexplicably thunderous roar, the windows rattled and the entire building shook. Everyone rushed out into the street to see what was happening. It was an incredible sight. Vesuvius had erupted.

We could see some smoke pouring from the cone-shaped mountain that dominated the plain about 5 miles from Naples. The roars became more regular and there was pandemonium all around. The volcano continued to thunder throughout the rest of the day, and after dark the peak was blazing with molten lava being thrown high in the sky and cascading down the sides of the mountain. Huge flames were shooting miles into the air, and the countryside was illuminated by the intensity of the fire.

The following day, people were leaving their homes as a tsunami of coals threatened to destroy everything in its path. I went with a group of people to help with the evacuation of some of the villages, whose residents were under threat. We moved them and their belongings as well as some of their furniture. We were near a church, and the lava was moving very slowly. I watched some nuns kneeling in the road in front of the burning rocks, praying for it to stop. Unsurprisingly, their prayers didn't seem to work. Some of the molten rocks would break off from the magma and burst into flames shooting 50ft up into the air.

The lava continued to flow steadily for the next few days, and the villages of San Sebastiano and Creaola disappeared under a 30ft wall of lava. Plumes of purple smoke were now billowing from Vesuvius, and the whole top of the volcano exploded, shooting ash 3 miles into the air. Cinders and ash were raining down and fell as far as Ischia and Capri. Traffic came to a halt, and everything had a coat of black soot. People were utilising any kind of protection to cover their heads; I saw loads of women holding saucepans over their heads to keep the cinders from hitting them.

The eruption, which was the worst for 200 years, lasted for nearly two weeks. Thousands were made homeless and villages were destroyed and many were left without food; it was easy to imagine the destruction of Pompeii in AD 79. About twenty people lost their lives due to collapsing buildings or asphyxiation from the ash. I'm glad to say there hasn't been an eruption since.

Naples had been one of the most targeted cities by the Allies for aerial bombardment up until its capture and was subsequently bombed by the Luftwaffe. In fact, the harbour was attacked nearly every night. John and I were in the city late one night near the docks when an air raid started. We had to take shelter in a little hut on the side of the road, lay down on the floor and cover our heads as best we could to give us some protection.

Unfortunately, there was a huge explosion nearby, and the hut literally collapsed on us. Neither of us was hurt, but we were filthy dirty and covered in muck. We eventually struggled out of there and made our way back to our billet, only to find out that the water had been cut off and so we couldn't wash. I remember going to bed, caked all over in mud. It was a very unpleasant, uncomfortable night, but I suppose it could have been much worse. My luck again. We later discovered that the hut was positioned very close to an anti-aircraft emplacement, which is what the Germans were trying to destroy.

I passed the officer training course with flying colours. It mainly involved paper exercises. There was no training in the field: I suppose because we had already done that for real. As far as I knew I was going to be sent back to England and be given some new posting with much responsibility. Anyway, on the final day, I discovered a message on the notice board, requesting that I should report to the medical office. I had no idea why they wanted to see me.

I was greeted by my commanding officer, a medical officer and a psychiatrist. They had been studying my notes that had been compiled while I had been undergoing the training. Although I had passed all the necessary tests, there was some concern that I was deemed 'unstable', which had shown up in the psychological testing. It was felt that the trauma of warfare had affected me more than I realised. The psychiatrist was apologetic, 'You've done so well on officer training, but you might break down under the stress and we can't risk it.' The shrink couldn't approve of me going back to England, becoming an officer and being put in charge of a platoon of men, who would very likely be involved in another invasion, on the second front. They said it would be unwise for me to lead men into action.

I was experiencing what was called 'battle anxiety' in those days but would now be termed 'Post Traumatic Stress Disorder'. Looking back, they were absolutely right. I was very anxious and would jump out of my skin when there were unexpected loud bangs. In fact, I still do. Not surprising really. I couldn't drink from a glass because my hands shook so much. I was in a bit of a state, but I suppose I just thought it was a natural reaction after what I had been through. There had been so much killing and carnage. I'd always been a pacifist, and I couldn't make sense of it all. I was frightened in battle, but somehow the adrenalin had kept me going. Although I had tried to kill myself, I must have had some instinct for survival along with a lot of luck. It was only afterwards that I could think clearly about what I had gone through. So many of my comrades were completely exhausted by the battle fatigue of a long campaign and would never be the same men who had sailed from Scotland those months before.

I had mixed reactions: I obviously wanted to prove myself, but in a way I was relieved. It was yet again the sort of serendipity I had enjoyed since joining up. I wasn't deployed to the front and so missed the horror of the D-Day landings – another very fortunate break.

There then followed a discussion about what they were going to do with me next. It was reiterated that, despite everything, I had performed well and could still be more than useful in 'doing my bit' in some way. My CO told me that they had had a meeting and, somewhat unusually, had come to the conclusion that I would be allowed to choose my next step, 'Give us some idea about what you would like to do and we'll arrange it for you.' I couldn't believe my ears. This was extraordinary.

Well, I didn't need any time to decide. I knew exactly where I wanted to go. I'd been having an affair with a very beautiful American boy,

Warren, who was absolutely gorgeous. He'd been posted to Allied Force Headquarters at nearby Caserta, and so I thought, 'That's where I want to be.' I wanted to be with Warren. I knew that the Americans and the British worked very closely together. So I said, 'I'd like to be posted to Allied Force Headquarters in the Intelligence Division. That's where I think I could make a difference.' Of course, I didn't mention Warren. Anyway, they seemed pleased with my suggestion and very soon it was agreed and arranged.

A few days later, I was collected by a despatch driver on a motor-bike to take up my posting in Caserta. Well, I took one look at him and thought 'mmm ... I'm in luck'. He was a great beauty. Anyway I climbed on the back of his bike and held him as tightly as I could around his waist. What with the vibration of the motorbike and a little frisson from such close contact, I'm afraid my hands just slipped down-wards and ... well ... what was I supposed to do? We dismounted, so to speak, and hurried into some woods where we had sex. I'd picked up a souvenir of a cock and balls silver necklace while in Pompeii, and I lost it in the ensuing passion. It was all very exciting, but I was disappointed about losing that cock and balls.

FIVE

CUNNING LINGUISTS

.

'The chalice from the palace has the brew that is true!'

The Court Jester

The Allied Forces Headquarters (AFHQ) had been established in 1942 and, during the North African campaign, was initially based in Algiers. In April 1944 AFHQ moved to the luxurious palace of Caserta outside Naples. The Royal Palace residence was larger than Versailles and housed over 1,000 rooms. Built in the eighteenth century for the Bourbon King Charles, it is now a UNESCO World Heritage Site but was then an extraordinary setting for the military and political administrations.

And it was in this astonishingly grand palace that I was sent to assist in setting up Counter Intelligence Austria. Initially, there were just a few of us: Commanding Officer Lieutenant Colonel The Honourable Henry Bolton 'Graham' Eyres-Monsell, a Major Knatchbull and a couple of other officers and myself – now a warrant officer Class 1, which was the highest rank up until officer level.

Our dual unit of both British and American personnel grew rapidly. Every week there seemed to be more and more recruits attached to Counter Intelligence, and these consisted of agents, linguists and those with special skills. Eventually we had to move to a billet in town. The main aim of the section at that time was the arrest of high ranking

Nazis and their sympathisers. We would eventually move to Vienna when the Austrian capital was in Allied hands and continue our work from there. By the time we left Caserta, the section numbers had swelled to approximately 120 officers and nearly 500 other men and women. I was responsible for much of the staff and accountable for welfare queries and allocating the work once identified by the agents. I was made aware of which Nazis we were targeting.

As well as my role in the pursuance of Nazis, the other reason for my transfer to Counter Intelligence was also to track down my American Jewish lover, Warren Myers. We met up again soon after my arrival, and he told me that he knew I was coming and had been to the PX – the American store where they sold lots of goodies. With his ration book, he'd obtained everything that he knew I liked, including a *huge* bar of chocolate. I hadn't eaten chocolate for years. It was divine. Warren and chocolate: what more could I want? He was marvellous, and we had a fabulous time. Although I had a bed in my office, I was billeted in the town in a large house belonging to a very nice professor, and it was here that Warren used to stay with me. Our close gay circle knew about our continuing affair, but obviously no one else knew.

Within the palace there was an opera house, a miniature model of the San Carlo, which was used for army concerts and other entertainments. In fact, there were so many people in the HQ who had some talent – actors, singers or musicians – so the people organising entertainments were well blessed.

There was one particular production that was quite unique and which Warren was involved in. It transpired that he was one of the staff under accomplished novelist and playwright Thornton Wilder, who was a lieutenant colonel in Army Air Intelligence and based in Caserta. Wilder's responsibilities while working for the MAAF (Mediterranean Allied Armed Forces) were the interrogation of prisoners of war, gathering and preparing Intelligence and briefing and debriefing Allied pilots.

In November 1944 the American service personnel urged Mr Wilder to let them perform one of his most celebrated plays, *Our Town*, and persuaded him to oversee the production. Initially reluctant due to his demanding workload, Wilder subsequently agreed and duly sent out a message saying that he wanted a personal assistant to help with the production and wished to audition possible cast members. Well, my lovely Warren, who had been an actor in civilian life, immediately registered to go to Thornton Wilder's audition, and I went with him because I wanted to apply for the job of personal assistant. And indeed Wilder did cast Warren as Joe Crowell, the newspaper boy in *Our Town*. The part was quite important because he cycled around the stage, throwing the newspapers like they do in America and casting light on some of the characters.

Mr Wilder agreed to have me as his personal assistant because he wanted somebody who spoke English too. The preparations took about a month. In Penelope Niven's biography of Thornton Wilder, *Thornton Wilder: A Life*, she writes that Wilder 'directed a group of soldiers and some WACs with very little theatre and professional experience' and that, according to Wilder, 'the amateur productions had their own share of underground politics and some very bitter feuds – they still served as a welcome relief from the demanding work and duty schedule.' I must say I remember that there were some professional actors involved in the production and can't recall any backstage dramas.

Thornton Wilder was a lovely man, and somewhat surprisingly, he was so nervous on opening night that he couldn't sit down, and we stood right at the back. He said to me, 'You stay with me Bruce.' I replied, 'Please don't worry too much: it's going to be a success. It's a wonderful story and it's yours! You've done a great job on the production.' And of course it was a riot; there were even standing ovations. I took Thornton's arm and I said, 'There you are. I told you so!'

The role of the stage manager, who fulfilled the function of a sort of Greek Chorus, was played by Sergeant John Hobart, former drama critic for the *San Francisco Chronicle*. He wrote about the production in an article in *Theatre Arts* magazine in April 1945. 'For exiled Americans overseas *Our Town* inevitably stirred thoughts of home and it also summoned a feeling of deep and honest pride. Grover's Corner has never seemed so wonderful a town or held so tangible a meaning.'

The town of Caserta was in blackout some nights because the Luftwaffe was still sending out the last of its bombing missions in attempts to target General Eisenhower, who was also based in the palace. During one of the performances, all the lights in the palace went out. Luckily everyone carried a torch for such events, and one by one all members of the audience shone their flashlights on to the stage so that a huge spotlight was formed, and at the end of the scene the main lights came back on!

Years later, in the early 1950s, I had an American lover called Charles Dufresne, who had homes in Chicago and New York. He was the executive for a top firm of travel agents, which took very rich Americans to Europe. Wealthy tourists always seemed to travel in groups in those days; they would never go anywhere on their own. Charles used to conduct these groups to London and Paris and other European capitals. Whenever there was a disparity in the numbers of women to men, which was quite often, he used to provide 'gigolos' to escort the women when visiting nightclubs in Paris. He would also pay for me to travel to Paris, and we stayed at the hotel The Claridge on the Champs-Elysées. I'd accompany an American lady for the evening and take her dancing to all the best nightclubs. I once went to a nightclub, and the Duke and Duchess of Windsor were there. It was really high style stuff. Incidentally, it was at The Claridge that I had snails for the first time.

One day Charles told me that he was going to meet some friends in the George V for drinks and then take lunch. I'd heard of the famous hotel but had never been there. We settled in the corner of a lovely luxurious lounge, which was pretty quiet. I looked across, and there was only one other guest, seated in the opposite corner of the room, reading a book. I thought there was something familiar about him. There was. It was Thornton Wilder. I got up and I walked over towards him, and he looked up when I was halfway there and he called out, 'Bruce, how wonderful to see you.' We embraced, and he came over and joined us for a drink. Thornton Wilder had remained in Caserta until the end of the hostilities and was still there when the Germans signed a surrender agreement at the palace there on 29 April. How extraordinary that the only one person in the bar happened to be him. I have had these lucky coincidences all my life.

One of the highlights of the Royal Palace was its formal landscaped gardens, which stretched out behind and comprised of hundreds of acres, bordered by forests. A series of reflecting pools and cascades, skirted by sculptures of Greek gods and goddesses, ascend a hill and culminate in a waterfall.

The entertainment officer thus decided to produce 'an aquacade' and notices were sent out to would-be participants. Being a strong swimmer, I naturally volunteered and was involved a great deal in the extravaganza. I featured in a number of scenes in the aquacade but most importantly I was cast as John Bull in the finale! I had a pair of swimming trunks that were red, white and blue, a sash and a hat, and I had to appear on the steps of the artificial lake, which had once been used to stage mock naval battles for the entertainment of the court. There was a large double stairway descending to the lake, and I was at the top with the serviceman playing Uncle Sam. On one side of the stairway was the British contingent and on the other side were the Americans. Music blared out, and Uncle Sam and I walked down for the huge finale. I was the last one down. Esther Williams, eat your heart out.

Unfortunately, my affair with Warren only lasted a couple of months, as he was taken seriously ill due to an internal medical condition. He was taken into hospital, where they discovered some kind of adhesion in his innards, and it was decided that he should undergo surgery in America. He was whisked away, and there was no time to say goodbye properly. It was heartbreaking as Warren was a big love, and I missed him terribly. I don't know what happened to him, as I lost touch and never had his address. I tried to track him down after the war but without success. He knew where I was, but I never heard from him. I suppose for him it was just a wartime romance and, like so many others during that time, was cut short cruelly because of the conflict. He may not even have survived. I'll never know.

I did have another lovely gay actor friend in Allied Force Headquarters, who was called Bud Turner. He was one of my American opposite numbers. He was terribly funny and had been in the movies – a bit player in Hollywood for years – and was about fifteen years older than most of us. He knew everyone in the movie industry, and although he would often only have a single word or one line, he was often in some big scenes when the stars were in a restaurant having a conversation and he was at the next table on camera. Such is the glamour of Hollywood.

Bud and I shared a billet in Caserta. There was a cesspit in the court-yard of this house, and once a week a young man would arrive with a cart to empty the cesspit, and the waste would be dumped into the cart. Of course, there was an awful smell and everybody closed their windows and doors for the hour that it took to clear the filth. Bud soon discovered that the young man that did the work was a great Italian beauty, stripped to the waist, and both of us used to watch him. Bud even used to go out on the balcony with a peg on his nose in order to gaze lovingly at this Adonis! Unlike Warren, I managed to stay in touch with Bud until his death about twenty years ago. He last appeared in an episode of an American television series, *The Littlest Hobo*, in 1981.

As I mentioned at the beginning of the chapter, my CO at Caserta was Henry Bolton 'Graham' Eyres-Monsell. He had been mentioned in despatches and recommended for the MBE for his services to security during the planning stages of Operation Torch. He was later awarded the United States Medal of Freedom. But the thing about the lieuten-ant colonel was that he was so absolutely gay.

During my time in the army, I soon discovered that nobody was as concerned about homosexuality as they were about rank. As a non-commissioned officer, I could not be seen with a commissioned officer in his chauffer-driven staff car. This class difference was maintained very strongly because so many working-class chaps were now doing so well and getting commissioned. This was something new in the army, as before that war no chap could become an officer unless he'd been to Eton or Cambridge and had the usual English upper-class background. Suddenly working-class people were becoming officers, and to preserve their status, the top brass made the divide even stronger than it had been before. But Graham Eyres-Monsell was wonderful. I loved him dearly and was very lucky I had such nice, special people always with me. He was a very clever man. And here was a man who in Civvy Street would have been humiliated, arrested and imprisoned for his sexual preferences but was treated like a hero in the army.

Most of us did indeed manage to adapt to the military environment without being turned in. Though it remained a criminal offence until the 1960s, for the most part homosexuality was unofficially tolerated in the armed services for the duration of the war. Although King's Regulations stated that 'confirmed homosexuals whose rehabilitation is unlikely should be removed from the Army by the most expeditious and appropriate means', this was got around by making out that the men were only seeking sexual gratification with each other as a substitute for women. It seems that formal charges were usually only brought against those who had committed a flagrant breach of discipline, especially between officers and other ranks or civilians. There is no question that some degree of acceptance was practiced because losing a number of servicemen would have seriously diminished the numbers of front-line troops.

On the whole we were protected by our comrades, and for some heterosexual servicemen, homosexual sex was considered preferable to going to brothels and catching a sexually transmitted disease. There is some evidence that homosexuality in the armed forces was far more widespread than in society as a whole. This was not just an important time in personal terms but, as John Costello wrote in his fascinating book *Love, Sex and War: Changing Values 1939–45*, the military experience of gays and lesbians in the Second World War 'chipped away some of the old taboos … servicemen living in close proximity were made aware that men who chose to have sexual relationships with other men were not suffering from sexual perversion, nor were they cowards.'

And there were, of course, some famous soldiers whose disputed homosexuality provided them with a little bit of glamour and charisma: Alexander the Great, Richard the Lionheart, General Gordon and Lawrence of Arabia among others. The myth that gay men were all effeminate or fragile and could not be masculine or strong was shown to be a lot of nonsense by the courage of those particular commanders.

During the war some lesser-known gay servicemen were decorated in the line of duty but had to keep their homosexuality a secret. Battle of Britain hero Flight Lieutenant Ian Gleed was killed when his Spitfire was shot down over Tunisia. He penned a memoir, *Arise to Conquer*, the year before, but his publisher, concerned about his status as a confirmed bachelor, created a fictional girlfriend called Pamela. He had to explain to the family that Pamela never existed, and as far as we know, his family never knew he was gay. His secret only came to light in the 1990s when a lover, Christopher Gotch, was interviewed on BBC television.

Over 5 million men served in the British armed forces during the Second World War. Based on national statistics, it's likely that at least 200,000 were gay or bisexual. In the *BBC History Magazine*, Stephen Bourne related the story of Dudley Cave, who was the same age as me when he was conscripted in 1941.

Dudley once overheard two of his comrades talking about him. One referred to him as a 'Nancy boy', while the other protested that Dudley couldn't be gay because he was 'terribly brave in action'. Their comments highlight a belief common at that time: that a man could not be both brave and homosexual, as the two things were incompatible.

Dudley Cave also told Peter Tatchell, the gay rights activist, that during the process of enlistment he wasn't asked any questions or given any warnings concerning homosexual behaviour, and this was my experience also. As Dudley said, 'People were put in the army regardless of whether they were gay or not and it didn't seem to bother the military authorities … with Britain seriously threatened by the Nazis, the forces weren't fussy about who they accepted.'

Soldiers having sex were never severely punished – let's face it, they would have had too many men on charges – and Dudley Cave stated that 'the visible gays were mostly drag performers in concert teams. Regarded with considerable affection, their camp humour helped lift the men's spirits.' Cave served in the Far East before being taken prisoner by the Japanese in Burma and recalled the following:

One man was renowned for giving good blow jobs in the mangrove swamps. He was well liked. Even supposedly straight men made use of his services. You could say that he did a lot to maintain the unit's morale. When a zealous sergeant attempted to charge him with being out of barracks after lights out, the commanding officer, who knew exactly what went on in the mangrove swamps, dismissed the charges. He had the wisdom to know that it was all harmless fun and a useful relief from the stress of war.

After Rome fell to the Allies in June 1944, I got a pass to go to the 'Eternal City' and was accompanied by another friend of mine, a Jewish master sergeant from Brooklyn with a quick-fire humour that only New Yorkers possess. In fact, looking back, he could have been the inspiration for most of the characters in Sergeant Bilko's infamous platoon!

We had a ball in Rome going to all the male brothels. These places were all out of bounds, but we crept into them after dark. We would have gone straight into prison if we had been caught in the out-of-bounds area. Rome had recently been liberated; it was an open city and hadn't been terribly badly damaged. We were some of the first to go to Rome when the Germans departed. And my visit wasn't purely for sex: I was also very keen to see some of the other beautiful sights.

I had heard that you must see the Colosseum at dawn, so I went in the dark and waited in the gardens opposite until the sun came up. It is one of the great sights of the world. It was breathtaking, and I was enjoying the experience so much when I heard a voice behind me say, 'So here you are, watching the dawn over the Colosseum. How splendid!' I turned around to see quite an elderly lady, sitting on a bench. We started talking, and she told me she was working as a tourist guide in Rome and had been for some years since her husband had died.

She was English and had married an Italian, but she augmented her income by taking English people on tours and so was very knowledgeable about Rome. So she took me round the city and gave me a private tour. Wasn't I lucky? She was a lovely, amusing lady and an exceptional conversationalist, and she took me to places that one wouldn't normally see – so many wonderful statues and beautiful pictures and all sorts of things. Gosh, it was a cultural feast!

There was an abundance of gay parties in Naples. The Caserta HQ had 500 rooms, which were full of Americans and British from every walk of life, and so by the law of percentages, a number of the officers were homosexual. I wasn't supposed to travel in an officer's car, but these queens were insistent on taking me to these gay gatherings; I used to have to lie down in the bottom of the staff car so that the sentries on the gate wouldn't see me.

I remember once going to a party that was being held at a very grand house in what was one of the better neighbourhoods of Naples. I rang the bell, and Graham Eyres-Monsell came to the door. He led me into the hallway, but there was no sign of any party going on. 'Where is everybody?' I asked.

'Oh, don't worry, my dear,' he replied. 'They're all out in the garden ... sucking away!'

Dear Graham used to say outrageous things like that all the time.

Graham knew an Italian 'peasant' lady. One night he smuggled me into the staff car with two or three other boys and we went off to this house in the country where this woman prepared the most wonderful food on the black market. We gave her some of the army rations and some money, and in return she cooked this most wonderful lasagne. With about seven or eight layers, it was like a cake, and she cut it into chunks. Delicious. It was the first time I had ever tasted it, and I haven't had a lasagne like it since.

After the war, Graham used to invite me to various events. He used to give lovely parties in restaurants in Soho, and he once took me to lunch at the Ritz. We were great chums. He was a lovely man, and I adored him. The last time I saw Graham I was driving through Eton Square in my little car, a Mini, and I saw him trying to hail a taxi. I stopped the car and called out, offering him a lift. I can't remember where I took him, but I expect it was somewhere nice to eat! On the death of his father, who was the First Lord of the Admiralty, Graham became Viscount Monsell.

I discovered that Patrick Leigh Fermor, who I adored as a writer, was attached to the Special Operations Unit and, although he was stationed in Cairo he sometimes visited the Caserta HQ. 'Paddy', as he liked to be known, was an extremely colourful character, once described as 'a cross between Indiana Jones, James Bond and Graham Greene'. He had become celebrated for his feats of derring-do. He spoke fluent Greek and worked with the underground in Crete and helped kidnap German general Heinrich Kreipe, the island's commander. He was awarded the DSO, and his exploits on Crete later became the basis for the film *Ill Met by Moonlight*, directed by Michael Powell and starring Dirk Bogarde.

Patrick Leigh Fermor visited us in Caserta quite often, and one of the principal reasons was that his girl, his future wife, worked there. She happened to be Graham Eyres-Monsell's sister, Joan, who was a FANY (First Aid Nursing Yeomanry). It seemed that all the upper-class nurses were FANYs. It was through Graham that I met Paddy, because he and Joan gave a party in Caserta to celebrate their engagement. Paddy and Joan remained engaged for years before they got married. I stayed in touch with them, and they used to visit me at The Establishment club in the early 1960s.

I remember being thrilled at meeting one of my heroes. The party consisted mainly of officers, and I was one of a few other lower ranked soldiers invited and getting a little light-headed on a glass or two of bubbly. Paddy continued to crop up in my life. Later on, after the war, when I came out of the army and worked at the Players' Theatre, I met an elderly lady who used to come in two or three times a week for a drink at the bar. Everybody loved her, and her name was Fudge Leigh Fermor. She was Patrick's mother. Her name was actually Æileen, but she liked to be known as 'Fudge'.

As the Allies continued to make inroads into Nazi-occupied Europe, the Counter Intelligence HQ moved from Caserta to Vienna, which had been overwhelmed by the Red Army troops on 13 April 1945 after a siege lasting ten days. The Austrian capital became a quadripartite zone; the four sectors were overseen by the Russians, French, Americans and the British.

We flew from Naples over the Alps in a plane designed to transport troops. There were no seats, and we sat on the floor in the middle of all the gear. We landed in a place called Klagenfurt in southern Austria, and we were there for a while until moving into our new HQ, which was in the former SS Barracks, behind the Hapsburg palace of Schönbrunn. It is now called the Maria Theresa Barracks, as the palace had once been occupied by the only female Habsburg sovereign, Maria Theresa, Archduchess of Austria.

The Chief of Intelligence was a schoolmaster turned Brigadier named Harry Hitchens. He had served in France with the 4th Hussars and then as an Intelligence staff officer at Bletchley decoding centre. Soon after I arrived, I met a very camp young man, Freddie Stephenson, who turned out to be Harry Hitchens' personal secretary. We became great friends, and he told me that Harry was also gay. I introduced myself to Harry, who was adorable – very witty and possessing a wonderfully ironic view of mankind.

There was still a sort of small lift, operated by a pulley system, in Harry's office in Schönbrunn; apparently the Empress Maria Theresa used to have food delivered by this lift when she was entertaining her secret lovers – guardsmen and the like. So that none of the staff found out about her extramarital affairs, meals for them would be sent up from the kitchen to the floor above. Amazingly, that contraption was still there after all those years, and Harry and I used to joke about what she got up to. It's surprising she had any time for lovers, as she and her husband, Francis I, Holy Roman Emperor, had sixteen children, one of whom was the unfortunate Queen Marie Antoinette of France. And if the story is true, it's possible that the emperor may not have sired all sixteen offspring!

Harry and I used to have secret meetings too. He used to come down to my office at the bottom of the grounds, and we'd shut the door so as not to be disturbed. These weren't assignations; mainly we just gossiped. I'd say to him, 'You've been here nearly half an hour. What will people think?' He used to say, 'Never mind what they think. If anyone dares to ask you, tell them we've been talking about "the men"', which of course we were!

Harry used to love us going to some very dodgy gay nightclubs together in Vienna. Because of his rank, I had to enter the clubs first and check that there was no one there who might recognise him. The clientele was mostly German deserters, great big beautiful men who had given up the fight against the Russians; the only way they could survive was to spend their nights selling themselves in these nightclubs. It was very sad, actually.

The stories about the Russian troops were horrendous. Rape and pillage were common in their thirst for revenge. But, strangely, despite these stories, the Russian soldiers I met seemed a different breed. I used to go into town to the main square and spend time with the Russian officers, who spoke English. I used to invite them into our club and got to know quite a lot of them. Believe it or not, they were much nicer than the Americans and the French to be with for an evening. There is no excuse for how the ordinary foot soldiers behaved, especially towards the Viennese women, but I couldn't blame them for pilfering things from their enemies. A number of the soldiers wore six watches, which they had clearly stolen, on their arms; some of them had probably never seen a wrist watch and would be returning to a life of poverty and deprivation under the Stalinist imperative.

Harry Hitchens was awarded the Legion of Merit Degree of Officer in August 1946, a military award of the United States Armed Forces given for 'exceptionally meritorious conduct in the performance of outstanding services and achievements'. On demob, Harry became a headmaster of Solihull public school and a friend of Field Marshal Lord Montgomery. Sadly, his life ended in tragedy: Harry committed suicide in 1963 at the age of 53 to avoid the shame of being 'outed' following the discovery of a gay tryst. This wasn't untypical of the gay men who had served their country with distinction during war: they were tolerated during the war but in peacetime were vilified, discriminated against and attacked for their sexuality.

I can't help but think of Alan Turing, who is very much in the news recently following his depiction by Benedict Cumberbatch in the much-lauded film *The Imitation Game*. Alan Turing, the founder of computer science, worked at Bletchley Park and devised a number of techniques for breaking German ciphers. He was a key figure in cracking the Enigma Code, and Winston Churchill was quoted as saying that Turing made the single biggest contribution to Allied victory in the war against Nazi Germany.

Although a hero during wartime, Turing was charged with gross indecency for admitting to a homosexual affair in 1952. He was given the choice of a prison stretch or being on probation; one of the terms of his probation stipulated that he must agree to hormonal treatment in order to reduce his libido. Alan Turing chose chemical castration by oestrogen injections as an alternative to a jail sentence, but he couldn't cope with the consequences of a life without love and took an overdose of cyanide two years later, aged 41.

On 24 December 2013, the queen signed a pardon for Turing's conviction for gross indecency. This was marvellous, although sadly, thousands of others convicted under the same law have never received pardons.

To provide administrative and secretarial support, the authorities had sent out about half a dozen girls who were highly experienced typists and experts in shorthand. One of these, Margo Gibbard, was a very sophisticated and bright woman who became a great friend and source of support. She would accompany me on hospital visits, which were sometimes quite tricky and emotional, to wounded soldiers. We got on so well, and we used to spend a lot of time together away from work and acted as each other's 'beard'. Margo was engaged to a Canadian medic in the forces, and being in my company would keep other would-be suitors at a distance, and those who didn't know I was gay would assume we were a couple.

In May 1945, during a period of leave, Margo and I went to Venice. I had a hotel room at the Grand Hôtel des Bains on the Lido, which was used as the location for the film *Death in Venice*, and Margo stayed at the YWCA. Seems a bit unfair now when I think of it! In any case, I collected Margo every morning, and we would go to the beach or galleries. I recall that the gallery in the Piazza San Marco held an exhibition of the paintings that had been hidden during the hostilities before being returned to their rightful galleries.

On our fourth day when I was visiting, Margo wasn't quite ready, and the English woman who ran the YWCA suggested I listen to a record while I waited for her. I found some records and put on a Glenn Miller disc. Margo arrived just as the track ended. I greeted her and said, 'Margo, you must listen to this tune. It's marvellous.' I put *Moonlight Serenade* on for a second time. As we were both listening, an Italian newspaper boy rushed into the hostel with the news that the war had officially ended.

Although Margo and I hugged and were very happy, we weren't as excited and moved as most other people in Europe would have been. Working in Intelligence, we knew that it was only a matter of time before the official announcement that the war had come to an end was made, and so we had been expecting this news. There was a strange sort of symmetry when I think back of how I had felt when war had broken out six and a half years ago. The news was expected and not shocking at all. We did, of course, feel very happy and celebrated by spending the day on the beach. We walked on air all day.

After the war Margo went to live in Vancouver with her doctor. We stayed in touch for years, and when she visited me in London, she told me how happy she was. I kept in touch with her until her death some years ago.

My duties in Vienna were varied, and although they were mainly administrative, I was once in charge of taking a group of German prisoners to the cinema to watch documentary footage of the liberation of a concentration camp. The Germans all stared at the floor, heads down, unwilling to accept the truth and even refusing to watch. We had to aim loaded guns at them and force them to watch. They didn't like it, but afterwards I could see that they had been greatly affected. I suppose many Germans did despise the Nazi regime, but by the time war broke out they were too subjugated or terrified to do anything about it. In any event, there was a great deal of anti-Semitism all over Europe, not just in Germany. I can remember people saying awful things about Jews when I was a child.

In consultation with Harry Hitchens, I was involved in directing field agents to track down Nazi sympathisers and supporters. I played a small part in the arrest of Herbert Von Karajan, the Austrian conductor. In later years he was famously associated with the Berlin Philharmonic, which he led for thirty-five years, and he was the top selling classical music-recording artist ever at one stage. But in earlier years, Karajan was a Nazi sympathiser, who had joined the party in Salzburg, Austria, in 1933 to advance his music career. Karajan was, by all accounts, extremely grandiose, petulant and full of himself. He was much disliked by his peers and aligned himself with anyone who he felt could advance his career, and whereas some conductors such as Klemperer, Toscanini and Kleber had fled from Nazism and Fascism, Karajan stayed in Germany and continued to work.

Documents from the National Archives, recently made available, show that, while based in Aachen in 1933, Karajan was an agent of The Sicherheitsdienst (SD), which was one of the oldest security organisations of the SS, and reported directly to Heinrich Himmler. The SD was the first Nazi Party information-gathering organisation and was given the responsibility with detecting and unmasking actual or potential enemies of the Third Reich. The agency employed thousands of agents and informants.

In 1942 the divorced Karajan married Anna Maria 'Anita' Sauest, who had a Jewish grandfather. According to historian Richard Osborne, 'Karajan's 1942 marriage to the quarter-Jewish Anita, which the composer cited in his defence after 1945, was more useful to him than harmful when the tide of the war was turning.' Karajan was arrested and detained briefly but never charged with any sort of war crime, although his undoubted link with the Nazi regime, even today, sullies his reputation.

At the end of the war, in May 1945, I was receiving a great many enquiries from civilians, who came to us to complain about the way the Russian troops and authorities behaved. I thought it would be beneficial to create a sort of ombudsman's desk. We set up an office, and any civilian who wanted to ask questions outside the normal remit could come and tell us their story.

I was on duty there one day when this lady came and introduced herself. 'My name is Willy Frölich,' she said, 'I am not a Jew, but my husband is Jewish, and I've protected him right through the occupa-tion.' Her husband was much older than her and had somehow survived, although he was demeaned by sweeping the streets and having to wear the yellow Star of David at all times. She told me the most terrible sto-ries about how the Germans had taken all the Jews out of the houses, lined them up and took them off to the camps. On one occasion they had shot a number of the men while their wives and families watched.

Anyway, this couple were once quite well off. Her husband had his own factory, but of course, it was all taken over by the Nazis. They had also been thrown out of their nice house, which was quite near the Schönbrunn Palace in an elegant part of Vienna. Mrs Frölich told me that they wanted to return to their house, which was now empty, but that the British had now commandeered it as a billet and no one was allowed to enter the property. She wanted to know if I could help pre-vent that happening so that they could move back to their home. I told her I didn't know if it was possible, but I felt that this action was the least this couple deserved, so I told her I would do my best to help.

Funnily enough, Anthony Dawes, who was a high-powered estate agent in Clevedon – his family were old friends of my parents – was stationed with me and happened to be the billeting officer. I got straight on the phone to him and told him the story. He knew about the house, and although there were plans for some of our troops to move in, he said he would make alternative arrangements and agreed that the couple could return to their home.

Willy Frölich was, of course, absolutely delighted, and both she and her husband broke down in tears when I told them the good news. She couldn't get over the fact that I had managed to get the house back and so much so that she actually asked me to move in with her and her husband. Although the Russians had vandalised their house, sur-prisingly most of their lovely furniture was still there. The property was much more comfortable than my billet, and so I readily agreed.

Food was very scarce, and Willy used to stand in queues for hours for her rations. I remember her coming home once and us viewing her shopping. She had been given approximately fifty little white beans for one exhausting outing. I was all right as I could eat at work, but the poor couple had such meagre rations that I bought extra food from the canteen and used to smuggle provisions to them, secreted in my battledress!

Unfortunately, Willy fell in love with me, and on one occasion she told me how she felt. When I advised her that I was homosexual, she wasn't at all happy; she wasn't very pleasant to me after that, but I think it was for personal reasons rather than due to homophobia. In any case, I moved out ...

After the war, Anthony Dawes returned home to Clevedon to work for the family firm of estate agents and had an affair with a younger man that was reported in the local newspaper when he was betrayed by the lover. Anthony came from a rather grand family who were shocked that he was gay. His brother-in-law was aggressively homophobic and wholly insensitive to the situation. The Daweses were outraged, scandalised and ostracised their gay son. As a result, poor disgraced Anthony drove into the countryside and shot himself. He was yet another casualty, not of war, but of the pressures of a homophobic society.

During my time in Vienna, I became more and more involved in the screening of refugees in the Displaced Persons Camps, which were placed on territory occupied by American, British and French forces. The camps aimed to provide shelter, nutrition and basic health care. There was very little medical care, and sanitary conditions left a lot to be desired, so the residents were likely to suffer from malnutrition and illness and were often lice-ridden.

The definition of a 'displaced person' referred to civilians who were not in their home country when the hostilities ended, and in the years after the war, when most citizens in Western Europe had been able to return home, displaced persons were those who refused to go back to their birthplace. This was mainly because their nation was under Communist rule. There were a number of Poles in this position who didn't want to live under Soviet autocracy and eventually came to live in the United Kingdom.

At the end of 1945, some six months after the war ended, I was taken ill and admitted to hospital. It was the Austro-Hungarian hospital, which is quite famous and situated on the edge of the Vienna Woods. The institution consisted of about twenty beautiful buildings, and we had control of one of them. My only symptom was a sore throat, but yet again I was told I had diphtheria. This time the diagnosis was correct. A number of other patients with the disease were seriously ill and some died. Yet again I was lucky. I felt fine, but swabs showed that I still had the disease, so I had to remain there being looked after by nuns.

I was on the second floor, and I could look down from my ward to observe the nuns arranging some of the beds outside in the sun. The wing next door was full of concentration camp survivors, but they were mostly dying. Some of them were pitiful and weighed next to nothing. They were beyond hope, and they were just about being kept alive. I used to go down and help the nuns pull the beds out into the sun so the patients could feel some warmth. Lorries used to pass by, piled high with dead bodies because there weren't any coffins. The deceased had to be buried in mass graves, like they did in the camps. To see all these dead bodies on lorries was grotesque and beyond belief. Total inhumanity.

There was a young man of about 18 in the hospital – one of the camp survivors. He'd suffered horribly, and he was just about able to walk around the grounds but was stricken with a mental disorder. He fell for me because I was kind, and he used to stand under my window. I used to look out of the ward, and there he was looking for me, and he'd wave. He was very beautiful. He died a few weeks later.

And of course there were over 10,000 gay men imprisoned in concentration camps during the Holocaust, many of whom died. Homosexuals were treated as deviants and forced to wear pink triangular patches to identify them from other inmates. A number died from beatings, some of them inflicted by other prisoners, and were subjected to inhuman cruelty from their German captors. Homophobic policies perpetrated by the Nazis before the war contributed to their treatment. According to John Costello, 'The Commandant of Auschwitz attempted to reduce homosexuality by dispersing them instead of confining them together – but this only increased homosexual activity.' SS Chief Heinrich Himmler wanted all homosexuals eliminated, and in 1941 it was stated that 'any member of the SS or Gestapo who engages in indecent behaviour with another man ... will be executed'. Nazi doctors used gay men for scientific experiments in an attempt to locate a 'gay gene' and to 'cure' any future Aryan children who were gay.

What the Germans did ... after all these years I have tried to forgive the Germans, but I just can't. I've tried so hard not to hate them, but I do. So many died and died so young, at 19 or 20. They were just the right age to be cannon fodder because they didn't know any different. In the First World War there were so many boys who died at that age, slaughtered in their thousands. And it's still happening. In the Middle East it's been terrible for a while and now in Ukraine. There is always somewhere where there is conflict, and the arms manufacturers love it; war wouldn't happen if it weren't for them. The Germans started it with their arms manufacturing, and we're just as bad. We sell billions of pounds worth and so do the French. So many countries all over the world are at it. Profit at any cost. How dare we sell arms? But we do.

When I was well enough to leave the hospital, I was transferred to a Red Cross institution. It was a convalescent home that was situated by the side of a lake, and it was a wonderful place. I took to the water daily and was also teaching some of the wounded soldiers to swim. I was ready for demob, and I could go back to England any time I liked, but the nice English Red Cross ladies wanted me to stay, convincing me that my presence was helping the boys to recuperate. They were, of course, referring to the swimming lessons ...

I remained there for about two months. I did actually have a lover down the road. His father had been killed by the Germans and had left him a stretch by the side of the lake which the family had run as an entertainment place with rowing boats and so on. He told me that he was going to get it set up again as a lakeside attraction and asked me to be his partner, but I refused because I had been away for so long and wanted to get back to England. I've sometimes thought about what that might have been like, as he was a charming young man and I would have had a very good job working in an idyllic lakeside setting, but it was not to be.

Ronald Benge came to see me while I was convalescing, and he was accompanied by a Polish woman called Irena Seirer who had fled from the Russians into the British zone. Irena had been married to a German soldier and together they had a daughter, Alfreda, who was then aged 6. The first I saw of Irena were her shapely legs alighting from Ron's jeep. And, as you can imagine, in a hospital for wounded soldiers I wasn't the only chap to notice the arrival of a very attractive woman! Ron wanted to marry Irena and bring her to England, and even though I was out of action I could still assist with some documentation and most importantly help pull a few strings. Ronald returned home in 1945, and Irena and Alfreda joined him a year later. Ron and Irena were married in 1947. Incidentally, Alfreda Benge is a well-known lyricist and an illustrator and is married to musician Robert Wyatt.

I had already given some thought to my future while I was helping the nuns with all those poor, desperate concentration camp survivors. Freddie Stephenson came to see me and asked, 'Do you remember that I was going to join a friend of mine in a flat in Earls Court?'

'Yes,' I replied somewhat vaguely.

'Well,' he continued, 'I'm not going there now as something else has come up, and I wondered if you would be interested in the flat? You'll have to pay ten bob a week rent from now on, but I'll give you a letter of recommendation and you'll have somewhere to stay in London.' I would be ready for demob when I had fully recovered, so I said, 'Yes, why not? That would be lovely.' It was to be one of the best decisions of my life.

SIX

HATTIE AND OTHER PLAYERS

'We're dear old pals, jolly old pals
Clinging together through all sorts of weather
Dear old pals, jolly old pals
Give me the friendship of dear old pals.'

The Players' Theatre anthem, music and lyrics by G.W. Hunt

I returned to England following my demob in June 1946 and immediately took a taxi to the address in Earls Court that Freddie Stephenson had given me. En route from Paddington station I asked the cabbie to drive me around Hyde Park. It was a beautiful summer's day, and I just wanted to enjoy some of the loveliest scenery in London. So there I sat in the back seat of the taxi, still wearing my tropical uniform, while my demob suit was safely packed away in my luggage.

I was back in London, a city I had grown to love, and was excited at the adventures that lay ahead. He duly drove me around, and when we returned to the beginning of the tour, I was enjoying myself so much that I asked him to drive me around again. He replied, 'I'm happy to drive you round all day as long as you pay what's on the clock!' It was during the second spin around Hyde Park that I decided on something that I have followed ever since: never be ordered about again – ever!

Six and a half years of obeying orders in the army was quite enough. I would try to be my own man from now on.

When I finally arrived to No. 67 Eardley Crescent, I was struck by the elegance of the large whitewashed Georgian house. I rang the bell and was really rather taken aback by the man who opened the door. Edgar Redding looked me up and down rather admiringly. He was quite clearly an old queen and rather unappealing. In fact, he was so ugly that if he'd sucked a lemon, the lemon would have made a face. Edgar rented a two-bedroom, first-floor flat in the house and led me upstairs, adding rather pointedly, 'All my stuff is in the spare room, we'll have to share one of the bedrooms. I hope you don't mind.'

'Here we go,' I thought. I have to say I was bronzed and lithe and must have looked rather good in my shorts and short-sleeved shirt; needless to say, during the night he pounced on me. I rejected his advances but had to sit up for hours consoling him; I didn't want to hurt his feelings, as he was a nice chap. He ended up telling me about the neighbourhood, where to go and all the local gossip. Edgar worked for Berman's, the famous theatrical costumiers, and used to throw drag parties. I'd never met a proper drag queen before. I remember the actor John Le Mesurier once rang the doorbell and Edgar answered the door in crinoline and a poke bonnet.

The following morning Edgar told me that he would introduce me to 'the girl', who was also the landlady and lived in the top floor flat. He seemed very fond of her and sung her praises. He told me that she was called Josephine Jacques, and just before he left for work he called up, informing her that I had arrived. She said, 'I'm just cooking breakfast. He can come up.'

I went upstairs, to see this remarkable looking woman, in her early 20s, wearing a tatty blue crepe evening dress, which she was using as a housecoat. She was hovering over a stove cooking a great big English breakfast, and she immediately asked me to join her. I was to discover over time that this gesture would be typical of her generosity and kindness.

She told me that she didn't like to be called Josephine – she hated that name – but was known by her friends and family as 'Jo'. That day, and most of the evening, Jo and I spent 'nose to nose', telling each other about ourselves and getting to know each other. She was so warm and friendly, and I loved her straightaway. Jo was an aspiring actress and was currently employed at the Players' Theatre – a music hall venue.

It turned out that Jo was known in the business as 'Hattie'. This was a stage name that she had acquired during a production that year at the Players', and she was to adopt it professionally for the rest of her life. Whilst appearing in a minstrel show, Jo had blacked up, and one of the backstage staff likened her to Hattie McDaniel, the rotund black actress in *Gone with the Wind*. (Although I always called her Jo, I shall refer to her as Hattie from now on for the sake of convenience.)

Hattie also explained that the house actually belonged to her mother, Mary, who lived in Gunnersbury but let out the flats and rooms. The ground floor was rented to a middle-aged man and his wife. I met them soon after and took against them. It wasn't personal – I just didn't like them. They were homophobic, which proved to be somewhat unfortunate in that No. 67 Eardley Crescent became a homosexual haven for years to come! The basement, which wasn't actually owned by the Jacques' family, was rented at that time by an elderly suffragette and close friend of the Pankhursts, a Mrs Richardson-Rice; she was, I think, related to the famous suffragette Mary Richardson, who damaged a painting and went to prison for her beliefs. She was arrested nine times and was most famous for slashing a painting (*The Rokeby Venus*) in the National Gallery with a concealed cleaver.

I hadn't yet seen my mother and father since demob, and so I travelled down to Clevedon to see them. It was a wonderful reunion, and they were as delighted to see me as I was to see them. Reg was still away with the RAF and Jack was still in the services, but the rest of the family were there gathered in the sitting room. Tom remembers me 'enthralling' them with some of my experiences of the war, although he and Di also recalled that I seemed a different person and clearly affected by what I had witnessed. Di had worked in a factory in Bristol until September 1940 when the factory was bombed, and then for the rest of the war she worked in the Folland Aircraft Company, a Southampton aeroplane factory. We thought the world of each other. Joan had given birth to a baby daughter, Elizabeth, during the war, and she and her husband had delayed the christening so that I could attend as godfather to Elizabeth. She had since had another daughter, Storm.

While I was in Clevedon I received a letter from Hattie. She had realised that it was going to be awkward for me sharing a flat with Edgar and so suggested I move into her spare room on the top floor. I was delighted, and when I returned to Eardley Crescent, I moved in with Hattie. Poor Edgar was a little disappointed as he still held some romantic aspirations!

It was a very happy time, and I was lucky that I didn't have to find a job straightaway; in fact, I was determined not to work for some time because I had this demob lump sum and I was okay for money. I'd worked from the age of 14 and then had been in the army throughout the war, so I felt I deserved a rest. However, Hattie took me to the Players' very soon after we met, and I used to spend a lot of time at the theatre, getting to know everyone. The Players' was a very successful club, and everybody went there. Many performers started their show business careers there, and the likes of Peter Ustinov, Ian Carmichael, Eleanor Summerfield, Clive Dunn, Bernard Miles and Daphne Anderson all went on to become very successful actors.

According to *Late and Early Joys*, a most marvellous book on the history of the institution, the Players' Theatre had its roots in Evans's 'Song and Supper Rooms' of the 1820s that first introduced Londoners to the joys of cabaret, 'singing the bacchanalian ballads of the time, over chops and ale'. Hot meals were served until the early hours accompanied by tankards of 'foaming ale or steaming glasses of grog'.

The Supper rooms closed in 1880, but a theatre club, based in Covent Garden, reopened in the 1920s. The waiters were actors and friends who either stage-managed, sold tickets or worked in the cloakroom. Following the outbreak of the war, the entertainment moved to a basement at No. 13 Albemarle Street, Piccadilly, and alongside The Windmill, the Players' was the only other theatre 'never to close' throughout the war. In 1945 the Players' moved premises again to the old Forum cinema, under the arches in Villiers Street.

The entertainment on offer was Victorian Music Hall, and as Hattie's performances became more assured, she quickly established a reputation as being one of, if not the most, popular entertainer at the Players'. A regular chant of 'We want Hattie' rose loudly from the audience, and she received habitual praise from the public and her peers.

Leonard Sachs ran the theatre and, along with Don Gemmell, acted as 'chairman'. The chairman introduced the acts and ran the proceedings. As *Late and Early Joys* recounts, 'Sachs' effervescent vitality and flow of repartee gave him a well-deserved reputation in handling the audiences and making them forget the blitz. That gave as much to the entertainment as did the artistry of the company gathered there night after bomb wrecked night.' Leonard Sachs was a purist when it came to running the theatre, and consequently the cast had to dress in exact period costume and have their hair styled in an authentic manner. In 1953 Leonard Sachs became the celebrated chairman of the BBC television show *The Good Old Days*.

It was Leonard who offered me a job at the theatre, cleaning and collecting glasses. I then worked in the bar, having learned the job from the current bartender. The work provided me with some nice spending money, and Hattie and I used to drift around the West End, sometimes going to very questionable clubs ... we used to have a lovely time.

Although I was enjoying myself at the Players', and despite my little nest egg, I felt I did need to find a proper job. Naturally there were millions of people who had just been demobbed trying to get jobs, and it was hard to find employment. However, I came across an advertisement for a job as a steward on an ocean liner. I thought that I wouldn't have any trouble and that they would want to snap me up for the job immediately. I was shocked when they rejected me! I'd never been turned down before in my life. I was furious and boarded a bus in high dudgeon. We got stuck in a traffic jam in Cheapside, and I looked out the window and saw the sign 'Army Resettlement Bureau'. These offices were dotted all over town and were akin to Labour Exchanges for out of work servicemen. I'd never been to one, but on impulse I jumped off the bus and went in.

I was told to take a seat, and eventually I was called into a cubicle where a man was sitting behind a desk. He introduced himself and said he would endeavour to find me employment. He then added, 'Your name, Bruce Copp, is very familiar to me. Is your father also called Bruce Copp?' I nodded. He became very animated and said, 'Bruce was my greatest friend for a long time but we lost touch several years ago. This is just marvellous. Well, Bruce Copp, I'm going to find you a very good job! Come back tomorrow and I promise to come up with something.'

He was lovely, and I can't help but think how lucky I've been with chance meetings and coincidences like this throughout my life. It's always been like that. Out of all those millions of people looking for jobs I happened, just by chance, to jump off the bus and get in touch with an old friend of my father's.

He was a man of his word, and the following day he told me about a position that he thought would suit me perfectly. Guy Elwes was a very highly regarded interior designer before the war. He had been forced to close the business in 1939 as all his employees had been called up, but he was starting up again. He wanted a young man in the office to help him – somebody who was personable enough to meet the clients and talk to them – and decided that I fitted the bill. It was a lovely job. I usually went with him as his assistant when people were choosing their curtain colours or whatever, but the very first customer I went to on my own was a lady who lived in a beautiful house in Brompton Square. She didn't actually live there but was just fixing it up before her marriage to Christopher Soames. She turned out to be Winston and Clementine Churchill's daughter, Mary.

I was very nervous about it because I knew she was very well known, but she was awfully nice. Strangely, we met many times after that: she used to come to one of my restaurants in later years and we would always have a little chat. Another resident of the square was Lord Farringdon, who took a great fancy to me, although we were never lovers and he was a good deal older than me. He used to take me out to smart restaurants and other places. He used to love spending his time with reasonably agreeable gay people from all sections of society, not just the world from which he came.

I'd been with Guy Elwes for several months while continuing to work some evenings at the Players' when Leonard Sachs approached me. He told me that the theatre's 'Supper Room' was losing money and, because of my hotel background, asked if I would help run the restaurant. It seemed to me ridiculous that the restaurant, which seated about sixty people, was not profitable. I replied that I'd never actually run a restaurant professionally, but I had learned so much from my father and the hotel business that I felt confident about 'having a go'. And there I was handed a restaurant on a plate, as it were. I was to be Charges D'affaires of The Supper Room.

Well, I have to blow my own trumpet and tell you that The Supper Room was making a profit within a month and for the first time in ages. I really enjoyed the work. I had a very nice Polish refugee chef, and one of the directors of the theatre had a sister who worked in the kitchen too. Gladys was her name and very good she was too. Another priceless member of my staff was my sister Di.

She had also come to London in 1946, lived in a hotel near Paddington station and found employment as a clerk for *Teleradio* in the Edgware Road. She didn't know anyone in London apart from me, and after a couple of weeks she looked me up. Hattie had opened the door and recognised Di straightaway as I had a picture of her. Di stayed for the weekend, and Hattie took her to the Players' and got her a job in reception, then in the bar and eventually as a waitress. She continued to work at the Players' on and off for seven years. Di later described me as a good boss and very fair to my staff. It was true that I did appreciate them, tried to be flexible and fed them well too. But at the same time I expected them to be professional at all times and work hard. Di used to tell me off if ever I became 'difficult'. I used to test new kitchen staff by getting them to make an omelette, which I thought was a good way of gauging culinary skills.

We used to do quite nice food, although we were very limited because to begin with we didn't have a meat licence. So I just did what I could with vegetables: 'cauliflower gratin' and that sort of thing. I used to go into Soho and get hold of anything I could 'off the ration'.

I went through the membership list, which contained lots of exalted names. One of the names on the list was the head of Lyons. I obtained his address and telephone number from the office and phoned him. I told him that I was running the Players' Supper Room but that we were in trouble and wondered if he could help with obtaining a meat licence.

It was a bit cheeky, but it did the trick, and he actually stood up in court and spoke up for me. We were able to procure a licence, so we started to have proper restaurant food, with escallops of veal, steaks and roast meat.

I used to make a soup I called 'Players' Broth', and jellied eels went down very well. It was a bit camp, but the diners used to pounce on them – they couldn't get enough. One of my mongers, Charlie Isaacs, used to bring them up from the East End in enamel bowls. I kept the menu very simple, and I always used to have skate because skate is a fish that is better if it is two or three days old!

Apart from The Supper Room, we also had a snack bar in the theatre, which was popular just before the show and during the interval. I used to sell huge piles of hot dogs. One day I was in Soho shopping round for bits and pieces, and I found some lovely prawns, which were quite rare in those days. I bought some and gave them to Gladys, who put together some delicious prawn canapés.

I decided to sell them in the snack bar. The girl that ran it was a very nice Jewish girl called Norda McPherson, who I loved. Sadly, she had been estranged from her Jewish family because she had married a gentile doctor called McPherson. She used to come in the most wonderful clothes, and I would say to her, 'Oh Norda, not another expensive new dress?' She would reply, 'It cost me £5, 11 and thruppence from C&A!' But you could clearly see it came from Dior. I loved Norda.

Anyway, I took a great trayful of these prawn canapés down to her, and I told her to have one herself so she knew what she was selling. I went down after the interval, and Norda told me that they had all gone. I asked her, 'Did you have one yourself?' She replied, 'Oh yes. I don't keep kosher. It was delicious … like God going down my throat in velvet trousers!' From then on I always had 'Velvet Trousers' on my menu in whichever restaurant I ran. Word soon got round that we offered such lovely food, and many of the members who wanted to dine there couldn't be accommodated, so I used to lay places in what we called the shelf – a little circle at the back of the theatre – and fit more diners in that way.

New Year's Eve was always a big thing at the theatre, and one of the directors, Don Gemmell, was Scottish, so we always had a special

Hogmanay celebration with Scottish dancing after the show. It always seemed to me that on New Years' Eve the problem was the timing of serving the food. It was a long evening, as people used to get to the theatre about 8ish and were at the theatre until 2 a.m. and needed feeding. So I suggested to the directors that I could serve the audience a proper supper while actually in their seats.

I got hold of some out of work actors and actresses, employed them as extra waiting staff and had them running up and down the aisles with hot plates of food while one of the directors announced from the stage which rows were about to be served. I did two or three courses and gradually served the entire audience of over 200 people. It was a huge success and everybody loved it.

And at home we weren't doing so badly in terms of culinary delights ... Hattie used to buy black market food from a shop in Kensington. I was a little disapproving, but she said, 'I've got some money, darling, and that's what I'm going to spend it on – some good food.' She used to get a dozen eggs, and you were only allowed one a week!

Hattie had learned to cook from her mother, and with my input, Eardley Crescent house soon became notorious for gastronomic treats. We managed to create mini banquets from limited resources. Apart from the food, Hattie also offered maternal nourishment. She was an extraordinarily selfless and giving woman, who would always step into the breach if anyone needed help. Friends in trouble would flock to Eardley Crescent.

Hattie and I always planned to write a cookery book together. The idea was that on one side of the double spread we would describe a dinner, party or gastronomic event that we had enjoyed or found interesting and on the other side we would describe the food that we had shared there and perhaps a recipe. Sadly, we never got around to it, and I suppose this book is the closest I'll ever come to that idea.

During the war, Hattie had embarked on a passionate affair with an American major, Charles Randall. She told me that her American Major Charles had been killed in a bombing raid, and in magazine interviews Hattie spoke poignantly of 'a fiancé' with whom she was very much in love and who had been killed in action during the war. In fact,

I later discovered that he had returned to the States after the war and never returned to Hattie. This was Hattie's way of coping with her loss; whatever the truth, she used to cover her pain by involving herself with a series of boyfriends. We were actually both quite naughty during this time and would occasionally find ourselves breakfasting with our conquests from the previous night. I seem to remember that our temporary paramours were mainly actors or models from the Rank Charm School.

It's such a shame that most people think of Hattie as being the large harridan of the *Carry On* films. Hattie was actually quite a flirt, beautiful and voluptuous – and very sexy. Even after she became quite well known, Hattie kept her name in the telephone book and would receive anonymous and obscene phone calls from men who liked 'large ladies'. Hattie wasn't one to take umbrage – far from it. Instead of slamming the phone down, if someone was talking dirty then she would give me the nod and I'd pick up the other telephone extension, listen in and then get hysterical. Instead of becoming cross or self-conscious, she used to go along with the callers, sometimes egging them on. It was hilarious. Eventually, she would call down the phone, 'Go away, you filthy beast!'

Hattie was very wise about gay life. As a child growing up in Chelsea, she had been used to seeing homosexuals and cross-dressers in the King's Road, and since then she had always felt at home with and had an affinity with gay men. They were sexually unthreatening, and she could always be herself in their company. And we, in turn, loved being with her. I could always confide in her, and she would never be shocked by anything. She gave unreserved support and was completely non-judgemental.

Towards the end of 1946, while Hattie was about to embark on a tour with The Young Vic Theatre Company, she, as generous as ever, told me that I could use her room if any of my friends wanted to stay. My old army pal Freddie Stephenson took up the offer and stayed for a few days, during which time Edgar Redding was hosting one of his drag parties. I wasn't the slightest bit interested in carousing with a bunch of old queens and had always politely refused Edgar's invitations. However, I felt I should go once so as not to offend poor Edgar. Freddie and I went to the theatre first, and when we returned to Eardley Crescent the party was in full swing. Edgar's flat was full of transvestites – all glammed up. We were asked to drag up but we refused. We looked around, and the only man not in drag was a guardsman, in full dress uniform. Freddie liked the look of him and said, 'I'll have him.' Even I was astonished. 'You can't possibly,' I replied, 'He's much too butch.'

Well he tried. Freddie brought the guardsman back to Hattie's bedroom but was unable to arouse him sexually, and so poor Freddie went to sleep. He was woken a little later by the guardsman, attired in Hattie's clothes and with huge erection. Apparently the soldier saw the open wardrobe door, rummaged around and selected one of her more rococo outfits. It was seemingly the only way he could get excited.

Freddie was horrified and not at all turned on. 'That dress belongs to Hattie. Take it off, put it back in the wardrobe and leave this house immediately!' He woke me to describe what had happened, which I must say I thought was rather amusing. When Hattie returned from the tour, I told her about the night-time frolics and she thought it all quite hilarious.

Hattie auditioned for a role in *It's That Man Again*, a BBC radio comedy starring Tommy Handley and which had begun in 1939. I was with Hattie when she received the call from her agent telling her that she had got the part. She was absolutely delighted. I'd never seen her happier, professionally at least. I knew the exposure would make her into a star, and she loved being involved in *It's That Man Again*.

The series started in the autumn of 1947, and Hattie duly joined the cast as Sophie Tuckshop, the schoolgirl with a voracious appetite who overate to the point of sickness only to report later, 'But I'm all right now.' I used to go with her to rehearsals at the Paris Theatre in Lower Regent Street. In the breaks we used to go to the pub round the corner, The Captain's Cabin, which has sadly been recently demolished for yet another West End development. We sometimes used to rewrite Hattie's lines – the things that didn't go well in the first reading. Hattie was brilliant like that, although I'm not sure what Tommy Handley thought.

I remember 1947 being a terribly cold winter. All those years in the war and all the hardships I went through and yet I almost suffered more that winter than I ever had in my life. Heavy snowfalls caused chaos all over, and the country suffered an energy crisis due to the shortage of fuel. Coal supplies, already low so soon after the war, were unable to be transported to power stations. Consequently, a great number of stations were forced to shut down and the government had to cut power consumption, severely restricting domestic electricity. I had neuritis in my face, and the pain was awful. There was no heating, Hattie was on tour with the Young Vic Company and I was alone in my freezing flat.

A man I knew in the army called Michael became the manservant of a Professor Edward Dent, a great man, an academic, author and man of music. Michael had taken me to his lovely apartment in Kensington and then introduced me to Edward Dent. Later, when the professor heard that I was ill, he told Michael to collect me in a taxi and bring me up to his flat. He even gave Michael a rug in which to wrap me during the journey. The old boy was able to heat the flat, and he put me in his spare room and surrounded me with heaters. I recovered in a week – thanks to him and Michael.

Edward Dent was a Cambridge professor and had access to every first night that took place at Sadler's Wells or Covent Garden. He was an opera expert and had translated a great number of Italian operas into English, some of which are still performed at London's Coliseum. He didn't always utilise his opera tickets and so gave them to Michael and I. We saw so many performances for free, and he always had the best seats in the auditorium. I remained very grateful to him for all he'd done for me.

I made a number of lifelong friends at the Players', including the Farjeons, who were a famous theatrical family. Herbert Farjeon was a writer and director and his sister Eleanor was a well-known author, who was a regular at the Players'. I got to know Herbert's son, Gervase, who later became one of the three directors of the Players' Theatre Club. Herbert had died some years before. It was awful. The family were supposed to be having lunch together. Herbert was in his office but hadn't appeared, and they were waiting for him. They called out, but he didn't answer. Gervase went into Herbert's study but found his father dead on the floor with a telephone cord round his neck. He must have been on the telephone and was accustomed to pace up and down while talking. He must have slipped and fallen down, and the cord had gone round his neck and strangled him. There was no question of suicide. It was a freak accident. Gervase adored his father and never really got over that.

Gervase Farjeon married Violetta, who was one of the girls singing in the show at the time. She came from a rather interesting family, and she was brought up in France in the Pyrenees, studying music at the Paris conservatoire. When war broke out, her parents were in England; Violetta fled Paris and travelled south to Vichy France, where she boarded the last coal ship leaving Nice for Tangiers. She arrived in London during the Blitz, aged just 16, and joined the Free French Army, becoming involved in Forces entertainment. She joined the Players' and met Gervase. Violetta was involved with the Players' until she was 75 and remains a very vibrant octogenarian and lifelong friend.

Actor Clive Dunn, later celebrated for his portrayal as Corporal Jones in that much cherished sitcom *Dad's Army*, made his debut at the Players' in 1947 and used to perform duets with Hattie. Clive was irascible and lovely company. Funnily enough, we actually had a link long before I met him. Clive's mother, Connie Clive, was a concert-party performer and appeared in summer season in Will Seymour's *Bubbles* at the Grove Pavilion, Weston-super-Mare. The pavilion was open to the elements and covered only by canvas on both sides of the stage. I would go along and peer through the temporary tent-like covering and was absolutely enchanted by the diverse variety acts. Connie Clive was described as 'the queen of the seaside concert party' and even had top billing above Will Seymour.

While at the Players' Clive Dunn needed some help in preparing his flat for a visit from his parents and asked me to do some painting in order to spruce up the accommodation. While I was halfway up a ladder daubing some gloss on the ceiling, the door opened and an elderly lady introduced herself. 'I'm Clive's mother … Connie Clive.' I immediately stopped working and, as paint dripped from my roller, told her how much I admired her and how much joy she had given me all those years ago. She immediately told me to climb down from the ladder and give her a hug, which of course I did. I'm not sure if the ceiling was ever finished. I remember Clive telling me that he used to watch Connie, who 'dubbed' the voice of Mary Pickford in silent films, standing below the stage and reading from the script loudly in an attempt to synchronise the on-screen action.

I became great swimming chums with the actress Margaret Courtenay, who was also a bit of a gourmand. She appeared in films such as *The Mirror Crack'd* and *Duet for One*, and I met her through a wealthy American friend of Hattie's, Alan Moreton Walker, who I was always convinced was a secret agent. Somehow Alan had the contract to supply the American PX (Post Exchange) stores in American military bases' establishments all through the war and so made a fortune! I was always suspicious about how he had managed to do that.

I got to know Hermione Gingold when she appeared in various revues. She was wonderfully funny and so camp. There's a lovely story in which she was invited to do a charity appearance in aid of New York's Carnegie Hall. She arrived very late, just before the show, and drew up in a large limousine, accompanied by four beautiful young men in white suits. She flounced to the top of the stairs, where she announced to all, 'I've come to say … I can't come.' Miss Gingold then descended the stairs very slowly and climbed back into her limo.

I do love stories about actresses. Another of my favourites is about Hollywood legend Ethel Barrymore. Barrymore had just started rehearsing a Broadway play, and on one morning a young actress had put everyone in the shade with an extraordinary performance full of passion and drama and in which she was word perfect. Fellow cast members were extraordinarily impressed by the talent, confidence and skill of this unknown ingénue. At lunch the director approached Miss Barrymore and was extolling the virtues of the new girl, saying, 'Isn't she marvellous? A revelation! She's going to storm Broadway.'

'Yes, she's quite something,' replied Miss Barrymore, 'What a pity she won't be with us after luncheon.'

One morning, while working at the Players', I was cleaning out the coffee urn when I noticed a devastatingly handsome young actor rehearsing. His name was Dennis Wood. Because there was only one entrance and exit at the Players', he had to make his way through the auditorium, and he stopped to chat with me. That was all I needed.

We soon forged a friendship and then became lovers. What a dish he was! It was quite an important affair in my life, and I was very fond of Dennis. Oh, I haven't mentioned that he was actually married to an adorable actress called Peggy Willoughby but was bisexual. She and Dennis had a flat in Soho behind the Globe Theatre, and I would sometimes sleep in the kitchen on a put-you-up. Dennis would sometimes 'visit' me in the middle of the night and we would carry on beside the sink and cooker. And I might say Dennis was very at home on the range. I'm sure Peggy knew what was happening but turned a blind eye to our cavorting, and it was never mentioned. I got to know Peggy very well and she became a close friend. In fact, I saw more of her than of Dennis, who later left Peggy and ran off with a man to America.

Dennis had lots of male admirers, and one of his friends was the master of the royal wine cellars at Windsor Castle. He invited me down there during Ascot week. His responsibilities were quite demanding in that he ran the wine cellars for all the royal houses, and so he had his own staff. We had lunch in the castle, and we were waited on by guardsmen. I sat in the window looking across the courtyard and observed the royals arriving from their various residences and then climbing into their carriages to travel to Ascot.

After lunch we followed on to the royal enclosure at the racecourse, but they wouldn't let me in. I had on an open-necked shirt with a silk scarf, which was quite normal in those days, but I was told that I wasn't allowed in without a tie, so I had to leave my friend and watch the races from a box in the grandstand. My box was the one above the one the royals were in, and just in case I attempted to sneak into the royal box, I wasn't even allowed to go out and make a bet – I had to send a runner.

In the summer of 1947 Hattie met John Le Mesurier, then an aspiring actor, who was visiting the Players'. He was quite taken with the vivacious and ebullient Hattie and asked her for a drink. Hattie came home that night and told me, 'I've met this man who's rather special.'

John was actually still married to actress June Melville, who was a very beautiful, erudite and entertaining woman but who had a drink problem and lost all those attributes under the influence and became much less attractive. Her elegant hat slipped to a jaunty angle and her make-up always became smudged. Poor June. I loved her. She could be the perfect hostess, enjoying a rather intense political conversation with a group of people here and a gay theatrical conversation with some other people there. But all the time she'd be drinking, and suddenly she'd keel over absolutely unconscious. She could be marvellous company right up to the moment she fell over.

Early on in the romance, the four of us went dancing at the Lyceum in the Strand, and despite June's presence John was quite overt about his admiration for Hattie, who was equally smitten. John and Hattie were completely oblivious to anyone else; surprisingly, June didn't seem to mind and suggested we leave them to it. June leaned over to me and said, 'They seem to be very happy ... why don't you come with me, and I will take you round the theatre. I made my first appearance on stage here in a pantomime.'

The Melville family had owned the Lyceum when it was a theatre, and accompanied by the manager, the two of us went off, hand in hand, on a private tour of the venue. We went backstage, and she showed me all the old dressing rooms and told me wonderful stories about the old days there. June just seemed to accept John's behaviour and felt that, in any case, she was powerless. In fact, this wasn't the first time that John had strayed, and Miss Melville was no innocent herself.

So, in the end, John left her. He had to for his own sanity. There followed an amicable separation, and June agreed to a divorce. The hearing took place at the Law Courts in the Strand and was brought on the grounds of John's adultery with Hattie. It was all terribly civilised. I was subpoenaed to be a witness in the divorce case, and it appeared that the case would be fairly straightforward. The only likely cause of concern was that of June Melville's appearance as a witness. June's solicitor drew me aside and said that if the hearing didn't take place until the afternoon then June was more than likely to refresh herself during the lunch recess with a few drinks. 'For God's sake, Bruce, keep an eye on her, and make sure if we are delayed that you don't let her near a pub.'

There were so many people divorcing after the war, mainly poor girls who enjoyed a quick liaison with some soldier and then realised it was all a terrible mistake, that it was very possible the court would be heaving with such cases. In those days, I think you could obtain a divorce if your husband or wife snored.

All through the morning there was a succession of these sad cases, and our hearing was delayed until the afternoon. Worse still, the lunch break was timed to last two hours. I took June under my wing then, and we went out into the plaza. The first thing she said was, 'Darling, I've got to have a pee. There's a bar which is used by all the barristers. We can go there.' When we got there we were told that there was no ladies lavatory, so June said, 'Oh well, never mind, let's have a drink while we're here. I'll just cross my legs and jump about. Get me a gin and tonic, darling.'

I thought, 'I can't stop her having one tipple, but that is all she is getting.' I would make sure that she didn't have another before we returned to court; I had promised the lawyer she'd be sober in the afternoon. I then considered where we could go for lunch that I could keep an eye on her. Maybe a pub wasn't such a good idea, but the Salisbury on St Martin's Lane was a lovely spot, where a lot of theatre people went, and they did a lovely buffet.

As we got out of the taxi, June said, 'Oh darling, just a minute, I've got to go into the New Theatre to see a friend of mine who's doing a matinee today.' Before I could say anything she'd gone to the stage door and into the theatre. 'Bugger it!' I thought. 'Oh well, she should be all right: she's with a friend who is about to go on stage, so they can't get up to anything.' So I went into the Salisbury and sat on one of the stools, saved one for her next to me and ordered lunch. They were carving the most beautiful turkeys and hams and things, and I was really looking forward to the food. Well, time wore on and on, and of course there was no sign of June. Eventually she tottered in about an hour later, completely blotto. She had been to see her friend but afterwards had also nipped into a nearby pub for a few more gin and tonics.

I poured her into a cab; I had totally failed in my minding job, and she returned to the court sloshed. But I have to say she was a true pro, and when she was called, she composed herself and delivered her testimony in a loud, clear manner. When she'd finished, the judge leaned over, congratulated her and told her that she was the only witness he'd been able to hear that day. I was called next and attempted to emulate June's projection in my best Shakespearian fashion, and when I'd finished, I was similarly congratulated and told by the judge we should all be thankful for my theatrical training! The divorce was granted to John, and everyone was delighted.

John and Hattie were married in November 1949, and I told Hattie that they must have the flat to themselves. Mrs Richardson-Rice had since passed away, and her sister, who owned the flat, only visited a couple of times a year. After some discussion, it was agreed that I could move into the basement flat, and as she was keen on helping ex-servicemen, I got the cut-price rate of 10s a week. She possessed some divine furniture, which she let me borrow, and when she died, she bequeathed me a lovely piece. I have part of it as my bedside table now.

During this time my mother came down to stay with me in Earls Court, and we had a lovely time, enjoying London life, going to the theatre and exhibitions and eating out. My father was already in failing health and was quite incapacitated, and during my mother's visit we received a telephone call that he had been taken seriously ill and she should return to Clevedon. Naturally, I wanted to be with them both, and so we took the night train to Bristol. Fortunately, while on board, we met a family friend of my mother's, who drove us to Clevedon. My father lived for a little while after we arrived but finally succumbed to heart failure.

As a young man my father had been diagnosed with scarlet fever, and his heart was affected. My mother was told by the doctor that he probably wouldn't live much beyond his 30s. He actually died at the age of 66, which wasn't bad I suppose, given his prognosis, although it felt a terrible loss at the time. My mother, who was devoted to him, was stricken, but she was as strong as ever, and the family rallied round.

Hattie was also cast in *Educating Archie*, another radio comedy, which was broadcast from June 1950 to February 1958 on Sunday lunchtimes and was extraordinarily popular despite the unusual premise of a ventriloquist act: Peter Brough and his doll Archie Andrews. A lot of comedians who were later to become household names appeared in the show, such as Benny Hill, Harry Secombe, Dick Emery and Bruce Forsythe.

I used to attend rehearsals and can remember Hattie teaching Max Bygraves how to use the microphone because he was so new to it in those days. Julie Andrews was then a schoolgirl with a wonderful soprano voice and appeared every week – she was already a star. Her mother and father, Barbara and Ted Andrews, were stage people, a very well-known comedy team in the musical hall world, and they pushed her quite a bit. Miss Andrews was later replaced by Beryl Reid, who I loved.

Tony Hancock was also in the show; I knew his first wife, Cicely Romanis, very well. We were quite good chums, and she used to come into the Players' and talk to me. Hancock was a very difficult man even then. While recording the series, Hattie was still working at the Players' and would return home about midnight, after which she cooked a very late supper. About an hour later Eric Sykes would arrive, wanting some help with finishing the script.

During this time, Hattie and John Le Mesurier were also filming *The Pleasure Garden*, a short 'movie masque', a classic piece of '50s Bohemia and set in the decaying edifices and tangled weeds and brambles of Crystal Palace. The film was quite charming, and I was actually employed as an extra, playing several bit parts. Sadly no major movie contracts followed.

In April 1953 rehearsals began for a show that was to put the Villiers Street venue well and truly on the map. Apart from the usual Music Hall shows, the Players' also produced pantomimes, plays or revues. At this particular time, they decided to put on a musical called *The Boyfriend*, written by the brilliant Sandy Wilson, who sadly died fairly recently. Set in the Roaring Twenties in the French Riviera, the action mainly takes place at the Villa Caprice, where a number of girls reside at Madame Dubonnet's School for Young Ladies. The most famous song was 'I Could Be Happy With You'. It was a lovely, charming show.

Vida Hope, one of the regulars at the Players', directed the show, and I was her assistant. I took notes while she was directing the rehearsals and also fed the cast when they wanted a meal. The lead role of Polly Browne was taken by a girl called Diana Maddox, who had a lovely singing voice. Sandy loved her and wrote the play with Diana in mind.

At the final dress rehearsal, three days before opening night, Vida did a whole run through before breaking for a meal. All the cast and backstage crew came to The Supper Room in great spirits. The 'dress' had gone very well, and everyone was very jolly. Vida then called everyone for a final run through and gave them a pep talk, saying, 'This is the last time you will do it before the public come in on Tuesday, so give it all and be on your toes.'

They returned to the theatre and were about to begin the performance, but no one could find Diana Maddox. She was nowhere to be seen. Above the office, at the front of house near to the entrance to the club, was a sort of box room that wasn't used very much, and I said to Fred, the car park attendant, 'Go up those steps, Fred, and look up there.' Sure enough an unconscious Diana was lying on the floor, in her full costume and covered in dust. We called an ambulance and she was whisked off to Charing Cross hospital where she was pronounced too ill to perform for several weeks.

So there we were on the eve of the production and with no leading lady. Vida was appalled because she had created a lovely production and everybody involved had made a positive contribution. 'The show must go on', of course, and so Vida suggested that the only thing to do was to carry on with the run through. Most of girls in the chorus had the odd line or bits of business but there was one of them who just had to sing and dance in the chorus and had no proper part to play. She was called Anne Rogers and had the least to do in the show, although she had played the lead in a national touring production of *Snow White and the Seven Dwarfs* when she was in her early teens. She had given up the business and had returned to full-time education, but she was now 18 and had left school and found work at the Players'.

Vida hadn't actually arranged anyone to understudy Diana but had actually asked Anne to study the lead part some weeks before, and so she decided to have the run through with Anne reading from a script. You can probably guess the rest. Anne read the part perfectly and even performed the lead's dance routines. She was wonderful, and we all cheered at the final curtain.

Anne Rogers was in as leading lady, but we had to get another girl into the chorus and several of the dancers had to move into different positions. Anyway it was all sorted by the Tuesday, and the show opened to a fabulous reaction. Anne received rave reviews, and although it seems such a show-business cliché, this time the old chestnut 'You'll go out there a chorus girl but you'll come back a star' really rung true. That was a line in *42nd Street*, a Hollywood musical in the '30s; Ruby Keeler was the girl. That is exactly what happened here at the Players'.

The Boyfriend was a huge success and transferred to the Wyndham's Theatre in the West End where it ran for more than five years with over 2,000 performances. The show moved to Broadway with several of the Players' stalwarts, and the American producers wanted Anne Rogers to star, but she couldn't because she was under contract to the London production. Dozens of girls auditioned, and the part was given to a certain Julie Andrews. It was thus in *The Boyfriend* that she made her Broadway debut in 1954 at the age of 19.

My friendship with Ronald Benge, forged in wartime, had remained as strong as ever. Ron resided with Irena and his stepdaughter, Alfreda, in West Kensington, which was conveniently close to Earls Court, and we used to see a lot of each other. I remember early on after demob an outing to the Proms. We hadn't been to a concert for years, and we went on the night they did Beethoven's *Ninth Symphony* ('Choral'), which was an unforgettable experience. Ron was extremely cultured, and we continued to share a love of theatre, music and books.

It was time to move on from Eardley Crescent, as John and Hattie had started a family. Robin was born in March 1953, and although not a formal arrangement, I was delighted to have him as my second god-child. Ronald and Irena were renting out bedsits, and so I moved in with them just before the coronation of Queen Elizabeth.

SEVEN

YOU ARE OFFAL, BUT I LIKE YOU

'To eat figs off the tree in the very early morning, when they have been barely touched by the sun, is one of the exquisite pleasures of the Mediterranean.'

Elizabeth David

As well as departing Eardley Crescent, I also left the Players' in the same year. As much as I loved working under the arches at Villiers Street, I realised it was time for a change. I had always wanted to run my own restaurant, and even in those days I possessed little glimmers of ambition.

I was offered such an opportunity following a business proposal from a psychiatrist, and I later discovered I should indeed have had my head examined to have considered his suggestion. Hilary James, a shrink at St George's hospital situated in Hyde Park Corner, and a regular customer at the Players', approached me about opening a French-style bistro. He rather admired my work, and he came to me one day and said, 'I'm going to open a restaurant in Elizabeth Street, off Eton Square in Belgravia. Would you be interested in running it for me?'

Le Matelot (the sailor) was actually the first really proper French-style bistro in London, and before long we were sensationally successful. I had built up a reputation and following at the Players', and we were soon filling the place with enthusiastic diners. Booking a table was a prerequisite if you wanted to be sure of getting in, and there was always a queue.

It was very hard work, but the restaurant was very successful as I made sure that all the produce was top quality. I used to walk to Soho to buy ingredients at Berwick Street Market. One day I was carrying heavy bags full of fruit and vegetables and trying to negotiate the streets, which were chock full of tourists who had come to the capital to see Queen Elizabeth's coronation festivities and decorations. It was just impossible to make progress and, struggling with all the produce, I thought I would just have a rest. It was near St James's Park, and I finally found a bench on which to sit down. As I stretched out and carefully placed the bags of shopping near my feet, I looked up and saw the street sign, which read 'Old Queen Street'. I chuckled loudly and thought 'how perfect!'

Hilary and I got on quite well initially, but once the restaurant was up and running I soon discovered a number of things that I wasn't happy about. Dr James was wont to pick up young men in Piccadilly, and he would sometimes bring them to the restaurant and invariably expect me to find them jobs in the kitchen. One morning, an unemployed Welsh boy, who Hilary had slept with the previous night, arrived at the restaurant. Hilary had felt sympathy for this poor boy and had directed him to Le Matelot. He was a nice young man, so I thought I'd give him a chance. I had Coquille St Jacques on the menu, so I said to him, 'You see that pile of scallops over there on the table? Well, I want you to slice them like this.' I showed him what to do and continued, 'Then just place them on that platter. There, that's all you have to do. There are a lot of them, but it's quite simple.'

The boy looked at me anxiously. 'That's fish, isn't it?' he said. I said, 'Well yes ... sort of. Scallops are seafood but they're a type of fish – shellfish.' The boy's expression changed from disquiet to dread, 'Ooh I can't touch fish. No, absolutely not. I've got a thing about fish. And if you don't believe me, my mother will tell you!'

So I said, 'Well in that case, you can take off that apron, put on your coat and fuck off!' The poor boy ambled off in shame. I found it quite amusing, but later Hilary had the cheek to tell me off about it and didn't find it at all funny. It was extraordinary that I was supposed to mollycoddle his rent boys in my kitchen while attempting to run a top-class restaurant.

However, the main problem with Hilary was that he wanted to fiddle the accounts so that we paid as little as possible, if any, income tax. He was earning good money as a psychiatrist and was from a wealthy family but always wanted more and more. No amount of money would be enough for him. I was outraged and didn't want to be involved in any such nefarious activity. I've never approved of that sort of thing in business.

I hadn't fought in the war to be involved in this sort of thing. His sort of people just didn't know about the real world and how some people had to live. I wondered how he could think of doing such a thing when people were starving. I just couldn't understand his mentality. Anyhow, I refused to do what he asked of me, and he got very angry. Sometime later I went to his house – a luxurious pad in Belgravia – to ask him for a bit more money for the kitchen staff, which he refused. I realised I couldn't work for him anymore, and although I had no alternative work to go to, I lost my temper and told him to bugger off!

I had no idea what I was going to do. I've never been very good with money and had very little savings put by. I'd become friendly with a Russian woman called Luba, who was a sort of 'Maitresse d'hôtel' at a rather nice restaurant in Chelsea, and I went for a drink with her one day. She told me that she was leaving her job and wanted to start her own place. Luba had discovered a little place round the corner at No. 19 Mossop Street, behind Brompton Road. It was currently a workman's café, but she was going to take it over and start a restaurant. She suggested that I catered for the lunchtime trade. It would be completely independent from her business, and I would be in charge until mid-afternoon when she and her staff would take over.

I was thrilled, but didn't have any money to help equip the kitchen and restaurant. Luba had a fridge, but I needed one for myself. Vida Hope gave me £100 to buy a fridge. The décor was very basic, and I hadn't changed it from a workman's room with long forms and refectory-type tables. In fact, the room was so cramped that if one of the customers wanted to leave then everybody had to stand up to make room. It was the first restaurant where, apart from waiting on table, I did absolutely everything, including the cooking, cleaning and even scrubbing the floors.

The menu consisted of very straightforward dishes like fried scampi, beef goulash and egg and prawn curry – things that would appeal to lunchtime clientele. My bestseller was the chicken and mushroom pancake: a great plateful of food for 4s 6d. I used to buy good quality boiling chickens, which you could get cheaply in England, because being old hens they were considered inferior. In Spain you have to pay double the price for them because they have this wonderful flavour, but the English still haven't caught on.

After my lunch service, the lovely Luba would arrive at three o'clock every day, and we'd share a pot of tea while recapping about the business and enjoying a good gossip. She'd then start preparing for the evening meals. I met lots of lovely people in Mossop Street, some of them rather grand, and they used to consider it frightfully amusing to sit on a bench in a workman's dining room!

There was only one entrance to the restaurant, and to get to the dustbins, which were in the backyard, the dustmen (who made a daily collection) had to tramp through the restaurant. In those days the bins were huge and metal and the men carried them on their backs. Every lunchtime – of course, it would have to be lunchtime – the dustcart would arrive and the dustmen appear. This always caused a bit of a commotion with the diners.

I had employed the actor Maurice Browning as a waiter. He was very efficient and equally funny. When he spotted the dustmen approaching, he would hold centre stage and call out, 'Ladies and Gentlemen, it's cabaret time.' He would then open the door and stand aside, and they'd enter and return moments later with the bins. The whole place was in uproar, and the diners would scream with laughter! The dustmen's foreman thought it was great fun, and I remember him telling me, 'You've got a nice place here, sir. You deserve to do well. And a very jolly crowd too.' Marvellous. Of course, I never told him why they were so jolly.

Soon after Maurice Browning, who was afflicted with polio as a child and had spent time in an iron lung, suffered a stroke and was very ill. Hattie had employed him as her personal secretary, and although he was no longer fit for work she continued to pay him. Typical Hattie. His mobility was seriously restricted; he was quite paralysed, and I felt sorry for him and thought he could do with a break. I asked him, 'What would you most like to do for a holiday, Maurice?' He replied that he'd like to go back to Corfu. I was rather hoping and expecting he'd say somewhere like Hove or Eastbourne. But Maurice had been to Corfu once on a previous visit and loved the Greek island. So I decided to take him there. I have to say the first part of the trip was an absolute nightmare.

I approached a travel agent to find suitable accommodation, and they assured me that there was a villa that had wheelchair access and would suit Maurice's needs. But the villa turned out to be totally unsuitable. There were loads of steps and no access to the bathroom. I had also hired a car, but Maurice's wheelchair didn't fit in the boot. Luckily I found a couple of muscle boys in the swimming pool down by the shore. They were English, rather beautiful and working there for the summer. I called them over and told them the story and they agreed to help; 'We're with you!' were their exact words. They stayed with us the whole time and carried Maurice everywhere. In a nearby villa there was a very kind English couple who helped a lot, and eventually we had a wonderful time and Maurice really enjoyed himself.

I was great friends with Johnny Heawood, a dancer and choreographer. Johnny was Canadian and had come to the UK on a troop ship that was torpedoed and had somehow saved himself. We had met at the Players', where he performed in a number of shows, and I remember he used to do a wicked drag act. Johnny choreographed the West End productions of *The Boyfriend*, *Guys and Dolls* and *Irma La Douce* and had gone on to work on Broadway. Johnny was very camp and obviously gay: wonderfully witty and waspish, with a lovely use of language.

One day I invited him to lunch. The day before I had been given a lovely bunch of camellias, and I put them in a little pot in the middle of the table. Johnny arrived rather late and a bit drunk. I told him to sit down while I finished in the kitchen. When I returned to the table with the starter, he'd eaten the camellias and said, 'Absolutely delicious darling but they could have done with a little more dressing!' Well I was a bit worried and telephoned someone to make sure that camellias weren't poisonous. He was so pissed he didn't know what he was doing. Poor Johnny was actually an alcoholic and drank himself to death some years later. It was very sad.

Johnny took me to see Marlene Dietrich in cabaret at the Café de Paris, Piccadilly. He knew Miss Dietrich as he had met her at a party in New York when he was doing *The Boyfriend* on Broadway. She apparently remembered him as 'a very amusing chap' and kept in touch with him. So at the end of the show, her manager suggested we go round and see her. I didn't need to be asked twice. We stood in the queue outside her dressing room, and I remember a slightly drunk Randolph Churchill also being there. We were the last in line, and eventually the door opened and Peggy, Marlene's assistant, opened the door for us and invited us in.

Marlene was so pleased to see Johnny and seemed very relaxed: she could talk normally to us about anything. She was really funny actually and still in the marvellous dress that she had just worn on stage. She went behind the screen and cast her clothes over the top like in the old Hollywood movies! She came out wearing a pair of black slacks and a black polo-necked sweater and had let her hair down.

We had a little chat, and she asked us to come back to the hotel for some supper. She was staying in the Oliver Messel suite at the Dorchester. Of course we both said we would love to join her, but Johnny said that his boyfriend, Ted Glennon, was also coming to meet him at the stage door after the show. Marlene told Johnny his boyfriend would be welcome too, and she immediately got on the phone to the stage door and told the doorkeeper to bring Ted to her dressing room when he arrived.

Ted was a merchant seaman and very intelligent; Johnny never consorted with fools. Of course he was shocked and thrilled when he got to the stage door and was told to come to Marlene Dietrich's dressing room! After a still somewhat stunned Ted arrived, Marlene said, 'Right we can all go to the hotel now, but I need to put this on – it's what the crowd will expect.' With that she donned a pure white ermine full-length coat, which covered her casual clothing underneath. She put me on one arm and Johnny on the other and told Ted to bring up the rear.

We walked up the steps to the street, where the police were holding the crowds back. Apparently it was like this every night. There was a limousine waiting with its headlights on and full of flowers. We climbed in. In those days you could drive from Coventry Street to Piccadilly, but when we got to the turning next to the famous store Fortnum & Mason, a car sped out and went into our side.

The pedestrians, who had witnessed the collision and then saw what had happened, recognised the famous occupant and started pointing and trying to open the car door – presumably to help but also because they were star struck. A look of panic came over Marlene's face. She was really terrified of being mobbed and had experienced this sort of thing a number of times before, when she had come close to being seriously injured in the melee.

The driver of the other car got out and wanted to argue about the accident, but Marlene wound the window down briefly and called to him, 'You know who I am. Follow me to my hotel and we'll talk about it there.' The man was certainly taken aback, and when the penny dropped he looked delighted. He was probably thrilled about the accident … it would certainly be something to tell his grandchildren! We drove on and reached the Dorchester safe and sound. Once there we were greeted by five uniformed commissionaires waiting. We were gathered into the foyer and then into a private lift where we entered her sumptuous suite.

We made ourselves at home, and Marlene made a call to room service, and very soon two waiters arrived with two trolleys laden with food, which we devoured. We talked for hours. She was wonderful company and, although such a screen goddess and known throughout the world, so natural with us. As it was just beginning to get light she asked me to join her on the roof. She told me she loved seeing London at dawn, so we went out on to the roof garden and watched the sun come up over the great metropolis. There I was, standing with one of my heroines,

Marlene Dietrich, with my arm around her waist and her arm around mine. Wow!

We left at about five in the morning, and Marlene told me she wanted to come to my Mossop Street restaurant, so we arranged a day and a time for her to come. We said our goodbyes, and later that morning when I stumbled into the restaurant and completed the lunch service, I thought I should telephone and thank her. I got through to her room, but Peggy told me Marlene wasn't there. About an hour after I had departed, she had left, after a short rest, on an early train to an American airbase in Yorkshire where she was entertaining the servicemen. Such energy that woman had.

A few days later she telephoned me, very apologetic, to say that she couldn't come to the restaurant because she was being mobbed everywhere she went, and she and Peggy had decided it wasn't safe. She did say, however, how much she'd enjoyed meeting me and that she'd had a lovely time. Imagine that. It was a marvellous evening, and my only regret is that I didn't ask her for an autographed photograph as a souvenir – and to prove to any doubters that I did indeed spend the night with Marlene Dietrich!

The business at Mossop Street was flourishing, but then, wouldn't you know, the landlord was offered a huge sum of money by some big property developer who wanted to build a block of flats on the site. There was nothing we could do, and so Luba and I had to close down. Although I do consider myself to have lived a charmed life, I do seem to have been dogged by misfortune when it's come to property.

One of our regular customers at No. 19 Mossop Street was Dorothy Green, the American wife of Philip Green, who composed film scores including *The League of Gentlemen* and *A Stitch in Time* and also won Ivor Novello awards for other soundtrack songs. The Greens were a lovely Jewish couple and owned a wonderful Georgian house in Regent's Park, which I used to visit. Dorothy had heard that Mossop Street was closing and told me she was in the process of opening a club in Fouberts Place, next to the Palladium. It was to be called the Key Club. She wanted to offer the sort of food I had been preparing at Mossop Street and asked me to run the food side of things at her club.

I accepted immediately and visited the Key Club, which was named thus because all members, mainly well-known actors and actresses, had their own key which they could use anytime during opening hours! I can't imagine members of the Groucho Club being afforded the same luxury …

The club was situated on the three levels. The restaurant was in the basement and the top floor housed the bar, which was run by actor Gerald Campion. Gerry was famous for his portrayal of the 'Fat Owl of the Remove', Billy Bunter in the 1950s television series. He later gave up acting and opened a very well-known club called 'Gerry's' in Shaftesbury Avenue.

I trained one of the waitresses, Kate Carter, to become a chef. She was a very pretty girl and flattered me by saying that she would love to work in my kitchen. I told her I would be delighted to have her alongside me, but that I couldn't pay her any extra. She was so keen that she offered to work for free during her time off. So I enlisted her to do lunch service with me one day, and she did a marvellous job. The only mistake she made was to serve some fish sauce with a veal dish. Fortunately the diners all thought it was a wonderful accoutrement and they all loved it. I later did a bit of research and discovered that the dish was along the lines of a classic veal dish accompanied by a tuna sauce.

Charles B. Cochran was an impresario, theatrical producer and talent spotter who had discovered new talents such as Gertrude Lawrence, Jessie Matthews and Evelyn Laye, among others, and made stars out of them. Another of his protégés was a very good friend of mine, Elizabeth 'Betty' Frank. Betty was a ballet dancer and, in her prime, the most beautiful girl. In fact, she was very attractive even when she was considered past her prime. She became a theatre and ballet critic for the *News Chronicle* (incidentally a marvellous newspaper – my favourite newspaper actually), and I used to attend first nights with her.

Before the war she was a member of de Basil's Ballet Russe, a company consisting mainly of exiled 'White Russians'. She fell in love with Alexei, one of the dancers, and at the end of a tour they found themselves in Marseille and unemployed. Alexei knew where they could get a meal and took Betty to a nearby community of refugee Russians in

La Favière, near Le Lavandou. Betty loved it and wanted to settle down there, so they decided to get married and look for somewhere to live in that lovely part of southern France.

They found a small villa for sale, but it was valued at £500, which was a lot of money in those days, and they were broke. Extraordinarily, just a few hours after they had viewed the property, Betty received a telegram informing her that a relative of hers had died and left her ... exactly £500! Betty bought the villa straightaway and ran it as a pension for a while.

At the outbreak of the war, Betty returned to England and Alexei joined the Maquis. Then, due to his language skills, he was drafted into serving with the US Army as an interpreter. He lost an eye when a jeep in which he was travelling crashed, and he was admitted to the US Army hospital in Southampton when after the war he was briefly reunited with Betty.

Meanwhile the villa had been used as the local headquarters of the Vichy French administrator and then taken over by the Germans. When they were forced to leave, the Nazis destroyed the house. I had also been told that the administrator was possibly a double agent, working for the Resistance, and so when the Germans discovered his identity, they actually blew the house up with him inside it.

At the end of the hostilities, Betty's villa wasn't a very high priority in terms of reparation payments – especially as it had belonged to an Englishwoman. For some years, nothing happened in regard to rebuilding her former property, but then a department of the French Government contacted her, stating that she was entitled to a war damage claim.

I went on holiday to La Favière in 1956 when Betty first mooted the idea of establishing a hotel. Betty employed an architect and asked me to join her in overseeing the project. Work was delayed as he was juggling a long-suffering wife with a mistress in Toulon and so was spending a lot of time away from the project. The villa was rebuilt using local stone and was pretty basic, but I loved it. The basement had actually remained intact, and I found some interesting items including an old Russian family bible and a truncheon with a viciously evil iron head, which I was to make use of in later years as my weapon of choice at The Establishment club.

I was still in touch with Peggy Willoughby after Dennis Wood had run off to America, and it transpired that she and Betty Frank were dancers together before Betty joined the ballet. Once the building work was completed, Betty suggested that Peggy and I run the restaurant, and she decided to name the hotel 'Le Coq d'or', a ballet in which she had once appeared.

We had about ten guests and cooked three meals a day. I had to go to the shops in nearby Le Lavandou for the produce as La Favière was only a small village. I had a bicycle and would cycle back with great baskets on the handlebars. I was very methodical and organised a fourteen-day menu, which included such delicacies as sautéed kidneys, *saucisson*, *pâté de campagne*, *terrine* of *foie gras* and *coq au vin*. Andouillettes are a French thing. They are tripe sausages, made from chitterlings – pigs' guts. They were one of my most favourite things in the world and something I still adore. When my niece, Storm, comes to visit me from France I always ask her to bring me an andouillette! I love tripe, and where I live now in Spain, every district has a different way of preparing the offal. In France they always had tripe on a Thursday in the butchers, and it was called *'Tripes à la mode de Caen'*. And actually tripe is very good for you – extremely nutritious.

Betty and I ran the hotel for the first full season, and we shared the profits fifty-fifty. I couldn't live in the villa because all the rooms were being used for guests, so I resided in a little hut, a small sort of bothy up the hill at the back of the guest house. It was rather nice actually because, of course, the weather was lovely.

The hotel, which was a bit of a London haven, was always full of interesting people as Betty's guests were mainly theatre and journalist chums as well as some of my contacts. The place was always buzzing. One regular visitor was Ellen Sheean, an actress whose parents were both writers. Vincent Sheean was an American journalist and author, whose most famous work was an account of being an overseas reporter, *Personal History*, which was the basis of Alfred Hitchcock's

1940 film *Foreign Correspondent*. Vincent Sheean served as a reporter for the *New York Herald Tribune* during the Spanish Civil War. I got on very well with Vincent as we shared the same political views. He once said that he had 'an ardent sympathy for the downtrodden'. Vincent was married to journalist novelist Diana Forbes-Robertson, daughter of the Scottish actor Sir Johnston Forbes-Robertson, and the two often travelled on journalistic assignments together.

Another guest was 'Vicky': Victor Weisz, the very famous political cartoonist. Victor was born in Berlin, and his cartoons took a very strong anti-Nazi stance; being both Jewish and left wing, he sensibly fled his homeland in 1935. He also worked for the *News Chronicle* where he had met Betty and had subsequently gained a celebrated reputation as a perceptive political commentator. One night at Le Coq d'Or, Victor found a melon seed in his starter and decided to plant it on the side of the terrace. I actually got a lovely melon from it. Sadly, he suffered from depression, and in 1966 he, like his father before him, committed suicide.

One day I was driving with Betty up in the mountains with my car stereo on, and we found ourselves listening to César Franck's *Symphonic Variations*. Betty used to do a ballet solo to a section of the piece, and when it came to that particular bit, I stopped the car by a patch of grass and asked her to dance for me. Betty was about 60, but she got out of the car and, with the radio turned up as loud as it would go, performed her old solo. She was still graceful and elegant, and it was absolutely wonderful. It is one of my most treasured memories.

Betty's mother, a darling lady called Amy Scorer, spent a lot of time at the villa, and I got to know Betty's daughter, Maroussia Frank, who later became a very distinguished actress and stalwart of the Stratford Royal Shakespeare Theatre Company. I used to go up regularly to Stratford and sometimes stayed in the flat that was kept for Peggy Ashcroft. Maroussia married that marvellous actor Ian Richardson, who sadly passed away unexpectedly in 2007. I am still in touch with Maroussia, who lives in London.

Lova and Lisa Obolensky ran a nearby stall from which I used to buy some of my vegetables. One day Lova Obolensky cricked his back.

He had to go to market every morning and load up all the things for the vegetable stall, including heavy sacks of potatoes, but because of his back injury was unable to do any lifting and so asked me if I would go with him in his lorry and help out. It was about 6.30 a.m., and the market was as busy as anything, and I watched in awe at all these men hauling great loads of vegetables around. Unfortunately, I just wasn't able to emulate them, and when it came to lifting a box of melons or a sack of potatoes I just couldn't lift them on to the lorry. He looked pityingly at me and told me to follow him. We went into a bar, which was already full of marketers, and he made me drink two large tots of Marc – a sort of brandy made from the residue of grapes. That's what they drank down there, and I have to say that I could feel the effect immediately. My muscles seemed to strengthen straightaway, and I went out and lifted the potatoes and the melons as if they were feathers! Marvellous tipple that.

The film *Bonjour Tristesse* based on the book by Françoise Sagan featured Deborah Kerr, Jean Seberg and David Niven. Some of the location shooting took place in a very glamorous villa near us. Betty and I went down to watch some of the scenes being filmed, and what I recall is that the production company had hired a very good chef to provide delicious food for the workers, but the crew were all moaning about the menus and wanted the chef replaced by an English cook! Perhaps I should have suggested they eat at our place.

After completing the first season in 1957, I decided not to do a second summer term although I did help a little with the administration. After Le Coq d'Or I was employed at another French gaffe, although La Popote D'Argent was actually situated back in London. In Marylebone Way to be exact. However, this was not a long engagement as after six months I discovered that the staff were selling pornographic photographs to the customers and stealing from the till. It was all absolutely hopeless, and the establishment was losing money hand over fist.

Vivien Leigh used to come in for lunch twice a week. She was very grand and used to arrive in a chauffeur-driven limousine and would sit there until a crowd recognised her and had gathered. Then, to the great pleasure and excitement of the crowd, she would give the driver a signal to open the car door. It was only then that she made her entrance into the restaurant.

My head waiter there, Emo, was a great fan of hers but was due to leave the restaurant and return home to Sicily. He asked me if I would approach Miss Leigh for an autograph. I agreed, and one day, after she had lunched and was sipping some coffee, we had a little chat and I asked her for an autographed photo. Two days later a publicity still as big as a television set arrived, and written right across it was, 'To Emo, my dear friend and the best waiter in London', and it was signed 'With love, Vivien Leigh'. He was absolutely delighted, and it was very nice of her. I felt sorry for her, as she was quite an unhappy person. Not only was she a drinker but she suffered from manic depression, which seriously blighted her later life, too.

I was involved in another rather disastrous episode during this time, having been approached by a friend, Dennis Arundell, to assist with a restaurant that he had opened. Dennis Arundell was a distinguished British stage and film actor, who had appeared in *The Life and Death of Colonel Blimp* and *'Pimpernel' Smith*. Dennis was a true Renaissance man who was also an author, translator and composer, but he was probably best known as an opera producer. I had seen his 1958 production of Wagner's *The Flying Dutchman* at Sadler's Wells; the production was famous for its faithfulness to the score but also for the imaginative design that employed the use of 'Magic Lantern' projection.

Dennis had a professional reputation of being difficult, and he certainly spoke his mind, but as far as I was concerned he was an absolute gentleman. He and his partner, a faded male film star, lived in a Georgian house in Islington that had seen better days. It was packed full of theatrical and operatic memorabilia, which had always held interest for me. Dennis was a warm and generous host of brilliant mind and conversation to match, and I had enjoyed some wonderful evenings in his company. The two of them had opened a restaurant in Camden Passage, Islington, but it was a hopeless arrangement as Dennis's lover had a terrible alcohol problem. To fund his addiction, he took money

My father in the driving seat outside the Clarence hotel, Ilfracombe. (By kind permission of Ilfracombe Museum)

Silver cars and charabancs – a different kind of horse power. (By kind permission of Ilfracombe Museum)

Grandpa Copp.

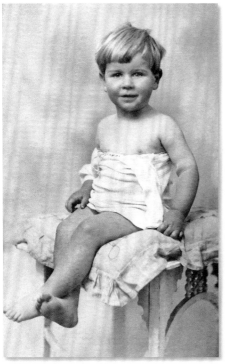

Anyone seen my nappy? The author, aged 2.

My darling sister Joan, cradling her dog Biddy, with cousin 'Tiny'.

Celebrating VE day with Margo Gibbard at the Venice Lido.

On the trail of Nazis, Caserta, 1945.

A fraternal post-war reunion in Clevedon with (clockwise) Reg, Tom and Jack.

In waiter's guise at The Players', while serving Hermione Gingold. (Athol Skipsey)

Ronald Benge and wife to be, Irena Seirer, Austria, 1945. (Alfreda Benge)

It's raining gags. Peter Cook outside
18 Greek Street, Soho, 1961. (Lewis
Morley. By permission of the Science
& Society Picture Library)

Checking the menus – a publicity pose for
The Players', 1948. (Athol Skipsey)

With the great and the good of 'The Establishment'.
(Bryan Wharton)

Vida Hope, actress and director of Sandy
Wilson's *The Boy Friend*.

Yours truly in reflective pose. (Athol Skipsey)

Johnny Heawood – always a queen but never
a drag.

A delightful night at Danny la Rue's club with Johnny Heawood and actress Joan Gadson.

The dangerous and charming Lenny Bruce performing at The Establishment.

Dearest Hattie and John Le Mesurier on their wedding day, Kensington Register Office, November 1949.

In celebratory mood with urbane John Le Mesurier and Richard Wattis.

Quaffing with Joan Le Mesurier, Sitges, Easter Sunday 2006.

My little sister Diana. (Andy Merriman)

The WIPS menu – a restaurant very much of its time.

With brother Tom at my cousin Philip's enchanting South Farm wedding venue. (Becky Duncan)

Daniele, the love of my life, on my La Floresta balcony in August 1988.

from the till and any remaining monies were spent at a nearby pub. The couple had been backed by various artistes, friends and actors, who gradually withdrew their money or attempted to get their funds back.

It was such a shame, but the place closed down and later became the site for Carrier's restaurant. I knew the American chef Robert Carrier quite well and taught him how to prepare a few dishes. I contributed to his book *Great Dishes of the World*, which in various editions sold over 10 million copies. Carrier made a fortune, with homes in New York, London and the country. I visited him in New York, and he arranged an extremely elaborate lunch in Manhattan for me and five friends. Bob Carrier was a roving queen if ever there was one, and his long-term lover, a writer, committed suicide I believe.

I had stayed with Ronald Benge and his family in West Kensington for about a year before moving into St George's Square in Pimlico with a gay friend from the army, Anthony Waller, who was an award-winning theatrical and later television set designer. We shared the apartment for a while until he came into some money from his father, Lewis Waller, a famous actor-manager, and moved out.

It was around this time that I met a lovely waiter, Ben, who was working in a Danish restaurant. He was beautiful, well educated and actually bisexual; he also had a girlfriend, an au pair also from Denmark. Ben and I lived together for two or three years, and then one day he just disappeared, leaving all his clothes and the few belongings he possessed.

I was naturally upset and concerned that something had happened to him – perhaps he had been involved in an accident or worse. I was very upset for a while. I had met his girlfriend and went to see if she knew what had happened to Ben. She didn't know where he was, but we had a lovely evening talking about him, how wonderful he was and how marvellous he was in bed. He had the most fabulous body and looked undressed even when he was fully clothed! The talk must have stirred us because I actually ended up in bed with her; she is one of the few women I have ever had sex with.

One night, about five years later, I was walking home to my flat and there was a young man walking about 200yds in front of me, towards

St George's Square. From the way he moved, I knew immediately it was Ben. I caught up and greeted him. He was delighted to see me, and I didn't feel any anger – I was just so pleased to see him. In fact, we were both so excited to see each other that I took him home and seduced him.

Afterwards, he told me what had happened. Ben explained that he regretted leaving the way he did, but he had met a wealthy, older man who offered him everything he needed – especially financial security. Ben decided that the only way he could leave and not upset me was just abandoning ship. It was immature, but I understood and wasn't at all bitter about it all those years later. Ben wasn't particularly happy living with the older man but had decided to stick it out. His girlfriend returned to Denmark. Ben's lovely mother gave me a pâté recipe, which I used later in one of my restaurants, so I always had something to remember him by.

My other long-term relationship during this period was with Patrick, a black man who hailed from the Seychelles. We had an affair that lasted quite a few years when he was in the Royal Medical Corps. He was the subject of a lot of racism and took to drinking too much. I had to pack it in. Without wanting to generalise, my personal experience of African or West Indian men was that they were much more laid back about relationships and it always seemed to be less complicated!

I used to meet so many people and a lot of gay men, so it was never a problem to find a casual partner. Sometimes I think I must have been in more laps than a napkin. I have to say that although we were never lovers, I did have a bit of a crush on Paul Danquah, an actor and lawyer and the son of statesman and one of the founders of Ghana, J.B. Danquah. I met him when we were both at a dance class. A friend of mine, George Erskine Jones, taught dancing, and although I wasn't that keen on learning, I realised it was very good exercise. I remember 'Modern American' being very demanding. I suppose I'm too old now to be considered for *Strictly Come Dancing*.

Paul was the most beautiful man you could ever imagine. His long-term partner, Peter Pollock, was a steel heir, who had served as a captain in North Africa and Italy and had been the lover of double agent Guy

Burgess. Before moving to Tangiers, the couple lived in Battersea and shared their flat with the artist Francis Bacon. Francis gave some of his drawings to Paul, and the Tate later exhibited them.

Working at night wasn't conducive to having a successful love life. I was so involved with my work that it was impossible to sustain a long-term relationship – a consequence that I've actually never regretted. Work was everything for me, and I loved it. Lots of my friends had lasting relationships, which was marvellous for them. I understand why some gay men want to legitimise their relationship in the eyes of the law and marry, but I can't understand why you'd want to have a formal wedding ceremony like some do nowadays.

However, I'm getting ahead of myself again. There was at this time, the mid-1950s, a court case that was to prove hugely significant in gay circles and was to sway public attitudes and eventually bring about a change in the law to legalise sex between men.

Edward Douglas-Scott-Montagu, 3rd Baron of Beaulieu, was jailed for a year, having been found guilty of homosexual offences at Winchester Assizes in 1954. Lord Montagu always maintained his innocence, but in an interview with a national newspaper admitted, 'I am bisexual. To describe it any other way would be dishonest. I remember feeling that I didn't have to apologise to anybody. I am what I am.'

Montagu was convicted along with *Daily Mail* journalist Peter Wildeblood and Dorset landowner Michael Pitt-Rivers, Montagu's cousin. During the trial, Wildeblood admitted that he was gay, which was very brave considering homosexuality was still a criminal offence. The offences had taken place in a hut on the Beaulieu Estate with RAF male nurse Eddie McNally and his RAF pal John Reynolds. McNally and Reynolds turned Queen's Evidence – what else? – and testified for the prosecution against the three defendants in court.

The arrests were part of a crackdown by Churchill's government during the height of Cold War paranoia, following the defection of gay spies Guy Burgess and Donald Maclean to the Soviet Union. I was lucky, in my work and the people I mixed with, to be mainly protected from homophobia and the virulently anti-homosexual atmosphere.

The then Home Secretary, Sir David Maxwell Fyfe, Viscount Kilmuir, had promised 'a new drive against male vice' that would 'rid England of this plague'. The police were ordered to clamp down on homosexual behaviour, and hundreds of gay men were locked up every year.

Meanwhile, Lord Montagu continued to protest his innocence, and the trial had caused so much commotion and controversy that the Home Office set up the Wolfenden Committee to consider changing the law. Of course Kilmuir, who was probably a closet queen – the vociferous homophobes usually are – led the opposition in the House of Lords to the implementation of the Wolfenden Committee, whose 1957 report recommended the decriminalisation of homosexual activity in private between two adults.

During the debate on the Wolfenden Report in the House of Lords the following was stated:

> Field Marshal Viscount Montgomery of Alamein rose to state categorically that he was quite convinced that no homosexuality had ever occurred among any of the hundreds of thousands of men under his command during the war. This statement produced a moment of astonished silence followed by suppressed snorts of disbelief and then an uproar of laughter.

Sadly, it took another ten years before consensual sex in private between homosexuals was approved by Parliament, and again in the debate 'Monty' was quoted as saying, 'This sort of thing may be tolerated by the French, but we're British ... thank God.' He urged the House of Lords not to legalise gay sex and warned that the 1967 homosexuality bill would be a 'charter for buggery'.

Methinks he did protest too much.

EIGHT

A MERMAID, A DAME AND AN OSTENTATION OF PEACOCKS

'Actors and burglars work better at night.'

Sir Cedric Hardwicke

Although I had left the Players' in 1953, they called me back again every few years until the mid-1960s because The Supper Room kept going into the red and they never got anybody decent to run it. After I'd left, they'd call me back in again. What is it with some people? They just don't know how to run a restaurant; a lovely little place like that and with a ready-made clientele, and yet it failed every time. I used to haul it together by having to sack staff, put new people in and get it all going again. Within a month the restaurant was making a profit again.

The actor and director Bernard Miles had been a regular performer at the Players'. I'd got to know him quite well, and he loved what I'd done there over the years. His daughter, Sally, had been a friend of mine for years and contacted me. She told me that her father had always wanted to run a public theatre and had acquired an old riverside warehouse in Blackfriars at Puddledock on the River Thames. The Mermaid was to be the first theatre built in the city of London since the Great Fire, and Bernard wanted me to run the catering side.

The basis for a new theatre actually originated in Bernard Miles' garden in St John's Wood. The schoolhouse was converted into a theatre that housed an audience of 200 and was used for concerts, plays and opera. I saw *The Tempest* there, in which Bernard played Caliban. There was also a celebrated production of *Dido and Aeneas*, featuring Kirsten Flagstad, a Norwegian opera singer and considered to be one of the greatest Wagnerian singers of the twentieth century. She and Bernard were very close, and he was actually at her deathbed when she passed away from cancer in Norway in 1962.

I went to see Bernard, who told me, 'I've got no money Bruce, I can't pay you anything, but I want you to set the restaurant up for me and we'll pay your expenses while you're doing it.' I didn't mind so much about the money: filthy lucre has never been my driving force, and the idea appealed to me, so I agreed to take it on. I arranged for somebody else to run Betty's villa, which by this time was running very smoothly. And so I started at The Mermaid.

I joined his team as the theatre was being built. My job was to organise the restaurant, which was behind the stage, overlooking the river. It had been the part of the warehouse where lorries were loaded and unloaded but was now to be at the centre of the theatre's food service.

There was no public money available, but Bernard was excellent at raising funds and had many wonderful ideas, so he enlisted the help of all his thespian pals. Bernard was incredibly persuasive and fearless about approaching anyone of importance. He was assisted by his wife, actress Josephine Wilson, who was always supportive and enthusiastic. He had Laurence Olivier and Vivien Leigh sitting on steps of St Paul's Cathedral with a pile of plastic bricks and calling out to passersby, 'Buy a brick for The Mermaid!' Members of the public would be so inveigled, and the famous couple would sign the plastic bricks. All proceeds would go to The Mermaid Theatre fund. Bernard would have dancers form the famous Tiller Girls running from the City to the Strand, publicising the new theatre.

During the building work, Bernard, Josephine and I erected a hut on the premises and invited prospective patrons to lunch. There was room for about six guests in the hut, and they were usually city tycoons, movie stars or famous stage people. After Bernard had persuaded the governor of the Bank of England to make a donation, the money flowed in.

We started off by providing super dishes with lots of English cheeses, and then I arranged that when one of the builders turned off his electric drill, I'd plug in one of my little stoves and cook them some hot food while Bernard kept them amused with a wonderful flow of stories and anecdotes. He was actually the best raconteur I have ever heard, and because he was so brilliant, I never tired of his stories despite hearing them numerous times. After lunch the foreman would come and conduct them around the building site and then the cheques would soon follow!

On one occasion, a well-known actress at the time called Margaret Rawlings was in the hut when the foreman entered the hut. He apologised for interrupting the lunch party but said that there was someone outside who had actually done the lunch and tour thing previously but happened to be passing and wanted to see Bernard. It turned out to be Dame Edith Evans, who, in my opinion, was the best actress in England at the time and possessed this marvellous voice. So she came in, and we all had to squeeze up. Everyone was delighted, of course, and not only because of her reputation but because she was so much fun. When it was time for the tour with the foreman, they all went out into the building site, but Dame Edith stayed in the hut as she had done the tour previously.

Just out of earshot of the guests, Dame Edith said, in a wonderfully theatrical tone, 'Margaret Rawlings, she's stage struck you know!' It was a lovely catty thing to say, but such fun. I loved her. I remember her being interviewed on Michael Parkinson's show once and telling the story about going for an audition in her later years when she had been in everything you could name. A young researcher had asked her, rather arrogantly, 'And what exactly have you done?' And she replied, 'Do you mean … this morning?' That put the upstart in his place!

We had donations and assistance from unusual sources. Walter Nell, the head of Express Dairies, gave us a huge amount of equipment, including a huge cold buffet counter, refrigerator and other vital pieces of apparatus. I once accompanied him on a trip around all the dairies and was very impressed that he knew everyone's name.

I was contacted by Marks and Spencer, who wanted to try out a new sort of cotton material and test how hardy it was and how well it would wear in everyday use before being produced in a bigger scale for general use. We agreed and asked the staff to wear the new slacks and shirts and had to record the occasions they wore them and how many times they were washed. It turned out to be very successful, and each employee was given three sets of the uniform by M&S!

Bernard also wooed a Signor Lucian Ercolani, the famous entrepreneur, whose 'Ercol' furniture was hugely successful and a household name in post-war Britain. The company had perfected the process of steam bending wood and, using elm, had produced a huge number of Windsor chairs. At its peak, Ercol manufactured around 3,000 chairs a week and their furniture had been featured at the 1951 Festival of Britain, feted as exhibiting the latest style and fashion in furniture design and manufacture.

Anyway, Signor Ercolani and his son came to lunch at the hut. I wasn't introduced, as I was busy preparing the frankfurters for their repast, and having listened to Bernard's pitch, they were shown round the site before returning to the hut, when it was expected that Ercolani's chequebook would be produced. Unfortunately, on this occasion, there was no sign of a donation. I introduced myself to Ercolani's son, also called Lucian, who told me that he was in the Air Force with somebody called Bruce-Copp, who was a rear gunner in his Wellington bomber. It turned out to be my brother Reg. They were great friends but had lost touch after the war. Wing Commander Ercolani had been a wartime bomber pilot and had been decorated several times for gallantry in operations over Europe and in the Far East.

Once he had established that I was, in fact, the brother of his friend, he had a word with his father. The Ercolanis subsequently gave Bernard and me a tour of their factory in High Wycombe, and after Bernard had charmed the management and staff, Signor Ercolani Senior told us we could choose what we needed for the theatre's restaurant. We needed no further encouragement and ended up being given thousands of pounds worth of furniture! They gave me a dining table for my own personal use, and it is now housed in my sister's residence in Shepherd's Bush, which I once owned. I gave Lucian Ercolani Junior Reg's contact details, and later they did see each other although Reg died a couple of years later, aged just 47.

Another family connection was the visit of my cousin Carol Lindsay-Smith, who was employed as a journalist by the *Daily Sketch* and had been sent to do a story about the opening of The Mermaid. It was suggested that she meet the man in charge of the restaurant; Carol recognised my name, and I greeted her immediately by saying, 'You must be Dozy's daughter!' (I wasn't being rude; Dozy was in fact the nickname of Dora, Carol's mother.) I was thrilled to see her and surprised by yet another extraordinary coincidence. Carol later asked me to do the catering for her wedding, and after the service at St Martin's-in-the-Fields, we held the reception at The Mermaid. I arranged a barrel organ to play them in.

One day, just before The Mermaid opened, I found myself sitting alone cogitating on all the things that had to be done before the big day. I was disturbed by two ladies waving from outside trying to get my attention. It was Peggy Ashcroft and Shakespearian actress Renée Asherson, Robert Donat's widow. They were terribly polite and apologised for disturbing me but said that they just wanted to look around. I gladly showed them around, and Peggy strode on to the stage and started reciting a monologue – she just wanted to test out the acoustics! It was a lovely moment.

Unfortunately, the theatre restaurant, in terms of my work, was very badly designed; I was furious with Bernard Miles for not letting me have more time with the architect before completing the design, because the kitchen was out of all proportion to the restaurant and possessed very little storage space. Cold foods and salads had to be kept in a small cupboard, and there was no wine cellar or cloakroom. Just inside the entrance was a large deep shelf, and all the coats, hats and outer garments of the customers had to be placed on top or below that shelf. In cold weather this amounted to a lot of clothing as the restaurant seated ninety-five people and was always full.

I had four bars at The Mermaid there, and trade was so successful that we put extra trestle tables up in the foyer, which was miles away from the restaurant and at the front of the house. We used to do 100 meals at lunchtime, although we were actually open all day. Bernard also opened the auditorium at lunchtime and put on old films or documentaries for free, and all the office workers from the City used to come in with their sandwiches. They'd all buy something at the bar too, and the place was bursting with people.

Eventually we opened the theatre in early May 1959. The first production being *Lock Up Your Daughters*, which was performed twice-nightly plus two matinées. Bernard wanted to keep the building open as long as possible during the day but also after performances. He had some crazy ideas, but some of them did work. After the second show of *Lock Up Your Daughters*, which finished at 11 p.m., Bernard felt that the audience needed a snack, so I agreed to do kippers and cocoa, and I must say the idea went down a treat. He also wanted me to serve mead, in keeping with the historical nature of the show, which didn't go down so well!

As a tribute to Lady Miles and all the help she gave me, we created a dish on the menu called 'Smothered Steak Josephine', which became a best seller. I also came up with a dish for Muriel Forbes, who was a theatre critic for *The Times*. I concocted a dessert in her honour – 'Mermaid Syllabub' – the ingredients for half a dozen portions included half a pint of double cream, several tots of rum and a pound of prunes ... we must have wanted to keep the customers on the run ...

I knew her quite well, and I think she rather fancied me for some reason! She was always inviting me to certain events. I remember attending the opening night of a wonderful opera at Covent Garden, and there was a huge party in the crush bar at the end. I remember I met Ninette de Valois and the conductor – his bloody name escapes me now although he was a very beautiful Italian. I never refused Muriel, as I loved going to these sorts of occasions when work allowed. I must say I was a bit of an old tart.

On one occasion Bernard told me that he had to give this special lunch party but didn't want to lose any customers, so he felt they could eat in the restaurant with all the other diners. So we reserved a table for ten, and the guest list included the Archbishop of Canterbury, the Lord Mayor of London and Dorothy Macmillan, the wife of

Harold Macmillan, who was actually much grander than her prime minister husband.

The arrangement was that they would all have drinks before lunch in the front of house bar in the foyer and would then come down to the restaurant for lunch. However, dear Dorothy didn't want to partake of a pre-meal aperitif and she came to the restaurant on her own. I told her that she was a little early and that they were serving drinks in the bar.

Lady Macmillan said, 'I don't want anything. I'd rather go and sit at the table now. Could you arrange that for me?' I said, 'Of course I can, give me your coat.' She had on one of those old-fashioned fur coats with actual fur buttons; it reminded me of one my mother owned. Anyway, she handed me the coat, and I hung it up on the hook, which was full of coats, and the bloody thing came away from the wall and crashed to the ground with a great cloud of dust. All the coats and hats, walking sticks and umbrellas cascaded down, and Dorothy stood there with all this mess around her feet. She barely moved, looked down and she said to me, 'Oh how very unfortunate. Never mind. Could you now show me to the table?' Terribly embarrassed, I sat her down and then persuaded the stagehands to clear the debris. It wasn't her fault, but that was probably the only time when I wasn't a friend of Dorothy.

In May 1961 Bernard put on the Wakefield Mystery Plays, and James Bolam was playing Jesus Christ. James was just starting his career and didn't have a speaking part. In fact, the main reason he didn't have a line was that in those days Jesus wasn't allowed to speak! During the run James was having dinner in the restaurant and found a nail in his spinach. He quietly said to me, 'Bruce, aren't you overdoing the props?' Bless him for not making a fuss. He's a wonderful actor – so under-stated – and I've always enjoyed his great success over the years.

The queen actually came to see this production, and I dealt with the refreshments when the royal party went to Bernard's office. I was advised that Her Majesty didn't like her champagne too cold, so I removed the bottles from the fridge and gave her a glass of room temperature bubbly. She was very gracious, but didn't touch a drop, so I must have failed my audition. I was mortified not to have made another queen happy.

Barbara Goalen, a member of fashion royalty, the queen of hauteur and one of the first supermodels, came to The Mermaid during London Fashion Week. She swept in looking so elegant and sporting a most wonderful hat. I said to her, 'Darling, where did you get that hat?' She replied, 'It's my husband's old army vest. I just put it together.' Barbara had suffered double tragedy while still so young. She was widowed at the age of 24 when her husband Ian Goalen died in a crash, and her teenage fiancé, an RAF bomber pilot, had been killed in action during the war. I met so many famous people during that time, including Agatha Christie and Luise Rainer. Boris Karloff is another name that springs to mind.

My sister Di hadn't just followed me to the Players'. She had also worked at No. 19 Mossop Street in the kitchen and as a waitress and was now with me at The Mermaid, initially as lunchtime manager in the restaurant and then as assistant manager during the evenings. One night, Princess Margaret was in the house and was totally engulfed by a crowd of admirers, and Di had to rescue her as her lady in waiting and a chinless aide weren't doing anything to help. Di asked her if she would like a drink, to which the princess replied, 'Yes, please. In the circumstances you'd better make it a double.'

Princess Margaret made another appearance that year when I had a pair of tickets for a very big ballet gala at the Royal Opera House. I had brushed up very nicely in a dinner jacket and biked to somewhere near Piccadilly Circus where I picked up Johnny Heawood, who was also in evening dress. We drove off to Covent Garden, and I went into the side street by the stage door where I knew I could park the scooter. As we climbed off there was a sudden warning cry. We looked over and saw it had come from a policeman. Two more bobbies rushed over and ordered us to stay where we were and not move. We didn't move a muscle and stood to attention just outside the stage door. We wondered what we had done wrong.

Then a very posh car pulled alongside, and I noticed the royal insignia on the bonnet. I thought, 'Bloody hell we've got into something here.' The police were upset because they were supposed to be keeping the road clear and they'd missed us. Princess Margaret got out of the car and she spotted us. She then started waving and called out, 'Oh hello Johnny!' Johnny waved back, and I looked at him in amazement. Apparently she liked *The Boyfriend* so much that she had requested that Johnny choreograph the dances for the private shows she mounted for all the Debutantes. She disappeared into the Opera House. The policemen's faces when the princess waved at us were an absolute picture. They must have wondered who we were, although they didn't ask.

Johnny and I visited Diana Churchill in the actors' home Denville Hall in Ruislip. Diana was married to Mervyn Johns (Glynis John's father). She was very frail, poor thing and unable to walk. Johnny was as lovely as ever and said to her, 'Darling it must be marvellous to be here when you put on a show. You can play all the wheelchair parts. Why don't you start with *A Little Night Music*?'

Bernard was difficult, but I understood him. He had no regard for commercial gain and insisted on putting on shows that were quality and of artistic benefit to audiences. Sally Miles used to say that if you really wanted to upset her father, you should just open the door to his office and shout 'Donald Wolfit!' (The rather hammy actor manager of whom Bernard disapproved). Poor Sally died of motor neurone disease in 1986 when she was only 53.

I remember once Bernard threatened to murder me because I got his wife, Josephine, to ride pillion on my scooter to the Mansion House. The traffic was so bad that it would have taken me an hour to drive my car to work, so I used a scooter, on which I could cut through the traffic – sometimes even riding along the pavement when necessary! Josephine had been invited to lunch with the Lord Mayor of London, and she couldn't get a taxi, so I said I would give her a lift.

Bernard saw us going off and told one of my friends in the box office to ask me to come straight to his office when I returned. My colleague warned me that Bernard was hopping mad, so I was prepared for a row when I went to see him. He was indeed furious. 'How dare you! Don't you ever put my wife on that dreadful vehicle of yours,' he said. 'Don't be silly,' I replied, 'I was actually doing her a favour. And what's wrong with a scooter anyway? I'll take you on it one day.' 'No you won't. Never!' was his response. And I never did.

Bernard and I did, however, fall out in a major way after I had been at the theatre for a few years. We used to lunch together once a week to discuss business matters. I mentioned that I'd got tickets for the Albert Hall concert of the world famous Russian father and son violinists David and Igor Oistrakh, and I was delighted as tickets were almost impossible to procure for the event. I had specially arranged to take the evening off.

On the night of the concert a few weeks later, and just as I was about to leave, I was asked to see Bernard, who wanted me to attend a meeting with the trustees. I wasn't usually invited to such gatherings, and so when I walked in the room, I asked Bernard what it was he wanted with me. He told me to sit down and he would come to it. Well, I waited and waited and time was passing. I thought that if I didn't leave in the next twenty minutes then I would miss the concert.

I suddenly realised that Bernard had done it purposely. For some reason he was being spiteful and didn't want me to go. He was like that on occasions. I finally got to my feet, went to the door and said, 'I'm sorry I can't stay any longer, gentlemen, because I'm going to this Oistrakh concert, and if I don't leave now, I'm going to be late.' The trustees were all sympathetic and, in fact, made it clear how lucky I was to be going. I managed to make the Albert Hall by the start of the concert, which did indeed live up to all expectations.

However, the next day Bernard made a terrible scene, and I thought he was going to throw me in the river. He was so angry and said that I had no right to walk out on the trustees and that I had been very rude. I'm afraid I lost it and told him what I thought of him and his ridiculous attitude. There was no reason for me to be at that meeting. I can only think he just wanted to show me that he was in charge. I worked day and night for him and took more money in the restaurants than he did at the box office; I don't think he ever forgave me for that! In any case, I had had enough of Bernard's behaviour and decided to leave. I just walked out on him.

Thanks to the success of The Mermaid I had gained a reputation for setting up restaurants in theatres. The politician Jennie Lee came to the theatre once to meet Bernard, and I was introduced to her. She was very friendly and was working for the Arts Council in those days before she became Arts Minister. The provincial theatre circuit, once successful, had gone downhill, and it was Jennie's brief, through grants from the Arts Council, to revive the theatre scene outside London. She was very impressed with The Mermaid and was keen that all the newly refurbished provincial theatres should have a restaurant.

Prompted by the financial success of The Mermaid, Jennie called me to her office. She wanted to know the secret of our success so that she could impart some of my knowledge to the theatre directors throughout the land. I warned her that The Mermaid was unique and told her, 'You won't make any money with the food in the theatres unless you operate like we do. We make more money at lunchtime with people who work nearby and pop into the restaurant for lunch than we do in the evening with the theatregoers. The theatre restaurants must be open all day.'

Of course, the artistic directors who were engaged to launch these new restaurants in their theatres didn't know anything about food and were mostly at a loss in knowing what to do. I had made my name at the Players' and now The Mermaid and so my expertise was in great demand. I went all over the country, starting in Sheffield, moving on to Liverpool and then somewhere a little more local – the Greenwich Theatre. The stage was moved upstairs and below was the foyer and the restaurant, which had been remodelled by an architect. I set it all up and then appointed staff and purchased the kitchen equipment.

I was on the catering committee for the Theatre Royal, Stratford, but decided against taking on the job of running the restaurant as it was so badly designed. While there, I once stumbled upon a group of actors having tea on the lawn outside the theatre. I said hello to the ones I knew, including Peggy Ashcroft, who I had worshipped since I had seen her in *The 39 Steps*, when she played the maltreated wife of John Laurie's crofter. I saw everything that she was in and was thrilled to bits when I first met her.

After Greenwich, I was asked to create a restaurant at the lovely old York Theatre Royal, which had been built in 1744 and was situated right opposite the famous Minster. York is such a beautiful city, and I lived in a small hotel near the theatre. I was there for quite a long time as it was a big job. A new wing had been constructed, which housed a cafeteria, a restaurant and bars.

It was here that I met Judi Dench, now a Dame and one of my dear friends. Her parents lived in the city and had close links with the theatre. Judi's father, Reginald, was a physician and attendant doctor to the theatre and her mother, Eleanor, was the wardrobe mistress. I used to see quite a lot of them, and they also came to the restaurant. Judi had been in the first three productions of the modern revival of the York Mystery Plays before making her professional acting debut with the Old Vic Company as Ophelia in Hamlet and embarking upon her glittering career.

The work on the new wing finished over the Christmas period, and its opening was to be marked by the production of a pantomime on Boxing Day, so I had to stay and supervise the restaurant and cafeteria. A lot of the people who worked in the team were local, but the architect and some others lived in London and so had to celebrate Christmas up north. There were about fourteen of us, and we decided we would hire a little unlicensed café on Christmas Day and have a conventional Christmas dinner there.

Early in the morning, about half past seven, I went down to the theatre to collect the wines and goodies that I had put aside for our party. It had been snowing, and as there was no one around, there were no footsteps in the virgin snow. The city looked even more picturesque than usual. And there, to add to the loveliness, standing at the bus stop outside the theatre, was a line of peacocks! They used to gather in the garden of an old building across the street from the theatre, and for some reason they were standing at the bus stop all in a row!

A little lady was scuttling along – a Mrs Mop type with a scarf round her head and clutching a handbag. As she came nearer I said, 'Are those real? My friends and I had quite a lot to drink last night ... am I seeing things?' 'Oh no!' she said, 'You ought to see them on Wednesdays in Woolworths at the sweet counter.' Apparently every Wednesday they were in Woolworths, and all the girls used to feed them sweets. How wonderful.

The pantomime duly opened on Boxing Day, and after the matinee, the restaurant was heaving with the audience wanting high tea.

Working and living in York was a lovely experience, but my work was done, and it was time to move on. I was offered a job at the Nottingham Playhouse, one of Britain's leading provincial repertory theatres.

John Neville, who was a West End idol of the 1950s and a foremost member of London's Old Vic Company, was now the theatre's artistic director and asked me if I would run the theatre's restaurant. I was excited about it, especially as Judi was employed at the theatre at the time, playing opposite him in a production of *Romeo and Juliet*. There is a nice story that Judi's proud parents often travelled from York to see her in the play, and one night, when she delivered the line 'Where is my father and my mother, Nurse?' her father apparently called out, 'Here we are, darling, in Row H.'

Anyway, my job at Nottingham was short lived. Well to be correct … it never actually happened. The town council had a very strong hand on the theatre and insisted on having a representative involved in some of the appointments. So consequently I was interviewed by a local politician (or a leader of the council or whoever he was).

His interrogation began with, 'Mr Copp, now tell me, are you married?' It was the first question he asked, and I thought, 'Ahaha, here we go!' Anyway he continued the interview in that vein. He barely asked me about my work or experience as he was totally fixated on my sexuality. He became more and more insulting and he made no pretence of his homophobia. He went on and on about how he couldn't stand homosexuals and that they should all be in jail.

After a few insufferable minutes I couldn't take any more and said, 'I don't think there's any point in going on with this interview. You're an impossible man and I don't want anything to do with you. Good afternoon.' And I got up and walked out.

I presumed he was yet another closet gay, but I was absolutely shattered by the experience. It wasn't as if I'd gone in waving a feather boa or singing a medley from *The Wizard of Oz*. It was the first time I'd ever come across the sort of prejudice that had a direct effect on my employment.

John Neville's assistant was present and had tried to back me up but to no avail. I later found out that this awful man had behaved badly on many other occasions, criticising the way John ran the theatre and interfering in everything that was none of his business. In fact, he finally drove John Neville out following a number of funding disputes.

After I had left Bernard, The Mermaid experienced mixed fortunes. There were successful productions, such as Noël Coward's musical revue *Cowardy Custard*, and an annual staging of *Treasure Island* in which Bernard reprised his role of Long John Silver. It was also in this show that Bernard gave Spike Milligan his first straight acting role as Ben Gunn. A somewhat dodgy property company, Gomba Holdings, bought the theatre in the mid-1980s, at which point Bernard's position as 'honorary artistic advisor' was brutally ended. The theatre was now in decline, and although there were various attempts to keep the theatre alive, The Mermaid closed.

I went to see Bernard at the actors' home some years later. I rang the doorbell and asked one of the staff if I could see Lord Miles. He'd been given a peerage by then and was only the second theatrical peer at that time (Laurence Olivier being the first). I was invited into a waiting area. The matron told me that she would go into his bedroom and tell him I was here. I overheard her say, 'Lord Miles, there is a young man to see you. His name is Bruce Copp.' 'Who?' Bernard queried. The matron raised her voice, 'Bruce Copp!' There was a moment's silence before Bernard gathered his thoughts, 'Oh Bruce Copp! Bring him in at once!' I was so pleased because I thought he was just going to say, 'Tell him to fuck off!' I had left him and The Mermaid because I couldn't put up with his nonsense any longer. But he didn't, and we had a nice chat.

Poor Bernard couldn't walk and was virtually bedbound. It was sad to see him like that. Bernard, or Baron Miles of Blackfriars as he was then known, moved back to his native Yorkshire but died in June 1991, a year after his wife, Josephine. He was aged 83 and impoverished.

In September 2008 The Mermaid was stripped of its theatre status, and although it is still standing as I write, there is a chance that the building will be demolished.

NINE

THE ESTABLISHMENT

'I've always been after the trappings of great luxury.
But all I've got hold of are the trappings of great poverty.
I've got hold of the wrong load of trappings, and a rotten
load they are too, ones I could have very well done without.'

'Sitting On the Bench', a sketch from *Beyond the Fringe*

One night I went to see *Beyond the Fringe* at the Fortune Theatre. The show had been running over a year or more, and I had never been able to go because my life was so bloody busy. I had a single good seat in the stalls, and I can't remember having enjoyed anything more in the theatre. In fact, there was a single man sitting next to me – we were probably the only two lone men in the whole place – and he bruised my side he punched me so much with glee. We had a drink together in the bar afterwards, and I never saw him again, but we did share the joy of the show.

The following morning at 8.30 a.m., while I was still in bed, the phone rang. I picked up the receiver, and a voice said, 'Hello. Is that Bruce Copp?' I said, 'Speaking.' 'Well this is Peter Cook.' I wondered who might be playing tricks on me at that time of the morning, 'Really? Come on, who is it? I'm not in the mood for all this.' The voice continued, 'No, it really is Peter Cook, I promise you!' I was eventually convinced and told him that I'd actually seen him on stage the previous evening. So we had a little chat about the show, and I then asked him why he had called me at this unearthly hour. 'I want to take you to lunch today,' was his reply. I was still rather bemused, but Peter Cook was a huge star, and I was very keen to meet him. I was intrigued and said I was certainly free for lunch. He suggested we meet at a French restaurant in Wardour Street that I happened to know.

When we met, Peter was accompanied by his fiancée and future wife, Wendy; once we had ordered, he gave the reason for our rendezvous. He explained that he and Dudley Moore had been planning to open a comedy and music club called The Establishment and wanted me to look after the restaurant. Although they wanted it to be in Soho, which at the time was a bit seedy with lots of strip clubs, prostitutes and frequented by villains, they thought they could attract posh clientele from Belgravia and Chelsea.

Premises had already been secured in Greek Street, just a few roads from where we were sitting, and the theatre designer Sean Kenny was involved in creating the décor of the club. I had worked with Sean (later of *Oliver* fame) at The Mermaid, where he had devised several sets including those for *Lock Up Your Daughters*. It was Sean who had suggested me to Peter.

Although he knew who the clientele would be, Peter wasn't very confident about the number of members he could attract. I was convinced by the venture and told him I thought it would be a huge success. 'You will have 25,000 members when you open,' I said, to which Peter replied, 'I think you've had too much wine.'

Funds for the venture were to come from two sources. A friend from Cambridge, Nick Luard, was a co-director and he had inherited some money on reaching the age of 21, through a trust fund set up by his grandfather. The other income stream was by soliciting subscriptions: three guineas for a year's membership, two guineas if paid before opening of the club and life membership for twenty guineas. To stress the satirical nature of the club, life members received a free pin-up picture of Harold Macmillan ...

Leaflets were inserted into the *Beyond the Fringe* programmes advertising membership details and offering special deals. None of the money could be touched at that stage and had to go into escrow. Within a week, 4,500 subscriptions had been paid. It was incredible that all these people were paying up front to be members of a club that hadn't yet opened. Huge money was pouring in, and I thought, 'I'm going to be rich for the first time in my life.'

The title of the club was, of course, somewhat ironic; it was a play on 'The Establishment' meaning the establishment of an institution and the term 'The Establishment' that had been created a little while earlier by *Spectator* columnist Henry Fairlie and described the power that controls British society. There was, of course, a further paradox in that members of The Establishment became the club's patrons. Peter Cook described it as 'the only good title I ever came up with'.

The property at No. 18 Greek Street had previously accommodated the club Tropicana (an all-girl strip revue) but had been forced to close following a police raid. It was very seedy. The chandeliers were plastic, the windows were swathed in oceans of red velvet curtains and there were discarded G-strings, used condoms and all the tawdry remnants of a former strip club.

The club had been acquired with property behind. You could go up the steps behind one house, and there was a sort of well between the two buildings. If there had been a fire, people would have been hopelessly trapped, so I put up these roll-up fire-escape ladders temporarily under each window; in an emergency, patrons could have lowered themselves down into the yard of St Martin's School of Art, which was behind us in the Charing Cross Road. I remember we used to see odd bits of sculpture lying around the yard there. Eventually we had to provide some permanent means of escape, and we had to spend £15,000 on proper fire escapes.

There was much media interest; The *Daily Mail* reported that The Establishment would be London's first satirical night club, and Jonathan Miller wrote the following in *The Observer*:

... the original idea was born in Cambridge, conjured out of the amber haze of an all night drinking session. Nicholas Luard, an undergraduate, was entertaining Peter Cook, who had already startled Cambridge with his bizarre contributions to the Footlights Revue. Cook had been fascinated, on his visits to the Continent, by the famous political nightclubs there. Luard shared Cook's interests ... Revue with its rapid montage of sketches and songs, seemed to offer the best form for the satire that Cook and Luard were aiming at.

The club allowed comedians and satirists to perform new material in a nightclub setting, outside the jurisdiction of the Lord Chamberlain, whose censorship of language and content had been a continuing dilemma for performers for over 200 years. It certainly freed them from the constraints of conventional theatre and chimed with the 'swinging London scene'. And indeed the revue format was one that I had been very familiar with at the Players', albeit in Victorian mode.

The stage entertainment from a regular team took place together with a star spot, which was taken by various singers and comedians. There was an hour's cabaret at 9.30 p.m. each night performed by resident company, who were so talented and constantly revised their material. The regular cast consisted of John Fortune, director of the 1960 Cambridge Footlights Revue; John Bird, then a Royal Court Theatre producer; actor David Walsh; and Jeremy Geidt, another actor and TV presenter, a wonderful straight man. Later on Eleanor Bron joined the cast, replacing Hazel Wright. Sketches were mainly written, but some were improvised although inevitably inspired by Peter Cook. Other performers included singer Carol Simpson and the multi-talented Jonathan Miller, who made short films that were screened between sketches. John Wells was teaching modern languages at Eton and had appeared with the Oxford Theatre Group revue in Edinburgh, and Nicholas Garland was imported from the Royal Court to direct the sketches.

Dudley Moore, who was still appearing at the *Beyond the Fringe* at the Fortune Theatre, used to play piano in the basement, accompanied by a bass player and drummer; although he was not paid very much, he was rewarded by being surrounded by a bevy of lovely young things and took great advantage of this arrangement, I seem to remember. Everybody loved to dance. 'The Twist' craze had just come in, and I remember dancing with Clive Dunn's wife, Priscilla, who said to me, 'Fancy an old square like you running a place like this.' Cheek!

Sean Kenny set to work, using the materials of wood, steel and glass. Besides the ground floor restaurant and bar was a small stage and upstairs library. Richard Ingrams, journalist and future editor of *Private Eye* and *The Oldie* magazines, designed all the signs for the club. On the wall of the bar hung a huge topical strip cartoon, about 16ft long and drawn by Roger Law, who Peter knew from Cambridge and who was to co-create *Spitting Image*. Burly Roger was useful on occasions in standing up to some of the gangsters or heavies that came to frequent the club and gave as good as he got!

The Establishment opened in October 1961, and we were only just ready! Every table had been booked, and there were long queues outside. The opening night was rather chaotic. There had been applications from people all over the world who wanted to say, 'I was there!' Most of the 7,000 members wanted admission, but we could only squeeze 500 into an area that was only meant to hold about 100 people. Bentleys, Rolls-Royces and other expensive cars jammed Greek Street, and so many people streamed in that the doors had to be shut. Those that couldn't gain entry angrily protested outside and were photographed by paparazzi and interviewed by reporters desperate for a story. The telephone system collapsed.

We had taken bookings on a first come, first served basis. And of course there were a few gatecrashers, including Margaret Campbell, the Duchess of Argyll, who was much disliked and had an awful reputation, as did her companion Dominic Elwes, a portrait painter and friend of Lord Lucan. Elwes was a well-known playboy. A real shit actually, very grand and from an aristocratic background.

They hadn't booked but had barged in and sat at a vacant table. When the members who had reserved that table arrived, this gruesome couple just moved to another table. They kept doing that until there was only one table left, and they moved there. Well, this table had been kept for a well-known peer. As you can imagine, I was desperate by this time, with all the pandemonium around me, and I was beginning to shake with nerves. Anyway, I went up to him and told him exactly what was going on. I said to him, 'I've got a very nice table for you but the Duchess of Argyll refuses to move.'

He smiled and surprisingly remarked, 'How wonderful.' The peer clearly relished the opportunity to get one over on her. He went over to the table and said something to her and Elwes. I never knew what he said to them, but they both blanched, immediately rose to their feet and left their seats. We didn't allow them to stay in the club and had them thrown out into the street. We cancelled both their memberships, and they never came back.

John Bird recalled that 'Socialites, cabinet ministers, fashion models, intellectuals fought to get in', and John Wells, in Humphrey Carpenter's tome on the satire boom of the 1960s, *That Was Satire That Was*, described a scene of indescribable chaos:

> Television arc lights blazed above the crush, rich girls in lovely diaphanous dresses wriggled and squealed in the crowd, their rock jawed escorts bellowing above the din, 'Hello Jeremy! Are you going to Antonia's thrash on Saturday?' Satire was in and they were damned if they were going to miss a second of it.

Subjects for satire on the first night included material about Harold Macmillan; Lord Hume, Foreign Secretary; Rab Butler, Home Secretary; and President Jomo Kenyatta of Kenya, founding father of the Kenyan nation. The opening night was reviewed in *The Sunday Times* by Harold Hobson, who complained about the 'sardine spirit', and in *The Observer* by the formidable Kenneth Tynan.

There is no doubt that the first night was a huge success, but backstage things were a bit different. A good half of the club was given over to the theatre, bar and restaurant, and the stage was at the far end of the premises. The kitchen was very limited: it was in the basement and very pokey, and there was one of those pulley-type lifts, a dumb-waiter, on which I had to send food up. The waiters used to collect food from this little cubbyhole, and we were limited in what we could cook because of the lack of space and also this archaic arrangement.

The first sitting in the restaurant was 7.30 p.m. before the early show at 8.15 p.m., and I was strict about keeping time: if people hadn't quite finished their dinner, they just had to wait to have their coffee. I wouldn't allow any clatter and carry-on during the show, and everything had to be cleared away before the show started. I told the waiters that the show was the most important part of the evening – not the food. The show lasted around an hour and a half and then a second sitting was served before the late show, which started at about 10.45 p.m. or later. Audience members and casts of West End shows used to fill the club at that time.

Drinks were available from the bar until 3 a.m., but licensing laws meant alcohol could only be served with food after midnight, so we had to provide some rather sad and ageing sandwiches in the upstairs bar, which nobody ate! Carmen Callil, the Australian-born future founder of Virago Press, was one of my waitresses, although they were mainly Italian men.

Because of the club's design, there were all sorts of other problems in regard to my work. I was in the middle of seating people when Reg, my assistant manager, came to me and said, 'I can't find the cheese.' Well, I had ordered it, so I knew it must be somewhere. A couple of people looked for the cheese, but we couldn't locate it. We asked one of the chefs, and he thought it was in one of the cupboards in the subterranean depths of the kitchen. This was a deep item of furniture, and he thought it had probably been shoved to the back with other objects shoved in front of it. And Reg, in his dinner jacket, had to struggle on his hands and knees and crawl into this cupboard, where he did indeed find the selection of cheeses. We made the cheeseboards up just in time.

Peter Cook would finish appearing at *Beyond the Fringe* and come to the club for the second show. He never bothered to find a parking place so used to park illegally outside the club and have his car towed away to a pound in Waterloo where a flunky would collect it for him – cheap at the price of £6 in weekly parking fines. He'd generally ask me how the evening had been going and what was happening in the club. Peter would always do a ten-minute spot at the beginning of the second show, and he always ad-libbed brilliantly, often mimicking someone he had just been talking to in the club. I don't suppose I would have taken the job if it hadn't been for Peter. He was so witty, extremely glamorous and very talented, but it was his charm that drew me to him. Although there was definitely an atmosphere of narcissism, I also felt that the club was trying to change things. The war had made me even more of a pacifist and had cemented my socialist leanings.

The other *Beyond the Fringe* stars, Jonathan Miller and Alan Bennett, also used to pop into the club, and I recall some lovely long conversations with Alan Bennett. In a newspaper interview, Alan once said that the food wasn't very good at The Establishment. I duly ticked him off! I have to say that despite that, and running the risk of sounding like Bruce Forsyth in *Strictly Come Dancing*, he was my favourite of the four.

It was wonderful to be involved with The Establishment – it was THE place to be of course. The whole town wanted to be there. Celebrity guests poured in every night, and I gave up trying to seat them when the room was already booked, so on the steps or standing at the back you could find Jack Lemmon or Eartha Kitt, Gregory Peck or Robert Mitchum! Eartha Kitt was so enamoured with Peter Cook she had to be restrained from coming in; she practically used to attack him. A posse of models, including glamour-puss Jean Shrimpton and April Ashley, were regulars, and Michael Caine and Terence Stamp propped up the bar.

Theatrical doyenne Joan Littlewood was a real character. Her lover was a wealthy backer, who had a mansion in Greenwich. She was often in the company of the incorrigible gay MP Tom Driberg, who used to come to the club and grab waiters by the balls. He was a total menace. Out of devilment, I always used to allocate the best-looking waiters to his table and, if goosed, I told the waiters not to think anything of it – it was just Driberg's normal behaviour. I had to throw the incorrigible columnist Jeffrey Bernard out of the club on more than one occasion when he was plastered.

One of my most thrilling memories of the club was an unexpected evening spent with my literary hero E.M. Forster. One night Peter told me that the great writer wanted to see the show. I reserved a table for him, and we had dinner together. I was so dazzled – it was one of the greatest moments of my life.

George Melly and his wife had their own table reserved for them. George came nearly every night and was very kind about the food, which encouraged me enormously because he knew about these things. There was a certain table, which was raised up on the side of the stage, he liked. All the big stars were there alongside all the rough-necks. Young actors used to come in every night because they could rub shoulders with famous actors and try to advance their careers with some serious schmoozing.

The writer and broadcaster Mary Kenny visited the club when she was very young. She once shared a table with some dignitaries, one of whom was an archbishop. (I wonder what he was doing in Soho, but there you are.) Anyway, she had hit the sauce rather heavily and tried to drink out of the cleric's glass. I was worried that an uncomfortable scene might ensue, so I approached her and said that there was a telephone call for her. I escorted her out and then had a quiet word in her ear. It was a ruse I used a number of times – thank goodness it was in the days before mobile telephones!

April Ashley was often at the club. April had just been outed by *The Sunday People* as she was the first known transsexual and had started to cross-dress when she was a man and known as George Jamieson. She underwent surgery in 1960 and became a successful fashion model. April was quite a girl – so courageous – and around this time she married cross-dresser Arthur Corbett, 3rd Baron Rowallan; he later divorced April on the grounds that she was born a man – which of course he always knew! In the 1950s she had moved to Paris and worked as a drag queen in a cabaret show at the Carousel Theatre.

April was absolutely gorgeous and the centre of a great deal of attention from men, including Peter O'Toole, who got into a bit of a muddle with her when he realised who she was! On another occasion, someone at another table invited April and her friend to join them for a drink, and she replied loudly, in her deep voice, 'Tell them to fuck off – they only want to buy me a drink because I'm a fucking freak!'

The ubiquitous Randolph Churchill was in one night, a little bit pissed, and told me that he wanted to go on the stage. I said I'd see what I could do and went to talk to Peter, who agreed to let him have a go. Churchill tottered up on stage and did a few minutes of stand up. John Fortune described it as follows: 'The Fleet Street columnist and drama critic, Hannen Swaffer had just died and Churchill got on stage and did a piece about Swaffer arriving in heaven. It was embarrassing but also quite thrilling.' I remember him also doing this joke, 'I have just undergone surgery for the removal of a benign tumour. So doctors have removed the only part of me that isn't malignant.' The audience thought it was rather novel because of who his father was, and he went down quite well.

If anybody in the regular team were ill and unable to appear, Peter Cook would tell me to send for David Frost. None of them liked Frost, but he was able to go up on stage and stand in as a sort of understudy. I used to ring up David and ask him to come in. He never refused, and I would pay him £5 in cash out of the till.

There was a room behind the stage, and in it was a locked filing cabinet in which Peter used to keep scripts that would-be writers had sent him. I sometimes replied to them on Peter's behalf. I had a key but wasn't aware that anyone else did. One day I was looking for something and discovered David Frost going through the scripts. He had somehow got hold of a key to the cabinet and was perusing the paperwork for ideas! I'm sure he stole some of the ideas. Peter may even have known about it.

I went to the Blue Angel club in Berkeley Square with Peter and Dudley. The cabaret was compèred by Rex Harrison's son, Noel, who introduced David Frost as the man who founded The Establishment. As if! It was incredible how Frost was treated as one of the gang although he was never really accepted by them. My friend Wendy Cook wrote a lovely book about Peter entitled *So Farewell Then*, and in it I was quoted as saying the following:

All Peter's friends regarded Frostie as something of a joke. They didn't despise him – they tolerated him. They thought he was a bit of an idiot and a bore – the worst thing you could be in that milieu.

Frost became known to the 'Beyond the Fringers' as 'The Bubonic Plagiarist'. The cast's resentment of Frost was voiced some years later at Peter Cook's memorial service by Alan Bennett, who admitted that the only regret he regularly voiced was that he had once saved David Frost from drowning.

At the risk of being accused of nepotism, I did employ several family members at the club. Before he went to Cambridge, my cousin Philip, who now runs a picturesque family wedding venue at South Farm in Cambridgeshire, waited on table and helped around the place, and my godson and nephew Neil Copp, Jack's son, was also a member of staff. (Neil became a hugely successful businessman and made a significant fortune by selling his company to Microsoft.)

I'd bought a house in Shepherd's Bush in the 1950s, which I initially rented out and where my mother now lived. She was beginning to become a little frail, so my sister Di moved from Dulwich in south London to look after her. I also found a job for Di, initially as bar manager and then as membership secretary. Di discovered that the membership section was run by pretty debutante types with double-barrelled names, who were absolutely clueless and didn't have an idea what to do. They were from wealthy families and had obviously been to finishing school but weren't equipped to work in the real world. The office was in a mess, and Di spent a year sorting it out.

On one occasion when Di was in the office sorting out the mess, a handsome, somewhat nervy youngish American burst in. He was working at the club and said to her, 'Hi. Hey would you mind looking after my bag?' With that he handed her a bulging carrier bag. Di looked into the bag and saw that it was stuffed full of banknotes. 'But you don't know me,' she protested, a little worried about the contents. 'That's ok. You probably know me.' She did. It was Lenny Bruce, who had been engaged to perform at the club for a month. Lenny ambled out of the office, and Di was left to keep guard of the bag. She was so nervous for the rest of the evening as she was convinced it was going to be stolen while he was on stage, and she didn't let the plastic carrier out of her sight.

Bruce had arrived in London in April 1962. He had already established himself in America as a hipster comic – controversial and challenging and hysterically funny. No topic was off bounds from his acute observational shtick, and he made an immediate impression onstage and offstage. Kenneth Tynan wrote, 'He roamed out on stage in his usual tormented derision ... ninety minutes later there was little room for doubt that he was the most original, free speaking, wild thinking gymnast of language our inhabited island has ever hired to beguile its citizens.'

He was certainly a menacing figure on stage, and his satirical routines and jokes about drugs, American big business, civil rights issues and sexually transmitted diseases usually offended someone in the audience. But it was a routine about cigarettes and lung cancer that elicited the exit of a very middle-class family and is beautifully described by Peter Cook in a television interview with Clive James:

> A very middle-class couple with their two daughters had sat through a torrent of four letter words but when Lenny started to talk about cancer, the father leapt to his feet and said, 'Cancer ... cancer ... Fiona, Caroline, Deborah ... out ... out!' Meekly, in single file, they marched out through the door.

Although he seemed physically well while at the club and was on good form throughout, Lenny Bruce was a well-known junkie and had a very upper crust female doctor 'administer' to him every day, but that wasn't enough to satisfy his habit. He needed more heroin to function. One of the waitresses recalled him removing a very stylish Italian shoe and expensive sock and injecting himself in the ankle.

I actually arranged for the waitresses to be driven home when the club closed so that they wouldn't be stranded in Soho in the middle of the night. After we closed, I used to deposit the takings in the night safe of a local bank, and Lenny would often accompany me. We would go for a wander around Soho. There was an all-night 'greasy spoon' near the Odeon Leicester Square that we used to frequent, and Lenny used to say that it reminded him of his early days in New York.

We sat for hours over coffee before he returned to the nearby hotel where he was staying. Lenny was the most disarming companion; in fact, I recall John Fortune, who Lenny liked very much, saying, 'He had more charm than anyone I've ever known.' Although he did talk about his life and chaotic lifestyle, Lenny didn't just talk about himself like most performers; he had a great interest in and knowledge about politics, social issues and life in general. He was very radical in his beliefs, which of course I found very appealing. He told me he was bisexual, and although he lusted after some of the men and women in the club, he behaved himself. He told me that he hadn't got laid once during his time in London! I liked him very much. He was very serious, shy and sensitive and had a haunting vulnerability about him. He never took any drugs when he was with me; he never even smoked a joint in my company. He was wonderful to be with, and on stage there was no one to compare. He was brilliant.

Singer Alma Cogan had a huge crush on Lenny and would ask me to reserve a particular table as close to the stage as possible. At that time the Café de Paris had just put up a plaque on the wall to mark the spot where Marlene Dietrich stood before going on stage so, at an amusement parlour, I stamped out a name plate 'Alma Cogan sits here' and then I put it on her table. At first she didn't notice it, but then she gave out a laugh that you could have heard in Shaftesbury Avenue. She threw her head back and screamed and asked everyone to come and have a look.

Barry Humphries had a brief spell at The Establishment, which he later described as his 'highly successful, five minute season', but unfortunately his Australian monologues didn't appeal, and Edna Everage hadn't yet received her Damehood – in fact she was still in her infancy. In any case, Barry took out a membership and could be seen propping up the bar after performing as Sowerberry the undertaker as well as understudying Ron Moody's Fagin in *Oliver*. He described some of the clientele beautifully, reporting that the club was 'patronised by girls with green fingernails all saying soopah – satire groupies loitered; pale faced girls with fringes pearlized lips and eyes like black darns.'

Some months after Lenny's appearance at the club, Peter and Dudley had seen comedian Frankie Howerd appear at an *Evening Standard* awards ceremony at The Savoy. Frankie had actually enjoyed a great deal of success previously but had gone out of fashion and hadn't appeared in the West End for years.

Poor Frankie was struggling professionally, very dispirited personally and was considering giving up the business. However, that night he was on top form. Peter thought he was marvellous, and the two of them were so impressed they invited him to appear at The Establishment. Frankie was very anxious but agreed to do a month's solo spot in September 1962.

He decided to do his own act in the first show and then topical material in the second half, but he was nervous about following Lenny Bruce, who had been the previous guest comedian. Before he went onstage Frankie was petrified, and both Di and I had to convince him that he could do it. There were occasions when we were on either side of him, holding his hands because he was so nervous. He was literally shaking with fear and would tell us that he couldn't go on. He was worried about his act: one or two jokes hadn't got laughs the previous night. 'Don't worry,' we used to say, 'the Audience love you! Go and do your bit. Bring the house down!'

And of course he was marvellous. Nicholas Luard, in Humphrey Carpenter's book, describes Frankie's performance as 'winsome, roguish, naughty lisping and flapping hands'. His routine was what we know now as typically Howerd. At the time Prime Minister Harold Macmillan's formidable wife Dorothy Macmillan was very well known and Frankie would say, 'You know it's Dot that runs the country, not Harold Macmillan. That Macmillan, well, he tells us we've never had it so good, I've got news for him – I haven't had it for weeks!'

Frankie kept the fact that he was gay very quiet in those days; it was just accepted in show business circles but never discussed and he was never 'outed'. Despite rumours of his promiscuity, he actually lived with wine waiter Dennis Heymer, his life partner for over thirty years. Frankie's career was reborn when he was seen at the club by director and producer Ned Sherrin and was booked to appear on the satirical television show *That Was the Week That Was* in April 1963. When his engagement at The Establishment came to an end, he was offered the lead in the musical *A Funny Thing Happened on the Way to the Forum*.

Frankie was a lovely, lovely man, and we became friends. At one stage he wanted to open a restaurant with me, and I actually looked at suitable properties. I found some lovely premises near Drury Lane, which had been one of the Lyons tea shops. It was naturally beautifully equipped but much too big for our purposes. I was on my way back to tell Frankie when I bumped into jazz singer Annie Ross's husband, actor Sean Lynch, who told me that he and Annie wanted to open a jazz nightclub. I told him I had just seen the perfect place for them, and they duly opened the club, which was called Annie's Room. (I never did open that restaurant with Frankie.)

Annie became a great friend of mine, and at that time she was trying to kick her heroin habit and had just married Sean Lynch. Poor Sean was involved in an awful car crash a decade later. It is a terrible story. They had a house in the mountains above Ibiza, and a friend was driving Sean through a village when they crashed. The car went through the wall of a house and killed a child. The driver was lynched by an angry mob, and Sean later died from injuries suffered in the crash. Soon after, Annie also lost her home and was declared bankrupt.

My friendship with Hattie had remained as strong as ever over the years; in fact, we were pretty inseparable. It was about this time that Hattie, while married to John Le Mesurier, became passionately embroiled with John Schofield, a voluntary driver who she had met while doing her endless charity work. John was separated from his wife and very good looking and charismatic, with a typical East End line in banter. He described himself as an entrepreneur, although John Le Mesurier's description of Schofield as 'A fast talking cockney who made a living, selling used cars' was nearer the mark. He was certainly skilled behind the wheel, and I used to say to Hattie, 'Darling, there's no question about it. John Schofield is a "getaway" driver.' Hattie had always been extremely self-conscious of her size and considered herself unattractive to men, so when Schofield paid her attention and declared his love, she became besotted with him. He actually moved into the Eardley Crescent house with Hattie while poor old, diffident John le Mesurier was consigned upstairs to the attic room.

But things were to get a little happier for John in matters of the heart. You probably won't have heard of Leota Bixby, although you may recognise the name Joan Le Mesurier. Ahh ... now there's a clue. You see I have referred to my dear friend Joni as Leota Bixby Gore for years – so long in fact that neither of us can remember why ...

I met Joan in 1962 when during the day she was working as a secretary in the complaints department at the toothpaste company Gibbs-Pepsodent and at night in the Queens Theatre bar. After work she used to haunt the 50 Club in Greek Street, which during the day was a gay hangout. She was a mutual friend of Johnny Heawood, who brought her to The Establishment.

John Le Mesurier happened to be in the club and Joan was introduced to him. They were listening to Dudley playing piano in the basement, and Joan asked Dudley to play an old and lesser-known number called 'What's New?' John looked amazed and said it was his favourite song and was impressed that she knew the tune. They discovered that they both had a love of jazz and hit it off straightaway. I played matchmaker again and invited Joan to a supper party that Hattie was hosting at Eardley Crescent. It could have been awkward as John Schofield was present, but Hattie and I made sure that John and Joan were seated close together. John was always so hesitant and sometimes deliberately vague, but I knew that he was quite smitten with Joan, and they soon began 'walking out'.

I subsequently offered Joan a job at the club and then she moved into my flat at St George's Square, where she stayed with me for about a year. We got on famously – so much so that some of her colleagues at Gibbs-Pepsodent thought we were an item!

Joan served drinks at The Establishment, and on her first night she was carrying a tray of drinks when someone jogged her arm, and Nick Luard, who was sitting at the next table, got absolutely soaked. Johnny Heawood, who was nearby, called out, while laughing, 'She's always great at auditions.' Despite this unfortunate debut we kept Joan on; she was absolutely marvellous other than one night some weeks later, when *The Man in Black* actor Valentine Dyall was in. He had knocked back a few drinks and convinced Joan and one of my other waiters, Bobby, to join him. Unfortunately, they all got pissed. Joan was extremely attractive and vivacious and used to get a lot of attention from the male customers. She would always have a couple of scotches to relax her and help her cope with the bum-pinching, groping and come-ons that she used to have to put up with. (Lenny Bruce flirted with Joan, and although he was very handsome and charismatic she thought him too dangerous.) In any case, she and Bobby were out of order, and I had to give them both a dressing down the next morning. They were both very apologetic, and it never happened again.

One night, the trumpet player Cat Anderson and a couple of other musicians from Duke Ellington's orchestra came into the club. Joan told me who they were, and I gave them drinks on the house and introduced them to Dudley, with whom they jammed later that night.

The Colony Club in nearby Dean Street, which we knew as Muriel's, was a well-known haunt in those days. It was a shabby afternoon drinking den and opened at 3 p.m. in the days when the strict licensing laws closed the pubs straight after lunch. That wonderfully acerbic writer Roger Lewis described it as 'a small, bright green chamber decorated with bamboo, mottled mirrors, leopardskin barstools and plastic tropical plants and was where you went to have fun and to have jokes when the rest of the world was working'.

The club was owned by Muriel Belcher, a Portuguese Jewish lesbian of Welsh extraction, who was autocratic, foul-mouthed and extremely outspoken. She despised anyone who was smug or pretentious and was a great supporter of the underdog. I loved her, as did some of her regulars, including Jeffrey Bernard and Francis Bacon; Bacon even painted her portrait regularly.

There was some friction and bitchy repartee with her camp barman Ian Board, who, it transpired, was doing his best to sabotage bookings at The Establishment. Aggrieved by the success of the rival club, he used to ring up and make bogus reservations. I worked hard on the seating plan every night, taking care not to sit people next to each other that I knew had an antipathy towards each other, so when people didn't turn up at all it caused a lot of difficulties. This happened quite a lot at one point, and we lost a lot of business before I discovered that it was Ian Board who was responsible. I went straight to Muriel, who was a tough old bird but had integrity. She also liked to bring her girlfriends to The Establishment! Anyway, she sorted it out, and there were no phony bookings after that.

I loved Soho, which in the 1960s was a fascinating place full of café bars, folk clubs and music venues – not to mention bordellos and strip joints. The government's Wolfenden Report had moved prostitutes off the streets and they were forced indoors. The area had been become the centre of a gangland struggle, and The Establishment was in a prime location, right at the centre of a turf war between gangs. Villains used to turn up and ask pointedly if we had fire insurance ... everyone was paying protection money apart from us.

It was fascinating to see how these posh Cambridge graduates coped with East End gangsters. Incredibly, Peter Cook had the confidence to deal with them, and one night when the heavies were really playing up, he threatened to put them on the stage where we could all see 'their act'. That soon shut them up!

I had a very nice but tough young man in the bar called Jason Monet, who claimed to be a descendant of the artist. He kept everything more or less under control, although the gangsters used to get in and try and sell dope, and the odd one used to get in and make trouble.

The truncheon that I found in the cellar at Betty's villa in France was absolutely lethal. I used to have it with me and carry it down to the basement and threaten anybody who was giving trouble to get them out. People used to smoke dope in the lavatories, and I'd leave notes for them that read, 'If you must smoke dope don't leave the roach lying on the floor. I don't want anybody finding evidence of it.' If anybody stole handbags they used to empty the contents and place the empty bags in the lavatory cistern.

The villains were in most nights, dressed very sharply in their camel hair coats and Italian shoes. Of course they didn't belong to the club and were always bribing members to sign them in. Regulars attempted to bring friends when it was a member's only club. Talking of which … one night the cleaning women found a penis in the gutter and told the police. I wouldn't say it was commonplace, but it was the sort of thing that happened in Soho in the 1960s.

My old dance teacher George Erskine Jones worked at The Establishment's front desk, and a man came in and demanded to be let in, even though he wasn't a member. He was one of these Soho wide boys, who thought he could bribe his way into anything, and he tried every trick he knew with George just to get in. George refused him entrance, and finally the villain lost his temper and said, 'If there's one thing I can't stand it's a box office queen.' George bravely replied, 'Well, it takes one to know one … next please!' And, surprisingly, the man hopped it.

The West End Central Police were very corrupt at that time, and if I phoned for help they would only co-operate and arrive in numbers if I named an illustrious customer – ideally a cabinet minister, who might be playing up. I once went to the West End Central Police station with a couple of crooks the police had arrested, and they wanted me to provide some more evidence. After leaving me alone for over an hour in a cell-like room, the policemen eventually returned and told me that they had to release the two villains and that I was also free to go. There was no explanation as to why they had changed their minds. I told them I had no intention of going out into the street with the villains probably waiting outside for me! I demanded to be driven back to Greek Street, which they did with extreme reluctance, and not a word was spoken by the driver or the escort all the way back.

Peter Cook described a visit from the Kray twins, one of whom, noting the expensive equipment, barked, 'Of course it would be dreadful if the wrong element came in and smashed the place up. We know these elements and we can provide you with people on the door to stop these elements from getting in.' A typically amusing anecdote from Pete, but not far from the truth as there were some quite scary times. One night I said to my sister Di, 'Don't look now but just over there are two gangsters who have threatened us for protection money.' She looked intrigued, but what I didn't tell her until much later was that one of them had said to me, 'If you don't pay up we'll kill your sister. We know where she lives.' I thought they were bluffing, but just in case I made sure that Di had a police car or another employee follow her home every night for a while after the club had closed.

In January 1963, the mental condition of my mother, who was in her 80s, had deteriorated, and she needed a great deal of care and support. Unfortunately, her home help left the front door of the Shepherd's Bush house open, and Mother had wandered out into the snow and tried to walk along the icy pavement. She inevitably had a fall, fractured her femur and was admitted to Hammersmith hospital, where she died soon after. We discovered after her death that she was actually five years older than the age to which she had always admitted! Despite our sadness, we all thought 'Good for her!' Di was devastated and still says it was the worst thing that has ever happened to her. She felt unable to work for a while and left the club's employ.

I also felt under a lot of strain. Apart from losing my mother, I was working from before midday until 1.30 a.m. the following morning, and what with having to deal with all the exertions of working in such an unusual environment … not to mention constant threats from gangsters and demanding members, I needed a bit of R and R and a haven from the hectic lifestyle.

I was thus fortunate to have access to a country retreat. My friend from the Players' Violetta Farjeon had been left an estate near Horsham in Sussex, which consisted of 60 acres of woodland, a lovely tennis court, extensive lawns, exquisite gardens and two wonderfully sized Elizabethan cottages, the roof beams of which were hewn from the ships of the Spanish Armada.

I used to go down there some weekends, and one day her husband, Gervase, and I were walking in the woods and I happened to mention that what I'd really like is to have a little cottage of my own where I could get away from it all and relax away from the hustle and bustle of London life. Gervase stopped in his tracks and said, 'Well you can have one here. We've got plenty of space. When we get home we'll have a look at some of my books.'

The Farjeons had hundreds of books, and Gervase found one on old English country cottages. The book had been written by an architect and there was a description and illustration of each cottage and, more importantly, the plans. We chose one called Teapot Hall.

Gervase had trained as an architect but never practiced very much because he decided he wanted go into the theatre instead. But he had maintained his knowledge and so adjusted the design and set to work designing my own little place! In fact, it turned out that it was too complicated to build an actual cottage, and my own Teapot Hall was more of a wooden hut.

With much help from friends to do the heavy lifting and digging, we actually built it ourselves. It was amazing. We had a proper little cellar with a nice wooden floor with a trap door in it, a bed and a wood-burning stove. A large picture window faced a little clearing in the woods, and I could sit there watching the birds – I was a bit of a twitcher in those days. Teapot Hall saved my life, and I used to go down there as much as I could.

Violetta has since sold the cottages but lives in a practical bungalow on part of the estate, and that's where I go and stay with her these days. She did her last show for the Players' at the age of 75. Now a vivacious nonagenarian, Violetta is a member of the University of the Third Age, where she is studying Spanish and painting. 'Someone wanted to buy one of my paintings recently. They must have cataracts,' she said.

Meanwhile the situation at The Establishment was getting pretty desperate. Peter and Nicholas Luard had become involved in setting up the satirical magazine *Private Eye* and had moved the office into the club's premises. Peter Cook bought 80 per cent of the shares in *Private Eye*, which was struggling financially. Profits from The Establishment club were being used by Nick Luard on *Private Eye* and other ventures, and I never did get the commission I had been promised in addition to my salary, which amounted to £25 a week.

Beyond the Fringe opened in Broadway, and while Peter and Dudley were being lionised in America, Nicholas Luard was left in charge. He behaved very badly when they went away and always overruled my wishes. He was quite bombastic, difficult and a drinker. I couldn't bear him. He met his wife, Liz, when she was a typist at *Private Eye*. I can't think what Liz married him for because she is lovely and very clever. (She now writes cookery columns for *The Oldie*). Despite his behaviour, Liz still talks of him fondly – she was always very loyal. Unfortunately the drink killed him when he was just 66 years old – even though he had had a liver transplant. Couldn't help himself, I suppose.

There were further financial shenanigans when Peter tried to bring Lenny Bruce back to the club. Despite the outrage of the press calling for his deportation at the end of Lenny's original month-long engagement, Lenny was a sensational success, and Peter requested him to come back to the club as soon as he could, to which Lenny agreed. Unfortunately, when he was booked to return, Home Secretary Henry Brooke announced it was not in the public interest to admit Lenny into the country, on account of his 'sick jokes and lavatory humour' and refused him entry. I had offered to meet Lenny at Heathrow Airport but discovered he was being kept in a room like some sort of prisoner by the Immigration Authorities. They strip-searched him before forcing him to return to the States (of course he later did a routine around this ignominious experience).

There was nothing I could do, and I was only grudgingly authorised to see him briefly by one of the officials. Lenny was allowed to put his head around the door at the end of a long corridor. I waved at him and he called out, 'Hi Bruce!' He was then ushered back into the room like a criminal and wasn't allowed to talk to me. It was awful. And that was the last I ever saw of him. He was subsequently deported and died a few years later from an accidental drug overdose at his Hollywood home.

Peter Cook and Nicholas Luard tried to bring Lenny Bruce back to the club, even trying to smuggle him back to the UK via the Irish Republic, but they were unsuccessful, and it cost them a great deal of money. In September 1963 Cook and Luard's company went into voluntary liquidation with debts of nearly £66,000.

There was further trouble in the shape of another villain: a large, clever and 'colourful' Lebanese character and businessman who called himself Raymond Nash. He was a very hard man – infamous actually – and there were stories that he used to nail people to the ground by their knees. Nash was a protégé and right-hand man of slum landlord Peter Rachman, who was at his most powerful in London at that time and wanted to take over The Establishment because it was right in the middle of his manor.

The club was becoming more and more dodgy and impossible to work in as the villains moved in and took over. It was time for me to get out, which I did just before Nick Luard finally sold The Establishment. Raymond Nash took over the running of the club, which continued to operate when the original cast returned from New York. The club now offered 'Jazz in the basement. Late night talking and drinking in the theatre bar. Gaming on the first floor. Mingle with renegade nuns, unfrocked prime ministers, and plain-clothes policewomen posing as both.'

Raymond Nash had a bodyguard called 'Speedy' who carried a gun. Hecklers were beaten up, there were fist fights and waiters were accused of stealing. Not surprisingly, members of the cast felt that they could no longer perform comedy in that kind of environment! Raymond Nash was refused entry back into the UK when he was caught coming in from the Middle East with something illegal, and he was eventually arrested in Japan for gold smuggling. Membership fees dried up, and the premises were sold to a Mr Jones, who turned it into a private gambling and dining club.

I loved being at The Establishment, and it's such a shame that it didn't survive. A few attempts to revive the club have also been unsuccessful. A few of the old haunts and institutions, such as Ronnie Scott's and Bar Italia, still remain in Soho. There are wonderful cafes and restaurants, the whole area is much more upmarket and there is a vibrant gay scene in Old Compton Street.

Zerbrano, a cocktail bar, club and restaurant, now occupies the premises where The Establishment once stood, although there is a blue plaque on No. 18 Greek Street which reads: 'PETER COOK, 1937–1995, COMEDIAN AND 'ONLY TWIN', CO-FOUNDED AND RAN THE ESTABLISHMENT CLUB HERE, 1961–1964.'

TEN

ANOTHER OPENING ANOTHER SHOW

'Memories are like mulligatawny soup in a cheap restaurant. It is best not to stir them.'

P.G. Wodehouse

The celebrated American playwright George S. Kaufman was quoted as saying that if you hook your audience in the first ten minutes, you've got them for the entire play. I realised early on in my career as a restaurateur that this also applied to customers entering my dining establishments, and throughout my professional life I have endeavoured to follow this philosophy. A friendly greeting and a warm, welcoming ambience must grab the diner immediately. And, of course, there's the food …

I used to say to new waiters, 'Why do you think people come to a restaurant?' And very often you were met with a sort of blank look.

It's because people are *hungry* and they need something to eat. So, in any of my restaurants when customers arrive, they are shown to their table and they are served with a basket of three different kinds of bread and a dish of crudités – nice chopped carrots and olives and other bits and pieces. So they had something to eat while they were studying the menu and so everybody was happy. I tend to find that when people are hungry they are very bad tempered and so if you want

170

to avoid scenes and rows you give them something to eat straightaway. And let's face it; they aren't going to order less because you've given them a bit of food.

My next eatery was WIPS. And before you get the wrong idea, it didn't have anything to do with that sort of S & M thing, although I don't know why it was given that name. The club, just off Leicester Square, was owned by a handsome young man in his 20s, who I knew as Tim but was actually Timothy Gilbert, Lord Willoughby de Eresby, son of Lord Ancaster. Tim was a bit of a playboy and had opened a club in Torremolinos that was very successful. He had purchased some land in Corsica for another club and had some property just off Leicester Square, and he wanted me to supervise all three clubs. I liked the sound of that, and as The Establishment was going down the drain, I agreed to join Tim's venture.

WIPS was rather plush and very 1960s; there was a lift decorated in deep purple that took diners to the top of the building and was the only way in and out. Looking back, it was as much of a fire risk as The Establishment. The entrance to the club housed a rather large fish tank full of piranhas. The restaurant had thick pile carpet, not only on the floor but also up the walls. There was a separate dance floor with a live band, supplemented by a disco. It was quite a big thing. I became quite friendly with Tim's mother, Lady Ancaster, who was a regular visitor, although her husband wouldn't be seen dead there. He thoroughly disapproved of his son's lifestyle.

I liked Tim a lot. He was very handsome but not gay, and I'd stayed one night at his house, having been invited to a party he'd thrown at his wonderful home in Knightsbridge. In his bedroom he had three pictures on the wall of himself, painted by a well-known artist. I admired these pictures very much, and I told him so, although I did say it was very narcissistic to have all three on show in the bedroom!

We'd opened in June 1963, and just a few weeks later we were already doing well and making some money. He came into the office and gave me one of the paintings from his bedroom. He asked me to put it on the wall and said, 'Hang it in here – so that it will remind you of me. I'm going away.' It was all a bit surprising and camp, even though Tim was very butch, but I was quite touched by his gesture. He said he was going to Corsica via Torremolinos and would be away for quite a few weeks.

Tim went down to Spain with a friend, and although he already owned a boat, he hired another craft for the voyage to Corsica and kitted it out completely. He knew the Mediterranean thoroughly but had been advised that storms were imminent and to postpone his trip. Tim ignored these warnings and set off. Well, Tim never arrived in Corsica and was presumed lost at sea.

Tim had a sister, Lady Jane, and she flew out to the Mediterranean and then hired a plane and flew around trying to find Tim's boat. Debris from about half a dozen boats that were wrecked in the storms were spotted, but not a stick was found from Tim's. The official story was that he died in the storms, but I'm convinced he never went out in that boat. I think he moored somewhere safely and never set sail. He was too much of an experienced sailor to be caught like that.

For years afterwards there were reports in *Private Eye* that Tim had been spotted all over the world – in Mexico and Brazil and other far flung exotic countries. I believe he was fed up with the disapproval of his father, who criticised everything he did, and wanted to cut himself off from the Ancaster side of the family. Tim was fabulously wealthy; Lady Astor was his aunt and she'd left him enough money to make him a multi-millionaire. He had money stashed in bank accounts all over the world, and so he just took off and has never been seen since. I think he just wanted to have a life of his own without his father interfering.

However, Lord Ancaster did accept the fact that his son had drowned and closed down all Tim's business ventures, including WIPS, which he put on the market. It was all very sudden, but I had to go; of course, in the circumstances there was no alternative. And I have to say Lord Ancaster did look after me: he actually gave me a car and paid me two years' salary. And I wasn't out of work for very long.

Although this is a Chelsea restaurant and has a great air of frivolity as far as diners are concerned, the food here, basically English, is very straight-forward and honest, with fresh ingredients and not a frozen vegetable in the place ... the interior has bench seating, green walls, lots of black and white checks on the floor and scrubbed pine tables and chairs. You will be pretty close to your neighbours but they are liable to be quite amus-ing. Upstairs there is a pie shop which sells pies to take away or eat over the counter for people in a hurry. Downstairs is a good place for a cosy dinner or for a family weekend lunch, the children will find the sort of food they are used to and the parents can keep their tempers with a good carafe of wine.

That's an extract from the menu of my next restaurant, Mrs Beeton's Hungry Horse. Bill Staughton, an Australian who ran Mrs Beeton's Tent, a restaurant in Greek Street, approached me and explained he wanted to open a restaurant serving classic English food and wanted me as his partner. It was just at the time that WIPS was closing so this offer was perfect timing.

The Hungry Horse was a windowless, oppressive and hot basement in the Fulham Road, and we employed Louden Sainthill, a celebrated Australian set designer, who among other venues had worked at the Royal Opera House and the Old Vic, to plan the restaurant. His early designs were described as 'opulent', 'sumptuous' and 'exuberantly splendid' and this was right up our street!

You have probably seen those horse butchers in France that have a beautiful horse's head outside their shops? Well, we went to France and got one of those horse's heads and we arranged for a potter on the King's Road to make a series of copies, which we placed all along the entrance and inside.

The Chelsea part of Fulham was really edgy in those days – a wonder-ful place to be – and I believe we were one of the first quality restaurants in the neighbourhood and so successful that others soon followed. Above the restaurant, on street level, we had a little pie shop selling steak and kidney pies, and puddings and chicken and mushroom pies. We always used the best meat too – very good beef and steaks from a very special butcher in Fulham. Some special customers bought the pies too, such as the Rolling Stones, who were then very young, and liked all the pies! It's amazing they stayed so skinny in those days. Mick Jagger still is.

The Hungry Horse became an 'in' restaurant, particularly for people in the theatre, and our clientele read like *Who's Who?*

I like to think I saved the life of the great Orson Welles; he once came to the Hungry Horse with some friends and told me, on arrival, that he had ordered a car to take him to the BBC for a broadcast afterwards. I was to let him know when the car arrived. Well I did, but I also had to inform Orson that the driver was drunk – staggering around and completely unfit to drive. I forbade the great actor from getting in the car and offered to drive him. He was very grateful and managed to wedge himself into the front seat of my Mini. I chauffeured him to the BBC TV Centre in White City, which was a bit of a way from Chelsea, and we had chatted all the way. To be honest I think he spoke and I listened while I drove, but he was very entertaining and a hugely charismatic presence. It was a very agreeable little interlude from the restaurant.

One night the artist Francis Bacon and a group of friends were being rather lively. Then a chair went over, there were screams and suddenly punches were being thrown. Our doorman went over, returned the perpetrator to his chair, carried him in it to the entrance and swiftly ejected him.

An American heiress who frequented the restaurant and used to spend a lot of money with us was shocked and approached me. 'How can you let such people into your restaurant?' she said. I apologised and gave her party free drinks, but I was worried that this incident might cause her not to return; I took Francis Bacon aside and asked him to make amends. Bacon introduced himself, apologised profusely and sat down at the American's table, where he charmed her and her fellow diners for the rest of the evening. She left very happy and continued to patronise us. I always found Francis to be very kind and considerate.

The gay writer and civil rights activist James Baldwin was in one evening and was seated at the little alcove table in a group of six people, which included a lawyer, Mark Lane, who had written a book, *Rush to*

Judgement, about the John Kennedy assassination. Lane was one of the first to espouse the conspiracy theory and take issue with the conclusions of the Warren Commission.

I had just read the book, and I sat with him and talked about it. He felt the murder of the president had been political and not simply the random actions of the sad Lee Harvey Oswald. There was so much evidence from people who saw the shots being fired from the grassy knoll and not just from the warehouse where Oswald had been positioned. So many of those witnesses disappeared, were run down or died that you can't help but be suspicious. I'm not a conspiracy theorist, but I was sure that Kennedy was not shot by Lee Harvey Oswald alone and that Jack Ruby was trying to keep him quiet.

One night, when the restaurant was packed and I was just having a little rest in the foyer, I saw some rather glamorous shoes come down the stairs. They were attached to the feet of April Ashley, who was dressed as if she was going to Buckingham Palace. In fact, she was dining at St James's Palace with the Duke of Leeds, who was her lover at the time. She entered the foyer and said, 'Come in the ladies loo with me, I'm going to have a slash!' So I went into the ladies with her, and while she was having a pee she said to me, 'I had to see you because it's your birthday isn't it?' I was amazed she remembered, and I nodded. April continued, 'I also remembered, not only that it was your birthday but the way you looked after me at The Establishment when everyone was being so rude. And because you looked after me so well, I've decided to bring you a present.' With that she presented me with a gold pencil and was then on her way to St James's Palace.

She was once waiting for a table and one of the customers greeted her by saying, 'Hello George, how are you?' I was seething at this disregard for her and, after showing April to her table, I confronted the man, 'Please leave my restaurant. You must never speak to April like that!' I said it very loudly so that all the diners could hear. I asked April, 'How did that chap know your original name was George?' She shrugged, 'I used to know him in the merchant navy and I never liked him then.' April was hilarious, but more seriously she has always been at the forefront of the fight against gender discrimination, and in 2012 she was awarded the MBE for services to transgender equality.

Elizabeth David, the cookery writer, was my heroine and the most amazing woman. I used to go and buy things in her shop for my restaurant. One lunchtime, at about 12.30, she appeared and told me that she was having lunch here with Robin McDouall, a fellow food writer, at 1.30 p.m. The clocks had changed, and poor Elizabeth was an hour early. 'Oh dear,' she said. 'Well, never mind. Show me to the table and I'll find something to do. Do you have any cookery books?' 'Yes, of course,' I replied. 'I've got some old ones in my office.' 'That's exactly what I want,' she beamed.

So I brought down my old tomes, and one of them she had never seen before. She was absolutely delighted, and she sat there quietly with a drink reading this book until Robin arrived. At the end of their lunch I presented her with the book as a gift. She graciously accepted. What a lovely lady, and how clever she was. She didn't miss a thing where food was concerned. Her books are quite extraordinary.

I know Princess Margaret has always had a bit of a reputation for being rather demanding, but whenever she used to come to the restaurant she was always very sweet. The princess was always accompanied by five or six people and inevitably a detective waiting in the foyer, keeping guard. The waiters stood to attention and would take her order first, which was always 'The usual, please.' Her 'usual' was a chicken and mushroom pie – a dish that that she loved, and she always devoured it all.

Fanny Cradock used to come in and make much more of a fuss than Princess Margaret ever did. Johnny, her husband, who she dominated for their whole married life, used to come in an hour before her and check that Fanny's table would meet with her approval. I used to say to him, 'John, I've booked a table as you asked me and that there is your table. I can't change it for you, as we're too full. You'll have to sit there, and if it doesn't meet with Fanny's approval then I suggest you go somewhere else.'

Fanny would always wear a cartwheel hat that shaded her face (very wisely in my opinion), and once she'd sat down, she would always say to the waiter, 'Would you ask Bruce to come and see me?' I always tried to avoid her – I couldn't stand her or her voice, but I'd reluctantly attend her table. She would never say, 'Oh do sit down, Bruce, and have a glass of wine.' I'd have to stand there to attention as if I was her butler, and she used to go right through the menu loudly and then order something that wasn't on it! And she used to go through this great long thing in that voice. The entire restaurant used to go silent and everybody put their knives and forks down and stared at her. She loved the attention.

There was a wet fish shop quite near Mossop Street, and every now and again, when I was short of something, I'd nip round there and buy it. Well, I was in there one day talking to the fishmonger and Fanny's car drew up. Interrupting my conversation, she shouted out her order from the car. I called out, 'Fanny would you mind just being quiet for a minute? I was here first and I'll finish my order. Thank you!' Only then would she shut up. That's what she was like. That was Fanny!

One night a well-known press photographer came into the restaurant. He was wearing one of those beautiful sheepskin-lined coats and on arrival handed it to the cloakroom attendant. By the time he left he had had a skinful so forgot all about his coat and went off without it. A bit later that evening he phoned me at the restaurant and said, 'I've forgotten my coat and I've got to have it tonight as I have an outdoor job early in the morning. Could you possibly get it to me? Send it in a taxi to me and I'll pay for it. I'm at the WIPS club.' So I decided to take the coat myself, as I wanted to see the old place and the staff. The doorman at WIPS was the very chap that I had employed, and he was so pleased to see me that he practically cuddled me in through the door.

When I went in, I saw the chap in a party of about eight or nine people sitting around, and I gave him his coat back. The music started to play, and they all got up to dance leaving this one woman sitting there alone. I thought, 'I'll just wait until the end of the dance and for the music to stop, and he'll introduce me to his friends, and I'll join in the party.'

After a few minutes I realised this was silly and I ought to ask her to dance, so I said to her, 'Would you like to dance?' She looked pleased and said, 'Yes, thank you, I would.' So we got up to dance, and I noticed a lot of people staring at her. She was very pretty, with long dark hair, but I had no idea who she was. When the music stopped, we sat down and I was introduced to her. It was Christine Keeler, who had just been released from prison, and it was only then that I discovered who she was. I always felt she had been cruelly treated in that Profumo business.

Bill Staughton was a drinker, and I always used to cover for him whenever he became hopelessly drunk. We arranged that we should alternate nights in the restaurant so we weren't there at the same time and one of us would always be on duty. This pleased me enormously, as he used to drink a bottle of scotch while he was on duty and became very difficult.

Rudolph Nureyev was dining one night with some dance friends, and Bill was drunk again. He knew someone in the party and so he joined their table. The conversation was mainly about ballet, of course, and Bill turned to Nureyev and pronounced, 'Christopher Gable is a much better dancer than you!'

The brilliant Nureyev had famously defected from the Soviet Union, so had obviously left the Kirov and joined the Royal Ballet. His arrival revived Margot Fonteyn's career because she was getting on a bit then, and they were wonderful together. They were late replacements for Gable and Lynn Seymour in *Romeo and Juliet* at Covent Garden, which Christopher Gable had never really got over and subsequently left the Royal Ballet, later to become an actor.

Bill's comment about Christopher Gable was, of course, a terrible thing to say and like a red rag to the volatile dancer. Rudi, enraged, stamped out shouting, 'You can keep your fucking restaurant!' He pulled every bank note from his wallet, tore them up and threw them like confetti all over the foyer of the restaurant and stormed out. The waiters picked up the pieces, and when the uproar subsided I stuck them together on a sheet of paper – patched up well enough for the bank to honour them. The amount I pieced together was far more than the bill, and so the waiters got a very nice tip.

I didn't want to be with Bill when he was in that state. He was also a terrible snob and was only interested in titles and upper-class people. He used to give Margaret Campbell, the Duchess of Argyll, with whom

I had crossed swords at The Establishment, the 'two handed salute' (ushering in with both hands in an obsequious manner), and when she came to the restaurant everybody used to wait for Bill because he always used to be the one to go to the door and greet her in that manner!

As Margaret Campbell, she had been one of the most beautiful debutantes ever seen, and she had then married into nobility. But then she became a sort of sex maniac and disgraced herself. She was now the infamous Duchess of Argyll, and in March 1963 she had just been involved in a huge society scandal. The Duke of Argyll divorced her for serial adultery, and some photographs had been taken of her in a compromising situation with two men – both of whose heads had been cut off in the snaps.

There was huge speculation about the identities of the headless men, but it has now been accepted that the two were Duncan Sandys, a cabinet minister and the son-in-law of Winston Churchill, and Hollywood star Douglas Fairbanks Junior. The divorce was granted, and the judge was quoted as describing the duchess as 'a highly sexed woman who has ceased to be satisfied with normal sexual activities and has started to indulge in disgusting sexual activities to gratify a debased sexual appetite.' I didn't care that the duchess had slept with eighty-eight men – I wasn't far off that figure myself – but it was the fact that she was such a dreadful woman that bothered me.

When I was doing the commando training in Scotland, we camped in the grounds of Argyll castle on Loch of Inveraray, the ancestral home of the Argylls. The castle had opening hours for the public to visit, but I could never get free at that time. One day I decided to try and look around that castle, so I went up there on my own. I donned my best battledress and made myself as smart as possible. I rang the bell, and the butler came to the door. I explained my predicament and asked him if I could come in. I'm sure he was about to refuse my request when I heard a voice in the background say, 'Wait a minute, Wait a minute!' The duke came to the door and directed me inside, 'Of course you can come in.'

He gave me a personally guided tour, and we had a wonderful time. We fell about laughing when he showed me a room in which, hidden behind sliding doors, were shelves sheltering a line of chamber pots. Each receptacle had a crest engraved on it and each belonged to a different nobleman, and as there was no lavatory nearby, this is where the men used to come for a smoke and to relieve themselves. The duke was a lovely man, but it was all terribly feudal. He ruled the village and wouldn't even allow the local shopkeepers of Inveraray to sell condoms!

Andre Deutsch, the publisher, had a table at the Hungry Horse and lunched about three times a week with clients. He once said to me, 'Bruce, if you ever write a cookery book, please submit it to me. You can't go wrong.' He continued, 'You know at Christmas there are so many millions of husbands in England who want to improve their wives' cooking that the bestsellers of all time are cookery books. Every book shop you go into has a front table with cookery books at Christmas.' Needless to say, I never got around to it – another way of making money that I missed out on ...

We did quite a lot of outside catering from the Hungry Horse. We usually provided three-course meals for people in their own homes. There was quite a lot of demand, and we were considered the most fashionable place to go to in those days. I never really wanted to do it because it was hard work and more complicated working outside our own environment in a kitchen we had never seen before. You had to remember to take everything to the house with you. I went to one place once and I didn't bother to take salt – everybody has salt – but they didn't have any, and I had to go out and buy some. A big house in Hampstead it was too!

We used to take our own staff, usually two waiters and a kitchen hand. It was very profitable because with outside catering you know exactly what has to be done. The clients decided what they wanted and we provided it. They kept anything left over – there was no waste and no overheads.

I had this gentleman's agreement with Bill that when the Hungry Horse was well established and making money, we would open another restaurant, and then we would end our partnership. Bill would run the Hungry Horse and I would run the new place, and we found lovely premises in the City, near St Pauls. It was also called the Hungry Horse, but unfortunately Bill didn't honour the agreement, as he wouldn't let me run it as my own.

We should have had something in writing, and in retrospect I don't know why I trusted him. I had some terrible rows and scenes with him and his accountants. I finally told him that if he didn't honour our verbal contract I was going to leave. I knew he'd never manage without me, but he refused and I walked out. Naturally the new restaurant failed. Bill was very good with food but bloody awful at running restaurants, and it was mainly to do with the drink.

It seems that I've been involved with drunks all my life! All my business partners, all clever people, have been drinkers and couldn't limit themselves. I suppose working in the restaurant trade you are expected to be sociable, and of course there is always booze on hand. I was always well balanced in this way, and although I liked the odd tipple, I didn't need alcohol as a crutch. And I was reliable and was sought after. The drunks knew that they could depend on me and I would carry the show.

I was now living in a mansion block off the King's Road. I could afford it because there were eighty steps from the ground floor to my flat and no lift, and so it was a bit cheaper than it otherwise might have been. The flat in Pimlico had been bought by developers, and Joan had moved in with John Le Mesurier. They were married on 2 March 1966 at Fulham Town Hall, and I was the best man. It was a quiet wedding; we had lunch at Tratoo in Kensington and John played their song 'What's New?' on the restaurant's piano. We all thought that was terribly amusing as this was John's third marriage.

I was still spending a lot of time with Hattie. We, with John Schofield, attended a charity event that Hattie had to open and make a speech. When she'd finished this job, which she always did voluntarily for charity, they presented her with an envelope, and when we opened it in the car it was quite a big cheque. We found that Maurice Browning, her secretary, had made a mistake and she had actually been paid for doing this job.

She was pleasantly surprised and said to us, 'Let's do something special. I've always loved those films where they fly to Paris for dinner. So why don't we just … fly to Paris for dinner?' Well, wouldn't you know that in real life that sort of thing doesn't work out? We rang the airport

181

but couldn't get a flight to Paris, so we decided to go to Amsterdam instead. Hattie booked us a very nice hotel; the city was quite wild and we had a ball!

I took her and John to a gay club, of which there were many in Amsterdam, but I knew a particularly nice one, and Queen Juliana actually came in. She was much loved and was known to hate royal protocol. She was known as 'the peoples' queen' and campaigned for peace and gay rights long before it became fashionable. She was a marvellous woman and so far ahead of her time. Of course, all these other queens from London who were in the club recognised Hattie and surrounded our table wanting to dance with her. I had a lover there, and I used to travel there regularly to see him. He worked in the airport on reception and sometimes in the city on the airport desk.

Sadly John Schofield was a terrible womaniser; no one was safe from his lascivious behaviour, and he tried it on with anyone that he could, including my own sister-in-law, my brother Jack's wife Joan, who was rather attractive. Hattie was oblivious to his unfaithfulness and remained devoted to him. The inevitable end of their relationship came in 1966 when Hattie was filming *The Bobo* in Rome with Peter Sellers and Schofield called her to say he was leaving her – he had met an Italian heiress with whom he had fallen in love. Hattie rang me from Rome. She was heartbroken. Absolutely inconsolable. I had never witnessed Hattie crying until she rang me to tell me that Schofield had betrayed her and was now out of her life. Poor Hattie was sobbing, sobbing, sobbing on the phone.

I was also upset because, for all his nonsense, I felt he was basically a good man, who did love Hattie in his own way. He was lovely with Hattie's kids. Robin now had a younger brother, Kim, who was born in 1956. But I do have to say also that Hattie was never quite the same again and lost some of her spark – her 'joie de vivre'. She put on a lot of weight and placed all her energies into looking after her sons, and she protected herself from future hurt by surrounding herself with a coterie of gay men, who all loved her but without the danger or complication of romance. I never wanted to be straight, but if I had been, Hattie would have been the girl for me.

Over the years, I had always spent Christmas festivities at Eardley Crescent, and they became legendary affairs. Planning began in November, and Hattie would hire a window dresser from one of the large department stores to design the backdrop. The menu was always prepared a long time in advance, and the actual shindig would last at least three days. I would arrive at Eardley Crescent at around 7 a.m., usually starting proceedings with six oysters and half a bottle of champagne. There were three kitchens in the house and so three large turkeys could be roasted simultaneously and then served with several types of stuffing that Hattie had concocted, a selection of vegetables, variations of potatoes, sizzling sausages and bacon and all topped by Hattie's famous gravy, which usually contained an extra ingredient – some ash from the ubiquitous cigarette that hung from her lips but which she barely inhaled!

Hattie always had about twenty people for the meal, and she had a special table made so that everyone could be seated comfortably. The Christmas cast list obviously differed depending on the era, but apart from close family members, there were various artistes from the *Carry On* company and in later years there were cast members of the stage show A *Hatful of Sykes*, in which Hattie appeared.

Kenneth Williams and Joan Sims never missed the event, and the two of them, in an impromptu double act, would dispense the presents, which were stacked in a large mound around a beautifully dressed tree that normally reached the ceiling.

Kenneth loved the occasion and described one such Christmas celebration in later years, 'I went to Hattie Jacques's house. She had a lot of friends round a groaning table and presided over the meal with that special warmth and affection which so endeared her to everyone. We all got a present – some even got two – but Hattie was given so many you couldn't count them.'

After splitting with Bill Staughton I was asked to set up the restaurant at The Royal Exchange Theatre in Manchester. The centre of the Lancashire cotton industry was the Manchester Royal Exchange, which traded globally in spun yarn and finished goods. It was a huge building, which now housed a theatre.

The artistic director was a lovely man called Michael Elliot, who launched The Royal Exchange with a team of three other artistic directors. Part of the entrance was converted to the catering department, so we had a sort of cafeteria on the ground floor and upstairs we had a restaurant, which I set up.

I was commuting from London, going to and fro, and Michael suggested that I could do with an assistant. 'I know just the girl. She's an actress friend of mine called Phyllida Law. She's in a play in London but has an antique shop and she's very good at furnishings. She'll be able to get you all you want in the way of carpets and furniture.'

Phyllida was duly employed and helped provide all the furnishings. I wanted a Victorian theme you see and there was very little money. I used to obtain kitchen equipment from a couple of chaps in London who specialised in second-hand apparatus from restaurant kitchens, and they would recondition it so that it was as good as new.

Phyllida was working in Peter Nichols' superb and challenging play *A Day in the Death of Joe Egg* at the Comedy Theatre in London. She used to commute to Manchester during the day and return to the West End in time to be on stage in the evenings. Sometimes she brought her girls, Emma and Sophie, with her, although I'm sure the train fares for the three of them were more than she was being paid! It wasn't until years later that her daughter Emma Thompson became a celebrated actress and screenwriter. Sophie is also a very talented and versatile performer, with lots of theatre, film and television credits to her name.

Phyllida provided everything from the Victorian period, including cutlery, which was extremely hard to find. She was told that she would have lots of help but discovered she had to search for these treasures single-handed! We gelled right away and made a great team, and while I was setting up the kitchen she managed to procure anything I asked for – all on a shoestring budget. She used to say, 'I know where I am with Victoriana', and I could always rely on her. Of course, Phyllida has never stopped working as an actress since those days and is still very much in demand. The restaurant was a great success, and The Royal Exchange was probably one of the most influential provincial theatres at the time.

I had been in Manchester for six months; shortly after I came home to London, I received a telephone call from my friend Stella Moray.

She said, 'I'm terribly sorry, Bruce, I got a bit pissed last night and I gave your telephone number to a man, who you probably won't like. His name is Peter Norwood.' I'd known of him at the Players', but our paths hadn't really crossed.

'Why won't I like him?' I said.

'Oh, never mind that – the thing is I met him at a party and he told me that he had found a space, which he wanted to open as a restaurant, but knows nothing about the business. Can you help? So,' Stella continued, 'I told him you were brilliant and could advise him. I gave you a big build up. So please talk to him.'

I duly arranged to meet him for lunch at a restaurant in the King's Road, and as he drove up in his car – I was sitting at a window table – I saw his 'PN1' number plate. Well if there's something I hate it's a personalised number plate! I regard that as the last straw of conceit and pomposity, and they are usually very expensive. I thought, 'Well that's put me off for a start.'

Anyway, he joined me and we lunched together. He explained that he had an antique shop in Windmill Row, Kennington, right between the Oval tube underground station and the Imperial War Museum. Next door was an empty shop that was in a state of some disrepair and the window covered in fly posters. It was apparently quite a mess. Peter had gone to the local council and was told that the whole corner was going to be knocked down in three years, so he could have the place for at least three years at £1 a week. The only caveat was that he would have to tidy the premises up. Thinking that this was an excellent deal, he immediately agreed to the terms of the lease and procured the premises with the idea of setting up a restaurant. Peter ran a business called Peter Norwood Displays and designed trade exhibitions and stalls and knew exactly what he wanted.

After lunch we went to see the place, and although it needed a lot of work, I thought it delightful and could see its potential. I had finished at The Royal Exchange, so I decided to take up his request. Peter had decided to call the restaurant Crispins, because he thought it was a nice English name and St Crispin's Day was referred to in one of Shakespeare's plays. He was very thorough and had already placed an entry in the telephone book.

When the work had been finished and the building renovated, I fell in love with it; it was the ideal little restaurant that I had always wanted. I couldn't have designed it better myself. The décor was extravagantly Edwardian in style, with a galleried entrance floor festooned with mirrors, pot plants and photographs of Edwardian actresses. Downstairs in the eating area the lighting was subdued, the walls dark and various partitions and pillars contributed to the cosiness. Unlike some of my previous kitchens, every corner was utilised in a sensible way. Crispins was wonderfully designed, and I was very impressed.

I had agreed to go into partnership on the understanding that the running of the restaurant would be entirely in my hands and Peter would play no part in that side of things. It all worked out very well really, although once or twice he did mess me about and I had a go at him, and then he stopped interfering.

We were full on the first night, and the restaurant was packed with people I didn't know. Usually it was my friends that would come to support me, like an actor on opening night, but this was different – these were strangers who were queuing up to come in. Around the back there was a very nice Georgian square where a lot of MPs lived and many of them used to come to eat. They could get to the House in time if the Division Bell was sounded. James Callaghan was one of our best customers. I used to keep a table for him and I'd ring him up and tell him what I had got in especially for him. Nice man. He'd often dine with his wife.

We were listed in the *Good Food Guide*, *Egon Ronay's Guide* and *Gourmet* magazine and so brought in plenty of discerning customers – one of whom was described by his biographer Michael Holroyd as being, in 1915, the most famous man in the world. Now, over fifty years later, Charlie Chaplin was in my restaurant. I didn't know he was there until one of the waiters came and said, 'I think that's Charlie Chaplin at table 6!' I had just read that he was in London staying at The Savoy, so I thought it really could be him.

Of course I scurried to the table, and it was indeed the silent screen legend. 'How nice to see you,' I said, 'and this is your old stomping ground.' Chaplin smiled and replied, 'Yes it is. That's why we're here. I came back today to have a look round the area. I used to live opposite here. It's where my mother died.' His old home was under a demolition order but local residents had erected a sign on the wall which read, 'Don't knock down this building. Charlie Chaplin lived here.'

I told him that I had an elderly cleaning lady, called Aggie, who knew him when they were children. He looked incredulous, 'I remember Aggie. We used to play together. Isn't she a little too old to be cleaning?' 'Yes,' I admitted, 'it's actually her daughter who does the work. She brings Aggie, who sits down and turns her hand at something easy, like the silver ... you know, she used to talk about you and how she played with you. Do you remember sliding down the cellar door of the pub next door?' He nodded, 'Yes, I do ... listen, I don't suppose you could get her here, could you?' It was far too late by then to knock on her door, but he agreed to come back the next evening for dinner when I would fetch her.

Sadly, he couldn't come the following night and telephoned me personally to say he wasn't feeling well and had been advised not to come out. So I never did unite Aggie and Charlie, and even if they had been too old to slide down into that pub cellar, it would have been lovely to hear them reminisce about it.

After performances at the National Theatre, which was up the road from Crispins, Laurence Olivier used to nip in and have a quick supper before he caught the train down to his home in Brighton. I'd known him over the years in a casual way, and we became quite friendly, and he liked Crispins. He'd just received a life peerage, the first ever offered to an actor.

One night he said to me, 'We're going to produce Hedda Gabler with the National cast at the Cambridge Theatre and Ingmar Bergman has agreed to direct it. The night he arrives, I'd like to give him a little dinner party here and we could introduce him to the cast.' Among others, the cast consisted of Maggie Smith, her husband, Robert Stephens, and Jeremy Brett.

Frank Dunlop, who was a director and one of the stalwarts of the Young Vic, had to go to the airport and collect Ingmar Bergman and bring him to Crispins. Lord Olivier wanted the little private room we had upstairs, which comfortably seated about eight or ten people. We were very busy but fitted the reservation in between our first house and second house. (Sometimes there was third house when the National Theatre emptied). I talked to Jimmy, our chef, about it and we worked out a menu, which Sir Larry approved, and wines were sent down from the National Theatre.

Well, the weather that night was beyond belief. There were storms, violent winds, blustery gales and driving rain. It was just appalling. How Bergman got over here in the plane and landed safely at the airport I don't know. Frank picked him up and brought him to the restaurant, where Olivier was already in the room upstairs, studying the Hedda Gabler script in readiness.

Maggie Smith was now twenty minutes late and there was no sign of her or the others. Jeremy Brett, a very sweet man, who was both bisexual and bipolar, arrived full of apologies and went straight upstairs. They were all still waiting for Mr and Mrs Stephens – even Ingmar Bergman was there on time and he had come all the way from Sweden!

Finally, forty-five minutes late, the front door of the restaurant was flung open and Maggie Smith entered and ... fell flat on her face.

Anyway, we lifted her up from the floor, while all the other customers watched aghast when they saw who it was. Miss Smith was followed by her equally drunk husband. I took them both outside into the back yard in the pouring rain where there was a sink. I splashed Maggie's face with cold water and told the waiter to bring some black coffee. We poured that down her, managed somehow to get her vertical and then took her upstairs to meet Ingmar Bergman.

She sat down and ordered soup, which the waiter ladled into her bowl. Her head suddenly lurched forward, and she was just about to do the classic thing of falling headfirst into her food, when I just caught her in time. She was as drunk as that! I caught Ingmar Bergman's eye. He was looking on, somewhat discommoded. I pondered on the fact that he'd got her all summer and I wondered what he was thinking ...

But of course, like so many true performers, when it comes to work, they are always, in my experience, so professional. Maggie Smith's skill, under strong direction from Mr Bergman, produced the performance of her life. I went to see the play twice; it was absolutely brilliant and the entire town was trying to get in to see it. Maggie Smith received fabulous reviews from the critics too. She has given up drinking to excess now. I expect it was mainly her husband's lifestyle that affected her.

Another thespian connected with the National Theatre at the time was Coral Browne, the Australian actress. She was wonderfully funny and outspoken. Well known for her 'colourful' language, somewhat surprisingly she became a devout Catholic. She was descending the steps outside the Brompton Oratory following Sunday Mass when an actor came up to her with some theatrical tittle-tattle about someone having an affair. Coral stopped him in his tracks by saying, 'I don't want to hear this filth. Not with me standing here in a state of fucking grace.'

Coral married Vincent Price and they both frequented Crispins. She was a marvellous looking woman, and she was always on the list of the Best Dressed Women of the Year awards – and sometimes at the top of it. She always looked divine. Some years before, she had come into the Hungry Horse, having booked a table for two. She was always on the arm of some young beautiful actor, who she would invariably seduce. While she was awaiting her companion, I sat her into the best corner table – dimly lit, which I knew she'd like! She was sitting there patiently when Joan Littlewood came in, and I had to show her to a table just beyond Coral's. As she passed the glamorous Miss Browne, Joan said, 'You look wonderful. Who lit you darling?'

Due to my responsibilities at the restaurant, I wasn't able to socialise much in the evenings. However, I was a big fan of the classical pianist Arthur Rubenstein, who was doing a concert at The Royal Festival Hall. Tickets were very hard to get hold of, but I managed to procure a marvellous seat in the middle of the front row. At the last minute one of the chaps in the restaurant was taken ill, and I had to cover for him. I didn't think I was going to be able to make it, but I somehow managed to take my seat just as the great man made his entrance.

Mr Rubenstein greeted the audience and seemed to be looking in my direction. He smiled and nodded at me, and then his gaze shifted to my feet. I always dressed nicely for such events, but when I looked down, I realised that, in my hurry to leave Crispins, I had completely forgotten to put on my socks! At the end of the concert some of the audience joined Arthur onstage, and so I decided to join him too. I shook him by the hand, and he said, 'Ahh ... you're the one without the socks!'

By 1973, and as warned by the council, the building Crispins occupied was due to be demolished, and we had to leave and open up the new premises. We had started work, but Peter Norwood had now become impossible. He was drinking heavily and had started spending way over our budget of £15,000. I'd told him not to go a penny over it, and then the next thing I knew was that he had spent double that amount on the new restaurant. I thought, 'I'm not working my arse off in a new place to pay off his huge debt.' I told him, 'You're on your own Peter. Who knows how much more you'll spend?' And that, sadly, was the end of Crispins.

I was in a bit of state, agitated and very anxious about my next move. I couldn't sleep, and I recall Joan Le Mesurier being worried that I was going to have a mental breakdown, and so I went to see my doctor. Patrick Woodcock had established his practice in a house in Pimlico. He was also Noël Coward's doctor, and the waiting room was always full of well-known performers. I once spent ten minutes chatting to Ken Dodd while waiting to see Patrick. Sometimes Woodcock was referred to as 'Timbertool' by his patients. Immature but amusing, I always thought.

Dr Woodcock was adamant. 'You're overdoing it and you must have a rest. Take a year's sabbatical. You've got the money, so go and have a nice comfortable year.' I almost expected him to say, 'If you can't stand the heat, get out of the kitchen.' His was an excellent idea, but the trouble was 'taking it easy' wasn't exactly how I'd lived my life, but I thought I could try. Of course I should have known that it would be impossible, and before long I was transported into a completely new world and one that I knew very little about.

ELEVEN

MI CASA ES
SU CASA

'For it was not into my ear you whispered, but into my heart. It was not my lips you kissed, but my soul.'

Judy Garland

After the war, my old army pal Ronald Benge worked at the St Marylebone public library in central London and had then become a lecturer in the librarianship department at North-Western Polytechnic. In 1961, backed by President Kwame Nkrumah, he set up a library school in Ghana, and in 1974 he was offered a job in northern Nigeria, to set up a similar institution. Ron was keen to move overseas but was concerned about leaving his elderly father, Charlie, on his own in London. Charlie had been a valet for the Astor family in Kent but had grown up in Fulham and was now living alone in a bedsit in West Kensington.

Ron thus asked me to keep an eye on his father, and I was very fond of old Charlie – he was a sweetie. I visited him regularly, and he used to go to the pub every day for his Guinness. I would occasionally join him and asked the pub's landlord that if ever Charlie didn't come in for his Guinness or he hadn't seen him for a couple of days to phone me.

Well, sure enough, wouldn't you know that the landlord was away on holiday when something happened? Fortunately a friend noticed that Charlie hadn't been in the pub for several days, so she went to the relief manager and told him to ring me. By the time I got a phone call and checked up on him, Charlie had been in bed for six days, in his own excrement and in a very sorry state. He'd been taken ill, and no one knew. His residence had been converted into a number of bedsits, and the occupants used to go up and down the stairs past his room every day and not one of them had bothered to look in and see if he was all right. Charlie was unconscious but still alive, so I sent for the ambulance. After Charlie had been admitted to hospital, the doctor told me he could never manage in his bedsit again and that I would have to arrange for him to go into an old people's home.

After some consultation with Ron, I got in touch with Social Services in Hammersmith and Fulham – a very good Borough actually – and they stepped into the breach quickly and efficiently. Charlie was admitted into this home that had once been a very old Victorian workhouse; it was a red-brick horror, although comfortable inside. I had to settle him in, so I went in every day for about two weeks to make sure he was happy. Luckily, Charlie loved it, which was a great relief because he was a strong character and independently minded, very much like his son. I used to take him out for little trips in my car and take him out for lunch. Charlie wasn't actually there very long before he was transferred to another residential home.

The home, 'Stewart Lodge', was near Battersea, and the matron was a lovely Armenian woman called Mida Flower. I continued to visit Charlie regularly and so became quite friendly with Mida. We used to chat about food and the meals served in the home. It was frustrating because they had a couple of very capable cooks and fantastic equipment but were still using frozen pre-packed food.

I watched about sixty residents shuffle off to the dining room for lunch and be served with a frozen chicken that wasn't thawed properly. I brought my concerns to Mida, and she actually asked me if I could go in for an hour a day and advise about the menus. I did this for a while and really enjoyed my unusual role. Eventually Mida asked me to join the staff, and they actually created a job for me as assistant manager. It was in those happy days when local authorities could spend freely and there was the possibility of being creative and imaginative.

The kitchen was equipped in a way I could never afford for a restaurant: it had everything, every imaginable piece of apparatus, and hardly any of it was used. On one occasion some frozen chicken had been placed in the oven, and when we removed it, I found that the lid was still on and stuck to the chicken. There was the most marvellous, rather large West Indian lady in the kitchen, who was actually a very good cook, and I told her that we couldn't possibly serve the dish – it could have poisoned the residents. I soon realised that she hadn't been able to read the instructions on the frozen chicken, which said to remove the lid before cooking,

I took her aside quietly and said to her, in an expression I had heard from some Jamaican friends, 'You haven't got the words, have you?' She admitted that she couldn't read, so I said to her, 'Don't worry, darling, this is just between you and me. Not a word of it will go elsewhere.' She was terrified that people in the home would find out. I told her, 'From now on we'll spend time together each week and I'll help you read and write.' In that week I started with very simple things, and I started to teach her some basic English phrases, especially cooking instructions!

What was ridiculous was that she was really skilled in the kitchen and was used to preparing food for her large family. There was no excuse for being forced to serve up this frozen muck. From then on we procured fresh meat and vegetables, and I asked her to prepare meals as if she was cooking for her family.

I formed a catering committee with some of the more compos mentis residents to find out what they wanted to eat, and we used to meet once a week in my office, and I'd take note of their suggestions. We started to serve up dishes that they actually wanted. We discovered that over half the residents wanted to eat tripe, and so we would put on two menus with a choice of tripe or sausages and mash. I was concerned with the individual needs of the residents and got to know all their likes, dislikes and favourite foods. There was no reason that, with a little bit of thought, we couldn't make their lives a little less institutional.

And this approach wasn't costing the council more; in fact, it was cheaper. In the first year at Stewart Lodge, I saved them £5,500 from the food budget. I got to know the Director of Social Services of Hammersmith and Fulham and told him that I could cut their spending in residential homes by a substantial amount if the catering was done properly and they stopped using this frozen rubbish. Fortunately, he was very sympathetic and not only listened to me but did what I suggested.

I'd been with Mida for a couple of years when she told me that there was a vacancy for a manager in another home. She said she would be sad to lose me but that I should apply for it, and she would support my application. The upshot was that I got the job and ended up running a home called Farm Lane, which was in Fulham.

I tried to imagine what it would be like if I was resident and ran the home on those lines. I wanted to make it as much like living in their own home as I could. I asked the residents to choose the menus and even got them to help a little in the kitchens!

I procured theatre tickets from friends in the business. One day I invited Gervase Farjeon to come to one of our parties that we gave periodically for the residents. An old lady came up to Gervase and shook hands with him and then pressed something into his hand. Gervase approached me showing his present, 'Look what I've been given.' He opened up his hand to reveal ... a tiny turd. A very hard, dry piece of shit. Quite hilarious!

With the backing of my ever supportive supervisor, Sheila Lycholit, we also endeavoured to get away from the traditional dining room arrangement, which was very institutional and meant that everyone had to eat in the same impersonal canteen-type room. Some residents also found it hard to get to the dining room because of restricted mobility, and in some cases they had to have meals on their own in their rooms. So we decided to arrange the residents into groups of friends, and those who wanted to be with each other could share rooms if they wanted. We changed the use of some rooms into kitchens and dining areas and others into small sitting rooms where they could sit and watch television in a much cosier atmosphere.

Members of the care staff were allocated to look after particular groups so that they would get to know them much better and their particular needs or interests. I wanted them to know the personal predilections of each resident, like which television programmes they were fond of or what particular type of music they liked listening to.

Apart from making the elderly residents happier, the girls also found much greater job satisfaction and would plan all sorts of things for their own groups as if it was their own family. The more mobile folk could go into their sitting room and make the tea, and I provided some nice cakes and bits and pieces.

After Fulham, I went on to another care home, Fairlawn, which was an old converted mansion overlooking Wimbledon Common. One of the residents was an old Polish gentleman who hardly had any English and wouldn't sit in the lounge with the other residents. He insisted on staying in the hallway. He did, however, make it known that he was at school with a certain Karol Józef Wojtyła – Pope John Paul II. We discovered that the 'Polish Pope' was visiting London in May 1982 and was actually staying for a few nights at the Apostolic Nunciature, an ecclesiastic office in Parkside overlooking Wimbledon Common and very near to Fairlawn.

Pope John Paul II's visit to the United Kingdom was the first visit to that country by a reigning pope, although his was a pastoral rather than a state visit. The trip was almost cancelled because Britain was then at war with Argentina over the Falklands Islands, but a diplomatic solution was found whereby the Pope would visit Argentina as well.

Anyway, I wrote a letter to the Pope explaining about our old chap; amazingly, I received a reply from the Pontiff that he remembered his schoolmate, and he duly invited him to tea in Parkside. I drove the man there and he stayed for two hours.

Another resident, Lilian Hopkins, had been blinded during the war in an air raid that killed both her parents. She was educated at St Dunstan's school for the blind on the south coast and she learned how to make furniture and coat hangers, which we used to sell to make money for the home. I still have a wooden and wicker stool that she crafted. David Niven told a lovely story about Noël Coward, who was a patron of St Dunstan's. He and his nephew were strolling along the seafront at Brighton, and on the walk they stumbled across two dogs having sex. One had mounted the other, and Coward's nephew looked on intrigued before asking innocently, 'What are those dogs doing Uncle Noël?' Coward replied, 'The little dog in front has just gone blind and his friend is pushing him all the way to St Dunstan's.'

I loved working with the elderly, and felt I was doing an important job. The only difficulty I encountered was some homophobia from the staff. Being in the theatrical world, which was full of gay men, I was very much protected from any prejudice. Social Services were a very different proposition. Some of the care assistants under my charge were homophobic, and of course when they realised that I was gay they treated me quite differently.

I hadn't experienced this since the early days in the army, when those who were fool enough to make it known that they were gay were discriminated against. Funnily enough, most of the antagonism came from white working-class women. I knew that in an East End back street there is usually one flamboyant gay boy, who everyone takes to their hearts. He is a figure of fun and a kind of stereotypical queen who presents no threat and is treated with amusement – a Larry Grayson or John Inman sort, like they may have seen on television. A nice camp young man was acceptable, but the actual sexual act between two men still seemed repellent to them.

Most of my staff liked me enough, but there was one girl in particular who was very unpleasant, and she used to try and stir it up with all the others. No one liked her or could do anything right by her. She always used to cause trouble in staff meetings and tried to put the knife in. I would get telephone calls in the middle of the night to wake me, and she would deliberately try to make me feel uncomfortable. Looking back, I should have been much more firm with her. I was the boss after all, but I didn't want to antagonise the rest of the staff by disciplining her. Silly really.

I've been to New York several times, and I made another trip during this time to research about residential homes as I thought they would be well ahead of us and wanted to compare their policies with the Hammersmith and Fulham homes. I found a most wonderful care home that was run by nuns. Even on a trip like this, I couldn't get away from Hollywood stars. On the same day that I was there, Greta Garbo was visiting a friend who was in residence. You can imagine her visit caused quite a stir! The home was stunning, and I told the Mother Superior how wonderful I thought it was. She shocked me by explaining that this particular home was a show-piece – and that the others in the group were all awful. There's no doubt that's why Garbo's friend was in that particular home – just in case there was any publicity about her.

My holidays weren't just for research purposes, and I managed to squeeze in a few trips away while I was working for Social Services; I had got to know the actor Richard Wattis, who was a great friend of Hattie's and also a keen gourmet. Along with Joan Sims, we all travelled on the cross-channel ferry on a day trip to France. Unfortunately, the day we chose was definitely the wrong day to sail: the weather was stormy and the sea very rough, resulting in some of the passengers being seasick.

Richard announced that the most effective remedy was several glasses of champagne. Well, we didn't need to be convinced, and we spent the rest of the trip getting pissed. When it was time to disembark in Boulogne, we couldn't find Joan, and only after a thorough search of the boat did we find her – semi-conscious … and in the gentlemen's toilet. Sadly, Richard died at the age of 62. Although much too young, he did pass away in a manner in which we approved. He collapsed, replete, in a Kensington restaurant, having tucked into one of his favourite meals …

In 1977 Hattie and Nigel Hamilton, an actor friend of Hattie's, and I went on a touring holiday in France, ending up in the Loire Valley. We smoked, drank and ate our way across, and apart from three siz-able meals a day, Hattie and I also planned snacks while we were on the road. Local boulangeries and patisseries were raided every morning before we continued on our journey. These titbits were referred to as 'tasty maisies' – a rather camp version of 'Mezes'.

We went on another trip to Ireland, but it was very sad to see Hattie in failing health. Her weight had ballooned since she had been dumped by Schofield, and she was now very breathless on any small exertion – even getting in and out of a car. We took the car ferry from Fishguard to

Rosslare before driving to Waterford and visiting the Ring of Kerry and the Dingle Peninsula. We alternated farm accommodation with hotel stays, and Hattie, such a cherished celebrity, was treated with great kindness wherever she went, and she, in turn, always sent flowers as a way of thanks. There was much laughter, and the holiday was a great success. Although Hattie enjoyed herself immensely, she was struggling physically. On the ferry on the way home Hattie stood outside on the bridge and was besieged by fans for autographs, to which she always patiently and kindly agreed. But near the end of the voyage, she put her hand on mine and said, 'You know I'm not going to live long.'

Sadly, she was right.

In 1980 I was staying with my sister Joan in Saffron Walden when I received a call from a friend of Hattie's to say that she had died. Hattie's son Kim had come in to bring her breakfast and found her dead in bed. He and his mother had had a row the previous evening, and he was distraught. I jumped in my car and drove to London. When I left Essex, it was a beautiful golden autumnal day. As I pulled up outside No. 67 Eardley Crescent, the weather had deteriorated drastically, and the heavens opened and the rain poured down.

The following day, lots of Hattie's friends appeared at Eardley Crescent, offering help but really wanting to be in each other's company and be together. The fridge was bulging as usual. There were cold meats and vegetables from the last meal Hattie had prepared. I felt that Hattie would never have forgiven us if we didn't use her food, so I made an enormous pan of soup for everybody and a plate of cold cuts and cheeses. It seemed important to care for and comfort anyone who needed to come over, just as Hattie had always done.

I retired from Social Services in 1984. Margaret Thatcher had been prime minister for five years, and there were huge cuts in public services, leading to the closure of many council old people's homes. Like Icarus, I now wanted to head towards the sun. I originally intended to spend time in the South of France, which I had come to know when running the guest house in La Favière, but prices in France proved to be well out of my range.

Ronald Benge invited me to holiday with his new wife, Maryvonne, and family near Barcelona. He actually owed me £150 and said he couldn't afford to pay me back but now that he and his wife and had relocated to Catalonia with their two children they would put me up in repayment for my loan. I happily agreed and had a fabulous holiday. I was immediately smitten with the area and told them I would love to move to that part of the world. I asked them to keep an eye open for anything suitable, and a few weeks later I got a call from Maryvonne, saying, 'Come out at once! I have found a wonderful place right at the top of the hill in the village of La Floresta with a view right out over the hills towards Barcelona. It's even got a swimming pool.'

La Floresta is, as the name suggests, a heavily wooded and rather eccentric suburb of Barcelona. It has a British feel, thanks to a builder and engineer called Fred Stark Pearson who was very influential: he designed the railway station based on English archetype and was responsible for developing the town. He put in electricity, developed a grand casino for visitors from Barcelona and there was even a well-known brothel in the town during its heyday in the 1920s, although I'm not sure Mr Pearson had anything to do with that ...

I had worked solidly for nearly forty years after leaving the army and had accrued some savings. My sister Di remained, but I sold the house in Shepherd's Bush for a tidy profit; although I couldn't afford to move to France, I was able to buy the house in La Floresta, with some money remaining to spend on converting the property into flats. I was going to live on one floor and had to find tenants for the other two.

There was a lot of work needed on the house, and I had some plans drawn up to improve the building. I employed an architect to convert the house into three flats, and a friend, Thomas, who is a skilled carpenter, did lots of work on the house for me.

I occupied the middle floor and let the top flat to Louis Lemkow, Professor at Barcelona University, whose father was Norwegian actor Tutte Lemkow and whose mother happened to be the Swedish actress Mai Zetterling, who I knew from the Players' – so I didn't need a reference! Louis, his wife and two children moved into the top floor, and it was marvellous for me when the Benge family decided to move into the ground floor. It was a lovely set up.

I had lost my dear friend John Le Mesurier in November 1983. His death notice in *The Times* was so apropos and typical of the man, 'John Le Mesurier wishes it to be known that he conked out on November 15th. He sadly misses family and friends.' There was a private funeral in Ramsgate followed by a memorial service a few months later at the Actors' Church St Paul's, Covent Garden. Fellow *Dad's Army* cast member Bill Pertwee gave a very amusing tribute, and the score to the Jacques Tati classic *Monsieur Hulot's Holiday* was played followed by a recording of John reciting an Indian poem, 'What is going to become of us all?' The tribute to John ended with Annie Ross singing 'What's New?' I concocted a buffet meal, and there was much drinking of wine and smoking of pot – something that John would have very much approved.

Joan lost her father at that time, so I suggested she come out to Spain for a holiday to stay with me in La Floresta. We attended a fete in La Floresta and Joan was immediately enchanted with the warmth of the people and the relaxed nature of the culture and lifestyle. The only thing missing was the sea, so a friend suggested we visit Sitges – a town known for historic houses and palm trees at every turn – on the coast. We stayed in a seafront hotel run by an eccentric large Belgian woman whose husband was as gay as a cricket.

Joan had had a passionate affair with Tony Hancock while she was married to John, and she was writing her autobiography, the wonderfully titled *Lady Don't Fall Backwards*, taken from a Hancock script by those marvellous writers Ray Galton and Alan Simpson. On the very first day in Sitges, I was sitting on a beach and surrounded by the most beautiful half-naked men, and she was sitting there on her sun lounger under her umbrella, scribbling away and so deep into her writing that she was oblivious of her surroundings.

I finally leant over and said to her, 'Joan have you noticed anything different about this beach?' She looked up and said, 'Well only that it is full of gorgeous men!' 'Too true,' I replied, 'It's the gay beach.' By chance it happened to be opposite this hotel, and I'd only just realised!

Sitges turned out to be quite a gay resort, and I later used to frequent discos and saunas there.

Joan loved it so much and told me she was going to stay forever, although she did nip back to the UK for what she described as a new pair of knickers! She rented a cottage in Sitges, and we used to meet regularly for trips to galleries and concerts. Before long she started looking for a permanent place to buy and found the most marvellous house, Casa Antigua (the Old House), in Sitges that was 400 years old and full of beautiful old tiles. It was ideally situated in the heart of the town and close to the beach, and Joan was marvellous at doing places up.

We came up with the idea of running a small guest house along the lines of Betty Frank's hotel in France. I chipped in about a quarter of the price – it was all the money I had in the bank – and so entered into the business as a Joan's partner. We had many connections and knew lots of actors, performers and writers in London who would flock here. Joan advertised Casa Antigua in the BBC bar and in the ITV studios and managed to attract the targeted clientele as well as her stepson Robin's musician friends from Rod Stewart's band.

Joan used to cook for them and do most of the work; it was her project really, and I was just helping out. I used to commute there from La Floresta, about a forty-minute drive. Joan provided breakfast and dinner and lunch if necessary. The trouble was that she didn't charge enough money, and there was a little friction between us at times: Joan wanted to run it as a kind of easy going, homely guest house for theatricals and provide basic food, and I, being a professional restaurateur, wanted to concentrate on the food and make dining the most important part of the visit for the guests.

Joan ran the guest house for seven years but became fed up with the cooking, and some nights, when she couldn't face several hours in the kitchen, she would suggest that she and all the guests repair to a local restaurant. And she would insist on paying for everyone! Needless to say, the business wasn't the most profitable, but we had a wonderful time. Eventually we both got a bit fed up with it, and I wanted to concentrate on getting my own property in La Floresta in order. We sold it at a good price, so we got our money back in the end.

During the time we were running the guest house, Hattie's son and Joan's stepson, Kim, was admitted to hospital in London with meningitis. Poor Kim had never got over his mother's death and continued to feel guilty for causing an argument on the day she died. He had become a heroin addict and was living the typically chaotic lifestyle of an addict. Joan visited him in hospital and brought him back to Sitges, where we thought we could 'rescue' him. Joan offered him accommodation and employment as an odd job man on the understanding that he had to 'stay clean'. Joan was adamant that she wasn't going to live with a junkie. I also helped him financially, and for a while the arrangement was successful.

Kim stayed for four years, and I must say he was absolutely adorable. Everyone loved him, and he was very attractive, so women were drawn to him. He managed to kick his habit in the physical sense but admitted the psychological dependency would always remain. He was a very clever musician and wrote a song, 'Fine Time', which was recorded by a female singer, got into the charts and made him some money.

All sorts of record companies wanted him in England; he was offered contracts and all sorts of financial inducements but always refused the money. I don't know why. Perhaps he thought returning to London's music scene would be too much for him in terms of his addiction. Sadly, this decision didn't save him. In a local bar, Kim met a woman who, unfortunately, was a junkie, and she turned him back on to heroin.

Our lovely gentle and good-natured Kim became surly and uncommunicative. We searched his room when he was out and found needles and all his drugs paraphernalia. Joan confronted him, and he admitted that he had gone back on the junk. He apologised but insisted it was just a temporary lapse. He then moved out of the guest house and into a grotty flat in a seedy area of Barcelona with his new girlfriend. He used to visit us and ask us for money. Of course we helped him and tried to feed him up, but he looked like a ghost, and it was obvious he was shooting up. We knew some of the funds were being used for drugs, but what could we do?

In 1991 Joan returned home to Ramsgate as her mother was ill. While she was there her granddaughter Emma, then aged about 10 and now actress and writer Emma Malin, received a phone call to say that Kim had died. Kim had been spotted by friends in a Barcelona bar, crying and clearly distressed. Some hours later he was discovered in his flat with a needle in his arm and a large amount of heroin in his body. All his instruments and demo tapes had been stolen. It was 6 October – exactly the eleventh anniversary of Hattie's death. He was aged just 35.

Darling Kim. Just before he died, I was trying to get him to come home, and I had given him some money that was supposed to be for his air ticket to England. I should never have given him that money because he just spent it on drugs. I loved Kim. He was an adorable boy. It was such a waste of life.

One night in August 1988, several years before Kim's death, Joan suggested that we go out for dinner with some friends to one of our favourite restaurants – a seafront place in Sitges. It was a particularly humid evening, and after we'd been there about half an hour the air conditioning broke down. It was absolutely stifling, and although the others seemed to be able to cope with the heat, I felt quite faint and stepped outside to feel the breeze. I bumped into an Italian friend, Mario Bellandi, who I had met at the gay beach. We were never lovers but remain good friends even to this day.

I was delighted to see him but even more taken by a young man shifting uneasily from foot to foot in the background. I took one look, that's all, just one look and was knocked sidewise by this dazzlingly gorgeous boy in his early 30s, dark and delicately featured. Mario introduced us, and I was immediately smitten. He had apparently seen me in a bar, and fortunately he liked older men – I was 68 at the time. Once he realised that Mario knew me, he asked to be introduced. Daniele was as lovely as he was beautiful, and I have to say I took him home that night. I fell in love with him immediately. I know it is a very clichéd expression, but it really was love at first sight.

Daniele was Italian and in Sitges on holiday with a friend and due to return to his home in Milan a few days later. We saw a lot of each other in that short time between our meeting and him going back to Italy. The day he was due to leave, I told Daniele that I couldn't come to the station because I hated goodbyes and was already besotted with him. We sat in a very nice café I know on the Plaza Catalonia in Barcelona and we talked. I told him I'd love him to come back to Spain and live with me, but I didn't want to be silly about it and make a big mistake. We could live together for a month and see how it went. I told him that I could afford to support him, but he didn't want that and said that he had money of his own and didn't want to be a burden or dependent on me. The main way that he supported himself financially was working as a male gigolo. He had been wined and dined and looked after by older gay men, but he told me that he would give that up and that our affair would be very different.

And that's exactly what happened. Daniele came to live with me in my flat in La Floresta. I felt immediately at home with him. He was witty and intelligent, and we shared so much. The month went very well, and I loved having him in my life. During that time he revealed that he had been a junkie. I was a bit taken aback, but it endeared him to me that he had been so honest. He wanted to stay with me, and I could think of nothing better. I'd never felt like this. I'd had plenty of lovers but nothing as deep as this. He was THE love of my life.

We were naturally both so aware of AIDS, which seven years earlier had been categorised as an official epidemic. By now there were over 100,000 reported cases in USA and many more worldwide, and so soon after we set up home together we underwent medical tests for HIV. To our relief the results were negative, so we settled into an idyllic life together. He worked occasionally as a teaching assistant at a local school and was a talented ceramicist. He loved to draw, and I kept all his sketches and doodles. He was the gentlest and kindest boy I had ever known, and I have to say it was the happiest and most settled time of my life. I believed we would be together for years to come.

It was during this time that I came to know a girl who lived nearby called Adriana. She was also Italian and well educated, but she had also been a drug addict. She neglected herself, and she didn't, or couldn't, cook for herself and so asked me to prepare meals for her on a regular basis for a small amount of money. She was charming but a little helpless, and I was happy to do what I could for her.

Soon after we got to know her there had been some concern in the neighbourhood of drug use going on, and a car that had been dumped in a nearby street was found to be full of syringes. Adriana became friendly with Daniele, and one day I found Daniele shooting up. I don't know why, but I wasn't angry. I was more disappointed and worried for him. I didn't know how long he had been back on heroin. Poor Adriana had also returned to using drugs and died from an overdose. She had collected a menagerie of stray dogs and cats, but she didn't look after them properly, and they all had to be destroyed after her death.

There had been warnings since the mid-1980s that avoiding injection drug use and reducing needle sharing would be effective in preventing transmission of HIV, and in 1992 Daniele developed a couple of worrying symptoms. He had lesions on his face, and his eyesight seemed to be deteriorating. He saw an oculist, but it was clear that something serious was going on.

I told Daniele that he must go and get checked out again. I took him to this very good clinic in Terrassa, a nearby Catalonian city. It was a traumatic day because we both knew what was happening to him. A few days later we received the results. I'll never forget how awfully shocked I felt when he told me that he was HIV positive. He looked like a zombie. I held him tight and then took him round the corner to a bar and bought us two large brandies; there we sat, somewhat dazed by the news. In a way, I suppose it wasn't such a shock as we had probably guessed the outcome. I tried to cheer him up, although I felt devastated. He was so young.

Daniele's father had died some years before, but he was incredibly close to his mother, Rosa, and his four sisters and three brothers, who all still lived in Milan. They were a rock-solid, working-class family, who were absolutely lovely and supportive. I had got to know them in the years we had been together, and without exception they had all welcomed me into their family.

We had to break the terrible news to them, but Daniele was too distraught to talk to them straightaway, and it was agreed that I would do so. With the help of a friend who spoke Italian, I telephoned his mother and told her what we knew. It was awful and one of the worst things I have ever had to do. It took me back to those days in Wark when I was writing those letters of condolence to the families of the soldiers lost in action.

The difference was that although Daniele was under a death sentence, he was still very much alive and initially he seemed fine. For a short while, we tried to carry on and live every moment, but his condition deteriorated very swiftly, and just a few weeks after the diagnosis he was admitted to an AIDS ward in a large general hospital in Barcelona. The infection spread to his brain, he developed a tumour behind the eyes and he gradually went blind. Daniele was in such pain. It was unbearable.

Nowadays, although there is no cure for AIDS or medication to reverse the damage to the immune system, there have been many advances that have dramatically improved the quality of life of people with HIV. More people are living longer with HIV than we ever thought possible, but in 1992 the medical profession was at a loss.

I recall talking to my cousin Carol Lindsay-Smith regularly at the time I was nursing Daniele, and we talked a lot about the virus. Carol worked for the children's charity Barnardo's, and the charity initially perceived AIDS as a gay disease, but Carol was insistent that the organisation take the dangers to young straight men seriously too. She advised the organisation of the dangers of AIDS and the need to act. Officials at Barnardo's duly listened and the charity was thus ahead of its time in that it appointed AIDS education officers in various regions of the UK. Carol worked as a counsellor and reported that the men she saw weren't afraid of dying but were more concerned with telling their parents and family that they were gay. And I'm sure that, tragically, this is still often the case today.

One day, while I was visiting the hospital, the doctor drew me aside and very apologetically said:

Daniele's condition is without hope. I am afraid he is going to die. There is nothing we can do for him here, and we are so overwhelmed with need for beds that I want you to move him if you can. It is best he goes home now and dies amongst his friends.

His words weren't shocking. I had known for a while that Daniele was dying, and so I agreed. There was no point in Daniele staying in hospital and preventing other patients from receiving nursing care they might need,

I took him back to my flat and did my best to look after him, but it was so awful. He used to get up in the night and wander about and defecate and pee on the floor because he was too blind to find the loo. One day he was sitting at the table on which there was a big bowl of fruit. I had stuck a lemon on top for decoration, but Daniele reached out to take a piece of fruit and took a large bite out of this lemon. He had terrible sores all over his mouth and screamed out in agony, and it was my fault. Although there were so many dreadful things happening like this during that time, I remember this incident terribly vividly.

Although I had lots of help from friends, it was getting too much for us to nurse him at home. Mario, who had originally introduced us, was wonderfully supportive but said, 'You know, Bruce, we must take him to Milan, so that he can be near his family. It's for the best.' Mario obtained Daniele's medical history from the doctors and translated it into Italian. He sat on my terrace, and it took him two days to copy it all out.

By the time we left for Milan Daniele was in a very serious condition and semi-conscious. Mario did all the driving and I sat behind Daniele, administering him the drugs he needed and giving him sips of water to make sure he didn't dehydrate. It was a nightmare journey, and to make matters worse there was industrial action by French lorry drivers, who blocked some of the roads. At one stage Mario careered across a field to find a way around the traffic. He was absolutely marvellous.

Normally the journey would have taken about two days, but this time we were travelling for about thirty hours. We went straight to the Milan hospital and arrived on 4 July – ironically American Independence Day.

It was a huge institution with extensive grounds. The AIDS ward was the furthest away from the entrance; we actually had to park the car and get hospital transport to get there!

A young doctor greeted us and said he wanted to talk to me. As I moved towards him, he stepped back and it was clear that he didn't want me to come too close to him. I had to stand apart from him because he was frightened of catching AIDS from me. Unbelievable. That was even how some medics behaved in those days – such ignorance. The terminology of AIDS being a 'gay plague' was still prevalent and sensationalising what was a global human disaster. Funnily enough, all I could think of was Diana Princess of Wales trying to convince people that you couldn't get the virus simply by talking to or shaking hands with somebody.

Despite this introduction, it was the most wonderful hospital, and the care they gave Daniele was the best he could have got. Unfortunately, it was situated right across the other side of town from where his family lived. I stayed with Rosa, Daniele's mother, and for six weeks drove across the city twice every day in heavy traffic, usually with Rosa at my side. And I have to say that Italian drivers are quite mad: they do everything but fly ...

Meanwhile, I met all the other patients; each of them had their own small private room. The awful thing about going to an AIDS ward is that everything is reversed. In hospitals, it is usually the younger people visiting the older ones, and the elderly are usually the patients. But this was the other way around in that it was a younger group of people who were in bed and gravely ill and the parents and frail grandparents who were the visitors. We used to crowd together in the lift together and travel one floor up to the wards. The other thing is that this all happened during the time of the Barcelona Olympics, and I'll never forget watching those beautiful young, strong and youthful athletes while these young people were all emaciated, weak and some barely unable to move.

One of the patients was a young, dark-haired Italian woman in her late 20s. She used to see me coming to see Daniele and would stand in the doorway, clad in her colourful pyjamas, to greet me. We would swap hellos every day. She bore a remarkable physical resemblance to Anne Frank, the brave young Jewish girl who died in Bergen-Belsen concentration camp. Eventually, I thought I should be friendlier. I couldn't always just say hello and goodbye: I must go and talk to her. So one day I stopped and went into her room and said, 'I still don't know your name. What is it?' She replied, 'Anne.' I broke down in tears straightaway. The two young women were now inextricably linked in my mind, and I couldn't help but think of the fate of Anne Frank. I visited my Anne Frank every day for a chat. She spoke a little English and told me how much she liked Daniele. She just loved to look at him in his bed because he was so beautiful, even though he was mostly unconscious.

The patients were treated very well. I used to feed Daniele, and one day one of the doctors – a lady doctor who I liked very much as she was especially kind in looking after Daniele – approached me. She told me that I shouldn't feed Daniele, 'There is no need.' 'Oh,' I replied, 'I love doing it.' She continued, 'No, what I am trying to tell you is that he is tube fed through his stomach, and I'd rather you didn't because solid food results in solid faeces ... in the bed usually, and I have to get special staff to come and clean the whole bed.' I felt awful and muttered, 'I am so sorry I hadn't realised.'

What was extraordinary was that the wonderfully sensitive staff had let me go on feeding him for a while as they knew how much I wanted to and how it gave me a role – even though it was causing all this trouble.

Daniele died on 6 August 1992 at 6.25 p.m. He was only 36 years old. When Daniele passed away, apart from me, 'Anne Frank' was the first person to see him. I saw her hunched over his body, praying for his soul.

Of course, in time she died too.

I returned to the hospital the next day with one of Daniele's sisters to sign the death certificate and collect his things. He was in the mortuary, and she told me that she wanted to see Daniele. I went with her ... I shouldn't have done because viewing him there left me with a terrible image, which has always remained with me. He was lying in a casket, looking like Dracula. His lips were drawn back, and all those weeks of having to wear an oxygen mask had discoloured his teeth. They had also dressed him in the most godawful black suit. He just didn't look like Daniele but someone else ... someone I didn't know.

The funeral was an absolute nightmare, although the family were wonderful to me. I tried to keep out of the way as I was still aware that there might be those present who would think I had brought shame on the family, but Rosa insisted that I should be one of the pall-bearers and told me that she wanted me to play an important part at the funeral as Daniele loved me so much.

The service was held in a Catholic church within walking distance from where the family lived. I was treated as if I was Daniele's husband and was given a prime position throughout. Afterwards we all got into coaches to go to the same cemetery where his father had been buried. Daniele's coffin was lowered into the grave by the pall-bearers and everyone took turns to throw a handful of earth on top of his coffin. I couldn't stop crying.

Later on, something astonishing happened: Emanuela, the wife of one of Daniele's brothers, worked in the hospital, and every day she lunched in the canteen with a friend, a nurse. One day, about two or three weeks after Daniele died, the nurse told Emanuela that she was a spiritualist and confessed that she had received a message, a clear voice telling her to seek out someone called Bruce. The message was, 'Let Go! Tell Bruce not to grieve and to let go. Daniele is quite happy!' I didn't know what to think, but I wanted to believe it. I had no alternative. I needed something ... anything to help me in my grief. I held on to that extraordinary communication for a long time. I still do, really.

He was the love of my life – there is no doubt. He loved me, and he was so kind to me. I still adore him.

TWELVE

SWIMMING
AND GARLIC

'I shall wear the bottoms of my trousers rolled.
Shall I part my hair behind? Do I dare to eat a peach?
I shall wear white flannel trousers, and walk upon the beach.
I have heard the mermaids singing, each to each.'

Extract from 'The Love Song Of J. Alfred Prufock', T.S. Eliot

Not long ago I was staying with friends and holding court at a dinner party hosted by my late friend the composer Peter Greenwell, and I suddenly had to stop in the middle of an anecdote. I told them that I couldn't remember someone's name. I simply said, 'Well, there you are. I can't carry on this conversation any longer.' There was a long theatrical pause, and Peter said, 'You're doing very well, dear, you've been here for forty-eight hours and you haven't drawn breath!' That seems to sum up my years, and I am only just now beginning to draw breath.

I've lived a rather charmed life, I think. I received the unconditional love of my parents and siblings, which provided me with an undeniably happy, secure and stable start in life. They always encouraged me to be who I wanted to be. I somehow survived the whole of the Second World War just about intact. I've seen history in the making and great strides in gay rights after having lived exactly half my life at the risk of being prosecuted for who I was. It wasn't until 1967, when I was aged 47, that the

Sexual Offences Act partially decriminalised homosexual acts between consenting male adults over the age of 21. (This didn't apply to members of the armed services, where the ban remained until January 2000.)

Unlike others, I have been lucky in that I have never had to become too politicised about being gay and have always been comfortable in my skin, but then I was in two professions – theatre and catering – where homosexuality was more accepted. And my friends have never just been gossipy queens. I've always had an affinity with women and never been completely home exclusively in the company of gay men.

I've seen some of the most charismatic entertainers perform on stage, such as Marlene Dietrich, Gracie Fields and Shirley MacLaine, who in my opinion is second only to the multi-talented Judy Garland. Garland was unparalleled. After singing and dancing up a storm, she would just sit on the edge of the stage and chat to the audience in an incredibly informal and intimate manner. She made all of us feel important, and we just didn't want her to leave.

There were memorable operatic and classical concerts that I still savour, and I've been witness to some of the best theatrical acting performances ever seen, given by Ashcroft, Olivier and Gielgud. Vanessa Redgrave, who is one of my favourite actresses, was magnificent as Rosalind in The Royal Shakespeare Company's production of *As You like It*, and her performance has stayed with me. She was married to bisexual director Tony Richardson, who died in 1991 from an AIDS-related illness. He used to throw gay parties, which I catered. Years later, I appeared in a television documentary, *The Unforgettable Hattie Jacques*. I'd told the director that I didn't want to be interviewed in a studio, so the production company arranged for one of the employees to use the drawing room of his Hammersmith house. When I arrived I felt a strange sense of déjà vu and realised it was the very house in which I had catered Richardson's parties.

Judi Dench was quite marvellous in *Amy's View* at the National Theatre. I didn't go round to see her afterwards. I never do that unless the actors are expecting me and want me backstage. I've seen too many actors trapped in their dressing room by people burbling at them when

212

they've done a matinee and an evening performance and just want to get home. Judi found out that I'd been in the house and was disappointed not to see me. We speak on the telephone regularly, and she very kindly sent me a hamper from Fortnum & Mason for my 90th birthday.

I may not have swum with mermaids, but I have bathed with a James Bond – Sean Connery was a regular at the Serpentine in the 1950s. I've had the privilege of being able to socialise with screen goddesses, theatrical knights and legendary comedians. I loved them for who they were, not what they were, but it was my friends and family who have always been the most important people in my life.

When the jazz musician Eubie Blake reached the age of 96, he was quoted as saying, 'If I'd known I was going to live this long, I'd have taken better care of myself.' I have actually taken care of myself physically, but my longevity has certainly created some financial pressures. I had to sell my house in La Floresta and now rent a small house, which I share with a dog and two cats but most importantly my live-in companion Danny Duch.

Danny looks after me and sees to my every need … well nearly; every now and again he will come and put his arm around my shoulder and give me a kiss and say, 'I love you!' I'm 95 and he is forty years younger. We're not lovers but great friends, and I don't know what I'd do without him, although sometimes he fusses over me too much, and I have to tell him to 'Fuck Off!' He understands me completely.

Danny is separated from his wife, has two grown-up daughters Christina and Sergi and is now a grandfather to a baby girl. Although things are changing, one of the awful things about being gay in my generation is that you don't have any children, and so I find it rather nice when Danny's family come and go. Fortunately, my own extended family has lots of children. I once went to stay with my cousin Carol in Suffolk. Her son and pregnant girlfriend, Sarah, were also staying with her at the time, and while I was there Sarah went into labour and came home from hospital with a 12-hour-old baby. I don't suppose it was the most ideal time for me to be around, but I took one glance at the anaemic looking Sarah and pronounced, 'I must get her some liver.' I didn't really think about whether Sarah wanted it or not … she needed it.

One of my dearest friends for over fifty years has been Philippa Potts, or 'Pip' as I call her. Pip worked for me as a cashier at the Hungry Horse until she became pregnant. She recently told me I was 'a stickler' for good practice and professionalism, which I suppose I was. And I have been wherever I've been in charge. I like to think I ran a very tight ship.

Pip separated from her first husband, Charles, and married Humphrey Potts, a very special man, who sadly died in 2012. Humphrey was a high court judge, who presided over the perjury trial of Jeffrey Archer. Humphrey and Pip had two sons, George and Jacob (Pip also has two sons from her first marriage), and the boys used to visit me in Spain, and I stayed with them at their family home in Newcastle. For reasons best known to them, they referred to me as their 'Gypsy Granny', who was a character in the children's book *Rupert the Bear*. I used to walk George and Jacob to school, and they actually introduced me to their teacher as 'Gypsy Granny'. I didn't mind. I've been called worse, although I wondered what on earth she must have thought!

The Potts now have a house in Hounam, a hamlet in the Borders, and I used to visit regularly. We were once having dinner with some neighbours who were farmers. The chap had just been shooting and announced proudly, 'I managed to bag a brace of blackcocks [black grouse]!' Well, of course, I couldn't resist that feed line and replied, 'Aren't you lucky? I've been waiting all my life for that to happen.'

I still see Joan Le Mesurier every year, and her stepson, Robin, has achieved great success in the music business. He was the lead guitarist with Rod Stewart for years and has been the regular musical director for French superstar Johnny Hallyday. My remarkable sister Di, who still lives in our old house in Shepherd's Bush, was married briefly but subsequently lived with an Australian woman Maggie, an antique dealer, for nearly fifty years until Maggie's death in 2004. Di told me it was a shame it took her so long time to realise she was bisexual!

When I visited Milan after Daniele died, I used to go with Rosa to see her husband's grave and then Daniele's resting place. I had provided a proper headstone and a photograph in a special weatherproof frame; it is still there. On another visit, the family clubbed together and actually bought tickets for Rosa and I to go La Scala, the greatest opera house in Europe. I had never been to it before. We went to see a wonderful production of *Anna Bolena* by Gaetano Donizetti. They paid for a taxi to take us there and back too. It happened to be opening night, so it was a wonderfully glamorous occasion – I've never seen so many furs and jewels. Daniele's family continue to be in touch. Rosa, his mother, has sadly passed away, but on my 90th birthday three of Daniele's adorable sisters visited, and we all had a lovely lunch together.

I can't speak Italian and they can't speak English, but my friend Thomas speaks a bit of Italian, and so every now and again we pick up the phone and he talks to them. I just say 'Hello', and we all laugh. I think they're surprised I'm still alive.

I still receive visits from a number of my friends I have mentioned earlier, but of course, at my age I have lost so many. Ronald Benge finally settled in St-Pons-de-Thomières in Languedoc and was married three times, so his family grew in number. I am still in touch with Maryvonne and Ron's daughter Eliza, who is one of my favourite people. Ronald died in 2009 at the age of 90. He was the most remarkable man and was quite rightly afforded several obituaries in national newspapers.

When Daniele died, I stopped going to funerals. Mind you, it is quite easy to avoid going to funerals when you are in Spain because people don't expect you to make long journeys. If I did I would be attending two or three funerals a year. I couldn't afford it now anyway. I don't really want a religious funeral myself. I would like a Humanist thing or something like that – it doesn't matter really. Ceremonies of that kind are so awful … when you get complete strangers, who maybe never knew the dead person, getting up and making a speech. I think that is ridiculous. I'll have a cremation, and they can scatter my ashes at sea. I love the sea.

I'm not keen on formal religion, although I was brought up in the Church of England. I was confirmed and used to go to church regularly, but as I grew older I drifted away from all of that and began to think for myself. I still wonder how anyone could believe in God after the ghastliness of war and suffering and what had happened in the concentration camps. My only spiritual interest is in Buddhism.

I have arthritis now, so any physical activity is difficult. However, I still manage to saunter down to a local café for the occasional lunch when I can afford it. I watch BBC television and love listening to music whether it is my favourite aria from *Tristan and Isolde*, a Chopin étude, a Gershwin song or a musical number. Fortunately, my eyesight still allows me to read avidly. I learned everything I know through reading. My parents were not intellectual, but they were educated and we always had a lot of reading material, especially reference books. I still use them a lot, and any new little thing I don't know about or don't understand I look up in my *Oxford Book of Music* or *Verse* or one of my dictionaries. I continue to learn something every day. I am content.

Whenever anyone asks me how I remain so well and fit, I simply reply, 'Swimming and garlic, my dear, swimming and garlic.' And in the words of Carlotta Campion, Stephen Sondheim's veteran performer in his wonderful musical *Follies*, 'Look who's here ... I'm still here.'

SOME SAVOURIES

*'I've known what it is to be hungry, but
I always went right to a restaurant.'*

Ring Lardner

Some people have suggested that at a different time I could have been a celebrity chef. I was watching Tom Kerridge on television recently and he started off saying, 'Well it's all simplicity in the kitchen – the vital thing is simplicity', and then he went on to tell us how to do the most complicated way of cooking asparagus I've ever heard and a duck dish that took four and a half hours and used twenty ingredients that would have been impossible to find. That's simplicity?

The only thing in my whole life that I don't like in the way of food is oeufs en gelée, which used to be on every French menu, and they are so clever with it. They take a glass container and they put pretty things in the bottom like parsley leaves and so on, then they include some aspic and eventually they put a soft boiled egg with runny yolk before adding more jelly and more decorations, and it is allowed to set in the fridge. When you order oeufs en gelée you get one of these turned out on a plate, and it's beautiful to look at; then you put your fork into it, and the yolk comes flooding out. When I first tasted the dish I actually had to run out of the restaurant into the road to be sick it revolted me so much.

But that's the only dish that I can't eat. Below are some of my favourite recipes, four of which (smoked chicken and lentils, smoked haddock and cheese bouchee, rabbit in wine and mushrooms, and port and prune fool) were included in the *Good Food Guide* in the mid-1970s. All serve four.

Smoked Chicken and Lentils (Crispins)
½lb of brown lentils
One chopped onion
Two carrots, sliced in roundels
One stalk of chopped celery
Thyme
Bay leaves
Black pepper
A smoked chicken
Lemon and parsley or watercress to serve

Soak the lentils in cold water for about four hours. Sauté the onion, carrots and celery in a little butter or oil. Drain the lentils and add to the vegetables, together with a good pinch of thyme and two bay leaves. Season with milled black pepper – but no salt! Cover with fresh water or stock and simmer for about one and a half hours. Divide the smoked chicken into four pieces and place in a pot large enough for all ingredients, then smother with lentils and liquid and bring back to boiling point for not more than fifteen minutes, as the chicken is already steam-cooked before the smoking process. Serve in deep plates, with generous amounts of lentils and sauce with each piece of chicken. Garnish with a wedge of lemon and parsley or watercress.

Smoked Haddock and Cheese Bouchee (The Hungry Horse)
1lb of best smoked-haddock (on the bone and not filleted or 'golden')
½pt of milk
Butter
Flour
Grated cheddar
Vol au vent cases
Black pepper

A pinch of cayenne
A pinch of grated nutmeg
One egg yolk
Cream

Bake a batch of bouchee (*vol au vent*) cases or buy four fairly large ones. Poach the haddock in the milk. Blend butter and flour for a roux, and add the milk in which the haddock was cooked together with a generous amount of good grated cheddar to make a strong cheese sauce. Meanwhile heat the pastry, season the sauce with milled pepper, a hint of cayenne and a scrape of nutmeg – but no salt. Remove the skin and bone from the cooled fish and combine with the sauce, adding, at the last moment, a beaten egg yolk and some cream. The consistency should be fairly stiff. Then fill the heated pastry to overflowing, set at an angle, sprinkle chopped parsley and serve on hot plates as a starter.

Rabbit in Wine and Mushrooms (my version of Civet de Lapin)
Two rabbits
Two coarsely chopped onions
Red wine
Oil
A bouquet of thyme, parsley, bay, crushed garlic and four cloves (all tied in muslin)
Stock or water
beurre manié
Croutons and button mushrooms to serve

Soak the rabbits in cold water, then wipe and cut as follows: two hind legs, one saddle, one breast, two forelegs. Marinade these pieces overnight in equal parts red wine and oil, together with the onions. Then sauté together with two sliced carrots, one cup of chopped celery and one cup of chopped bacon in a little oil and butter in a deep saucepan. Lightly brown the wiped rabbit pieces in a separate pan and add to vegetables, and then season with salt, pepper and nutmeg. Put in the bouquet. Add marinade with onions, then stock or water to cover. Simmer till tender. Reduce if necessary, and then thicken the liquid with *beurre manié*. Serve with fried croutons and sautéed button mushrooms.

Port and Prune Fool (The Mermaid)
1lb best Californian prunes
$^1/_2$pt double cream
4tsps port
One lemon
Biscuits such as *langues du chat* to serve

Soak the prunes and then poach them till tender in just sufficient water to cover, adding a good piece of lemon zest. Cool, remove the stones and then blend them in a liquidiser with enough port to make a thick purée. Then combine the purée with sweetened whipped cream – proportions to your taste. Chill and serve in stem glasses and with a suitable biscuit such as a *langue du chat*.

Fresh North Sea Cod and Caper Mayonnaise (The Hungry Horse)
One whole fresh cod
One lemon
One stick of celery
Salt and peppercorns
$^1/_2$pt of mayonnaise
A handful of capers
Caper juice

Buy the whole fresh cod on the bone, weighing about 6lbs. Make a good fish stock with the cod's head and bones. Add some peppercorns, a lemon cut in half, salt and a *bouquet garni* of bay leaves, celery and mixed herbs. After boiling this stock for twenty minutes, put the whole fish on to a tray of the fish kettle and then simmer gently in the stock with the lid on. When cooked through, remove from the fish kettle and allow to cool. Remove the skin, and with a large palette knife, remove the flesh of the fish from the bone in the form of fillets – be careful not to break the fish into small pieces. Make a mayonnaise and add plenty of capers. Then thin the mayonnaise with some juice from the capers until it becomes more like a sauce. Pour over the prepared fish on a platter and chill slightly. Garnish with twists of lemons and some crisp hearts of lettuce for decoration.

Soupe Au Pistou (Crispins)
1lb kidney beans
One onion
One celery stalk
One turnip
One potato
One tin of tomatoes
1tsp savory
Pistou

Soak the kidney beans overnight, drain, add fresh water and savory and simmer until tender. After one hour add the sliced onion, celery, turnip, carrot, potato – or indeed any root vegetable available. Add the tin of tomatoes, season to taste and pass through a *mouli legume*. Liquidise if you like, but this gives too fine a texture. This is basically a thick bean soup. Serve very hot with the *pistou*, one teaspoonful in each soup dish.

Pistou
Combine ¼pt of good olive oil with grated Parmesan, crushed garlic, fresh or dried basil and a few pine nuts (optional). Mix to a thin paste. This mixture will keep for weeks in the fridge.

Lamb and Chestnuts (Crispins)
One small leg of lamb
½lb of green bacon
One glass of brandy
Parsley
Thyme

¼lb mushrooms
One lemon
One gill of double cream
½lb dried chestnuts

Soak the dried chestnuts overnight or go to the trouble of scalding and peeling fresh ones. Simmer in a little salted water till tender. Trim and cut 1in cubes of lean meat from the leg of lamb. Dice the green bacon. Fry the bacon till the fat runs and add the cubes of lamb; fry till lightly browned. Pour off the surplus fat, add a small glass of brandy and ignite. Add a bouquet of parsley and thyme and the sliced mushrooms and then moisten with chestnut water plus the juice of one lemon. Season carefully and simmer till the lamb is tender. At the last moment, before serving, add the cooked and drained chestnuts together with sufficient double cream to thicken the sauce and then boil for a moment before serving. Generously sprinkle with freshly-chopped parsley.

Crepe a la Reine, or Pancake Stuffed with Chicken and Mushrooms (No. 19 Mossop Street)

Simmer the boiling fowl gently. Remove the skin, and take all the meat off the bones. Make a very strong chicken-flavoured sauce with the stock. Sauté some mushrooms and put them into the thick béchamel sauce you made with the stock. When cold, the sauce should be solid enough to go into the pancakes as a filling. Now fry the pancakes gently in butter until they are crisp on both sides. A nice crisp pancake with a creamy chicken and mushroom filling and rice on the side; this is a very filling dish actually. Serve with rice.

Piperade (Crispins)

Piperade is a kind of very elegant scrambled eggs with red pepper, green pepper, onion and tomatoes. It is very simple. Sauté the vegetables until they are soft and edible and then stir in a lot of eggs over a very gentle heat.

INDEX